On the Search for Well-Being

On the Search for Well-Being

HENRY J. BRUTON

Ann Arbor
THE UNIVERSITY OF MICHIGAN PRESS

First paperback edition 2001
Copyright © by the University of Michigan 1997
All rights reserved
Published in the United States of America by
The University of Michigan Press
Manufactured in the United States of America
⊗ Printed on acid-free paper

2004   2003   2002   2001   4   3   2

A CIP catalog record for this book is available from the British Library.

Library of Congress Cataloging-in-Publication Data

Bruton, Henry J.
    On the search for well-being / Henry J. Bruton.
        p.   cm.
    Includes bibliographical references and index.
    ISBN 0-472-10791-7 (alk. paper)
    1. Economic development.   2. Developing countries.   I. Title.
HD72.B78 1997
338.9—dc21   99-40106
                                                                CIP

ISBN 0-472-08716-9 (pbk. : alk. paper)

For Frances

Contents

Preface

In this book I discuss those issues about development economics that I have found of particular interest, and that I believe to be of great importance in understanding why some nations are rich and others poor. I wish to emphasize that I do not seek to cover all aspects of this area of inquiry, nor have I sought to make a thorough literature review. Neither do I seek to cover all sides of the issues that I do address. It is genuinely a discussion of topics that I have worried with for some time in a way that I found helpful, and that are, for me, just plain exciting to study.

Why some nations are rich and others poor is, of course, one of the profound questions of our time, on a par, I would claim, with the physicist's great question, why is there a universe. It raises many theoretical issues that cut across numerous disciplinary boundaries, it has political implications that cover an exceedingly wide area, and it creates many policy matters with which decision makers must wrestle. On the real bottom line however, it is a great moral issue. A world in which some people have so much while millions of others spend most of their life starving is a world which few would defend. I trust that the discussion in this book—limited though it is—may add a bit to the understanding of this great question.

The world is messy. It has been said by many that the only theorem in economics is that there are no theorems in economics. In addition to messiness, there is great ignorance at every turn. Still the economics profession continues to like rigor and elegant models which usually require "perfect knowledge" of some kind or other. I do not object to elegance and rigor, but I push the idea, as strongly as I can, that the world is messy and ignorance is ubiquitous. Economists must, I suggest, seek to capture this messiness and ignorance in theories and arguments if we are to illuminate great questions. I have tried to illuminate, to the extent that I can, and accept the necessary messiness. And I recognize ignorance at every step in the argument. I acknowledge that I may well be unnecessarily messy and inelegant, but if that helps with illumination, it is a small price to pay.

I put considerable store on my "vision." This rather potent word, maybe even pretentious word, is meant to distinguish between the details of my various arguments and the basic approach within which these arguments fall. I try to establish a way of thinking about the great question, and then I explore, examine, probe, and worry my way through a range of specific issues. This, I think, is a fruitful way to think about development. I hope that the reader finds it so.

It was noted above that the present effort is not to be looked upon as a review of literature. This should not be interpreted as meaning that I have not read. I have been reading development economics since President Harry S. Truman announced the United States foreign aid program in 1949. I have tried hard to indicate my debt to specific authors in those cases where I borrowed directly an idea or argument or data. More importantly, I am in debt to the great (and always rising) flow of books and articles for insights and observations and hints and models and histories and numerous other things that have been so crucial in the shaping of my thinking.

My more precise debt is to my colleagues in the Williams College economics department where I have taught and studied for more than three decades. Those who came and stayed for a long period and those who stayed only a few years have helped me enormously. Innumerable lunches, department seminars, office conversations, casual meetings in front of the mailboxes, and so on, have all taught me much. I have tried out much of what is here on my colleagues in one way or another. Much of what is helpful in this book is due to them, but none of the mistakes and weaknesses. The latter are all mine. I note this last not to be modest or perfunctory, but simply because it is true.

I am also grateful to the University of Michigan's Press's referees. Their suggestions, queries, doubts, were exceptionally helpful and led me to modify and rethink a number of issues. They too of course are not responsible for remaining weaknesses or errors.

CHAPTER 1

Economics and Economic Development

Economics is the study of the relationship between the production, distribution, and consumption of goods and services on the one hand and individual and social well-being on the other. Growth economics is the study of how output increases and of the relationship between the increasing production and increasing well-being. Development economics studies why the economies of some countries have been unable to achieve and maintain economic growth, why they have been unable to perform in a way that contributes to sustained increases in individual and social well-being.

The Great Question

Since early in the nineteenth century, the output of goods and services per member of the population in a small number of Western European countries and, beginning a bit later, in northern North America, and, still later, in Japan has increased in a fairly sustained way. Conventional measures of total output per person in these nations have multiplied many times in the course of the last 175 or so years. It is less certain, but still seems appropriate to say, that this continuous increase in the availability of goods and services has, in fact, contributed to the enhancement of well-being of the peoples of these countries. More cautiously, one might say that these increasing availabilities of goods and services have made possible increased well-being. Caution is dictated until the notion of well-being can be made more explicit.

In the great majority of nations, with an even greater majority of the world's population, however, there had been—before 1950—little or no increase in gross domestic product (GDP) per capita. In numerous instances per capita output did rise for a bit, but clearly there was no long-run sustained increase in the availability of goods and services. In a number of countries per capita output was lower in 1950 than in 1900 or even earlier.[1] In these countries, we can say with great confidence that their economies have contributed very little to enhanced well-being over these many decades. We speak of poor countries or less-developed countries as a matter of convenient expres-

---

1. See Maddison (1970), Reynolds (1985), and Kuznets (1971) for data on levels and growth of GDP per capita in the century or so prior to 1950.

sion. The level of per capita income in such countries has been very low compared to that required for health and longevity and compared to the level in the "North." It is emphasized that the reason that these countries are poor or less developed is because they have not achieved—have not been able to put in place—an economy which, as a matter of its routine operation, produces rising output per capita.

We may now rephrase the definition of development economics in a more specific way. Development economics studies the question, why have not the economies of all countries contributed more or less equally to the well-being of their populations? Why are not all countries equally poor or equally rich in the availability of goods and services?[2] Since they are not, then we may say that the ultimate policy objective of development economics is to identify the means to modify the economies of these countries in such manner that they, in the course of their routine operation, contribute to growing well-being. It is worth repeating: Economies that now provide large amounts of goods and services per member of the community are able to do so because they have, over the past century or more, increased their productive capacity year after year after year.[3] The economies of low-income countries have not been able to do so. Why?[4] I emphasize strongly the importance of this question: Why did not all countries begin to grow more or less at the same time? Such a question is not only of historical interest, but bears directly on present approaches to development.

There is a still more specific question that is part of development economics. Since 1950–60 some few countries, with low per capita incomes in the 1950s, have achieved extra-rapid rates of growth of output over the decades of the 1960s, 1970s, and 1980s. Why only a few? If some could, why not all? More deeply, why did the functioning of the economy in a few countries suddenly become able, in the 1950s and early 1960s, to make, or have the potential to make, sustained contributions to well-being, while in other countries no such economic metamorphosis took place? This question is of interest in itself, and it is relevant to the policy objective stated earlier, namely, how might an economy that has long not contributed significantly to enhanced well-being be converted into one that does?

---

2. Easterlin (1981) asks a similar question and answers it largely in terms of education.

3. Many economic historians have documented that the industrial revolution had its roots deep in the twelfth and thirteenth centuries. Kuznets (1971, 303 ff.) distinguishes between "what makes growth possible" and "the way it actually happens." The former refers to the changes that occur over a long period of time in the deep-seated characteristics of the economy and society that make it possible for a growth process to be initiated and maintained in place. See also Braudel (1984, 591 ff).

4. It is important to recognize that a substantial number of the countries now classified as less developed did, in fact, experience substantial growth of total output in the century or so before 1950. Output per capita, however, remained fairly constant, and, as noted in the text, declined in some countries over substantial periods of time. Reynolds (1985) has studied this early growth in some detail.

Why some handful of countries have grown steadily (more or less) over at least a century, while others have not, is to be kept distinct from the question why an even smaller number of countries in the latter category have grown rapidly after the 1950s and others have not. There are several reasons to insist on the distinction. Nations that began to achieve significant rates of growth of output in the 1950s and early 1960s have done so in a world already dominated by a small number of rich and powerful economies. Although the world is "smaller" now than 150 years ago in many ways, the "distance" between the North and South is, in many ways, much greater than it was earlier. Distance refers to per capita income, to the complexity of technology, to the range and quality of goods and services available, to the range of questions that a nation must address (e.g., the role of women, kind of health services to be made available, choice of technology, environmental concerns, etc.) and to a great variety of other things that directly affect everyday life. The effort to imitate, to borrow, to catch up is much more severe now than it was when per capita growth first began. Thus the international environment is quite different now from what it was two centuries ago. The fact of being a latecomer matters in a variety of ways in the analysis that follows.

The most common explanation of the differences in growth performances among developing countries in the post-1950s is in terms of the policies followed in the several countries. It is difficult however to make a case that policies in *all* countries of Africa, Asia (save Japan), and Latin America had been wrong for the 100 years prior to the 1950s and then suddenly became right for a few. Surely there was and is something else—in addition to policies—that matters and that has mattered over the years. What mattered in an earlier century may, of course, be quite different from what has mattered in recent decades.

I have placed emphasis on the question, how does the production, distribution, and consumption of goods and services contribute to well-being? This means of course that well-being must be explored in some detail, and this I do in the following chapter. Two basic points may be made here to justify this emphasis. The first is that there is no such thing as *economic* well-being.[5]

---

5. This is a frequently made point. See for example Lionel Robbins (1935) and I. M. D. Little (1957). Joseph A. Schumpeter (1934) begins with the following statement.

> The social process is really one indivisible whole. Out of its great stream the classifying hand of the investigator artificially extracts economic facts. The designation of a fact as economic already involves an abstraction, the first of the many forced upon us by the technical conditions of mentally copying reality. A fact is never exclusively or purely economic; other—and more important—aspects always exist.

John Stuart Mill makes a similar point:

> Political economy, in truth, has never pretended to give advice to mankind with no lights but its own; though people who knew nothing but political economy (and therefore knew

There are however economic sources of well-being. These sources are encompassed in the production, distribution, and consumption of goods and services that are generally included under the heading of GDP, leisure, and extra-market activities similar to those included in GDP. I include production as well as consumption because, as argued in detail later, employment—the kind and content of one's work—is a major source of well-being. The usual textbook argument that work is a source of disutility while leisure is a source of utility is to be rejected. Similarly, the usual statement that consumption is the "end" of economic activity is rejected. The end of economic activity is a contribution to individual and social well-being. Consumption is one part of that contribution, but only one part.

The other basic point is the more conventional one that economic activity affects other sources of well-being. There are externalities of the textbook sort, of course. More fundamentally, however, economic activities take place in a larger institutional, cultural, social, religious/traditional environment. These characteristics define the environment within which the economy functions. These institutions, this culture, these traditions are also sources of well-being. If the economic activity that leads to an increase in the availability of goods and services violates these other sources of well-being, then evidently the gains from the increased output are reduced. I will argue later that much of the tension and unrest and instability that prevail in the world now, and that have prevailed in the recent past, can be attributed to the arguments discussed in this paragraph.

This argument may be made clearer if we can conceive of an equilibrium with respect to (say) sociology and ethics and tradition and psychology. Such an equilibrium would be internally consistent, but built on the assumption that the "economy" is performing in a certain way. These several equilibria have to be consistent, and where they are not, change is forced on the community: at least one of the equilibria has to give. An economy cannot exist in isolation. Fernand Braudel (1984, 45) observes that the economy's "territory and expanse are also occupied by other spheres of activity—which are constantly reacting with the economy, either to help or as often to hinder its development."

Consider a simple example. Social norms define some sort of boundaries for social behavior. If all members of the community adhere to these social norms, we may say that there is equilibrium in this category of behavior.

---

that ill) have taken upon themselves to advise, and could only do so by such lights as they had. But the numerous sentimental enemies of political economy, and still more numerous interested enemies in sentimental guise, have been very successful in gaining belief for this among other unmerited imputations against it, and the "Principles" having, in spite of the freedom of many of its opinions, become for the present most popular treatise on the subject, has helped to disarm the enemies of so important a study. (Mill 1873, 237)

See also the remarks of Kenneth Arrow and Robert Solow in Swedberg (1990) and Arrow (1951, chapter 3).

Suppose, as an example, that this social behavior does not allow workers to bid down wages in the presence of unemployment. So unemployment prevails because the society is adhering to the social norm of not bidding down wages. If the community insists on full employment through wage adjustments, then there is inconsistency between the two categories of behavior, and something has to give. In a very real sense there is no equilibrium in this case because of the inconsistency between the two objectives—full employment and adherence to social norms.[6]

A second example refers to the possibility of economies of scale in some of the activities of an economy. The population may well object to large-scale units for any number of reasons: they can create power and power is always dangerous; they can create traffic problems and pollution. Jobs in huge enterprises are more likely to be dull and dulling than they are in smaller units, and so on. In this instance there would need to be intervention in the market in order to prevent the existence of economies of scale from leading to a firm size larger than that which the community prefers.

These two examples illustrate two additional points that emerge from the approach studied in this essay. The first refers to a situation—such as the labor market/unemployment example—in which a market mechanism cannot work, that is, cannot solve a given problem, because of some practice or convention that the community accepts. So then the labor market must be supplemented or modified in some way or other in order to (try to) achieve full employment. In such a situation as this, it is inappropriate to say that wage earners are "not rational" because they do not bid down wages in order to capture what appear to be rents. The community gives weight to a social arrangement that forbids bidding down wages in the face of unemployment, therefore other, or additional, means must be relied on to achieve the employment objective.[7] This argument enters in a significant way in the analysis of search in later chapters.

---

6. The first edition of Schumpeter (1934) published in German in 1911 contained a chapter 7 which was omitted from all later editions. Yuichi Shionoya (1990) discusses the content of this chapter. He quotes from the chapter as follows:

> It follows from our entire thought that *a dynamic equilibrium does not exist*. Development in its ultimate nature consists of the disturbances of an existing static equilibrium and does not have a tendency to return to a previous or any other equilibrium. Development alters the data of a static economy . . . Development and equilibrium are opposite phenomena excluding each other. Not that a static economy is characterized by a static equilibrium and dynamic economy by a dynamic equilibrium; on the contrary, equilibrium exists only in a static economy. *Economic equilibrium is essentially a static equilibrium*. (lst German ed. 489; italics added)

7. Lance Taylor (1991) discusses a similar argument in the context of macroeconomic issues. He asks on page 30, "How can the macroeconomic system adjust to satisfy a number of plausible restrictions that might be imposed upon it, such as an investment function independent of saving, an exogenously fixed level of employment or capacity utilization or a pre-determined

In the increasing returns case, a market outcome is assumed to be rejected by the community for legitimate reasons. Here, too, the government must act if preferences of the community are to be respected.

These examples illustrate how the market outcome is often unacceptable to a community when the analysis is extended beyond the conventional limits, that is, when it is appreciated that social and institutional arrangements are also sources of well-being. Both examples illustrate how reliance on the market, in one case even where it works "perfectly," will not yield the desired situation. A "perfect" market is not perfect from all standpoints.

All these considerations point up the crucial burden that falls on the capacity of the individual and society to make choices. The preceding arguments, in effect, increase the range of choices and the list of constraints beyond those usually recognized by economists. The notion of efficiency therefore becomes fuzzy. Indeed, it is often the case that constraints become known only as activities are undertaken, not before. The notion that economic activity can be described as a constrained maximization problem is therefore inappropriate. There are many examples to illustrate this notion: publicly owned firms that hire more people than are "needed"; subsidies or tariffs for agriculture to achieve food security; policies to accommodate ethnic diversity; paying off army generals to maintain social stability; activities that recognize social, cultural, and religious commitments; nationalistic feelings toward foreign investment, foreign advisors, foreign products; and many more. All of these considerations can affect well-being as much as or more than the level of GDP can, and they make clear that the notions of efficiency that are common in the textbooks must be greatly expanded. They are also issues on which it is obviously inappropriate to assume that "preferences" are given and known, so that the economist's role is to trace out the consequences of their existence in the presence of limited resources. Rather, they are issues about which the community must learn as they arise.[8]

Such matters are emphasized because they matter so greatly in an economy undergoing, or seeking to undergo, rapid and far-reaching changes. In particular, the link between ethical issues—issues of justice, issues of meaning, issues related to the question "How should one live?"—and the production of goods and services is relevant to the study of development economics, as this study was defined in the first paragraph of this chapter. This is so because virtually all societies, no matter how poor in terms of goods and services, have existing ideas and beliefs that constitute fundamental sources of meaning. Where such ideas and beliefs are undermined or even threatened, well-being is also threatened.

---

wage rate." Taylor refers to this issue as the "closure" question and his book studies numerous models in which this issue is crucial.

8. Charles E. Lindblom (1990) has some extremely enlightening things to say on this issue.

The discussions in these last several pages lead to a fundamental conclusion, one that will permeate the argument in the following chapters at every turn. It may be stated thusly: That which motivates development is the recognition on the part of the population at large that search for enhanced well-being is both feasible and can indeed be accomplished. Households can be a source of development by explicitly recognizing that their well-being can be enhanced. Life can be better, not just in terms of more things being available, but in terms of greater understanding, greater involvement in increasingly subtle and challenging ideas.[9] It has been noted by many people that human beings are the only category of living creatures who can distinguish between what is and what ought to be or can be. The exploitation of this uniquely human trait is an essential part of the development object, the enhancement of well-being. The population therefore becomes willing to accept the responsibility of searching to realize this greater well-being. Another side of this argument is that the greatest cost of severe poverty is that wants must necessarily be so very primitive. I emphasize the distinction between this motivation and that of simply wanting to imitate the North—to have what the North has. The essential difference between the two motivations is that the latter one will not work, while the former will.

These ideas are becoming increasingly commonplace in the literature in a variety of contexts. Amaryta Sen, for example, has reminded us recently (1987a) that economics was long looked upon as part of moral philosophy. Adam Smith was, of course, professor of moral philosophy, and until recently economics at Cambridge University was a part of the "Moral Philosophy Tripos." Sen reminds us further that Aristotle emphasized that while economics was concerned with the pursuit of wealth, it was, at a deeper level, linked up with the assessment and enhancement of more basic goals. Clearly, in Aristotle, the more basic goals take precedence over accumulating wealth; and therefore, to seek, as economists often do, to study economics with no reference to the more basic goals is to misunderstand the nature of the way society is organized and works.

This position of Adam Smith is especially relevant given the frequency of reference to his statement about the invisible hand and the fact that bakers and other producers do not pursue their tasks because of affection for their fellow humans. There are many instances in *The Wealth of Nations* when Smith emphasizes that the functioning of the market in the way that would yield the results sought depended on the virtue and justness of economic actors. Jerry Evensky (1993) notes that after the publication of *The Wealth of Nations*, Smith turned his attention back to *The Theory of Moral Sentiments*

---

9. This point is made, among other places, in Bury (1932, passim) and in Charles Beard's introduction to this edition of Bury's fine work.

and made significant changes in the earlier edition. In these revisions, Evensky says (202) that Smith pushed hard for all citizens to put the well-being of their society ahead of personal or factional interests. Werhave (1991) documents this argument of Smith in full detail. Smith, as did Mill and Marshall (in the early books of his *Principles*), Schumpeter, and, in my view, Keynes, recognized the dangers that the conditions that allowed the market to thrive and expand could also have adverse consequences on the very cultural and social arrangements that were necessary for it to function effectively, that is, contribute to national well-being.

Albert Hirschman argues in a similar way. In his essay "Morality and the Social Sciences," he argues that it is not fruitful simply to add issues of morality onto our hard economic analysis. Economists must, he insists, incorporate into their arguments all such basic traits as "the desire for power and for sacrifice, the fear of boredom, pleasure in both commitment and unpredictability, the search for meaning and community, and so on" (1981, 303). Two pages further on Hirschman elaborates: "Morality is not something like pollution abatement that can be secured by slightly modifying the design of a policy proposal. Rather, it belongs into the center of our work: and it can get there only if the social scientists are morally alive and make themselves vulnerable to moral concerns then they will produce morally significant works, consciously or otherwise."

The strong link between economics, viewed as simply the production and distribution of goods and services, and general ideas of ethics and social organization is illustrated in arguments in Kenneth Arrow (1974). There Arrow considers the trust and confidence that prevail in a society to be an externality of the usual sort. Trust and confidence and understanding of the appropriate rules of conduct can add efficiency to certain kinds of production processes. Resources are in effect freed from enforcing many laws and rules by virtue of the strength of the commitment to the prevailing morality of the society. Where they prevail over wide segments of the community in specific forms, supervision costs are less, shirking is less likely, free riding is minimal, litigation infrequent, prisoner dilemma problems solved effectively, and so on. Trust and confidence are produced, just as meat and potatoes are produced. They are produced, but produced independently of the market, or outside of the market. They are produced by experience, by history, by community living and community acceptance of rules of conduct and procedures.

These nonmarket demands are expressed and enforced in many different ways, including social and personal conscience. They then affect how the market performs at the same time that they are sources of well-being. And they affect preferences. They constitute agreements, often implicit, among members of the community, and as such are very difficult to change, even when it is recognized by almost everyone that such arrangements have outlived the role that they evolved to perform. That this is the case arises from the apparent fact, noted by Arrow (1974) and others, that social arrangements, socially arrived at routines are much more difficult to modify than are individual decisions. In addition, such changes are difficult to effect in specific ways. Amitai Etzioni (1988, 68) notes that "the more individuals act under the influence of moral commitments, the more they are expected to persevere (when circumstances change)." Learning might therefore appear slow and adaptation resisted. This is a different argument from the more common one that some groups are simply bound by tradition and cannot or refuse to change. Even where new formal institutions are established, they often do not work well because they have yet to find their place in the general social system.

There are of course many other observers who make similar arguments.[10] The point here is to note that the widening and deepening of the economic perspective beyond that reflected in the usual formulations of maximization subject to given preferences, technology, and so forth, is common in early and recent literature.

All Countries Should Have Equal Labor Productivity: An Argument

There is a set of assumptions widely employed in economics that lead to the conclusion that it is impossible for labor productivity or GDP per capita to be different in different countries. It is useful to review these assumptions briefly at this point as to do so will help illuminate the approach that I am trying to establish.

The argument begins with the assumption that technical and organizational knowledge is a public good, frequently free, but always available. Technology is the same in all countries as the Hecksher/Ohlin theory of international trade explicitly posits. Then the isoquant maps in all countries are the same. Financial capital moves rapidly and without impediment to all areas of the world in search of the highest rates of return. The prices of tradable products are the same in all countries in all parts of the world. There is free trade in all commodities. The composition of demand is similar in all countries. With these assumptions wage rates and rates of return on capital will be equal in all countries.

That these assumptions will produce equal labor productivity is virtually self-evident and needs little elaboration. Suppose a two-economy world with trade, but no capital movements between them at the outset. One country has a labor plentiful and high capital-cost economy, and the other a high wage,

---

10. Robert D. Putnam (1993, 167 ff) and J. S. Coleman (1990, 302 ff) are especially pertinent to the argument in the text.

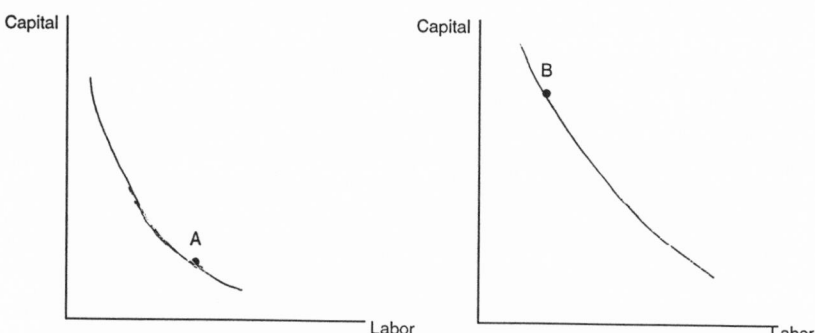

Fig. 1. Why labor productivity could be the same in all countries

low capital-cost economy. Competition prevails in both economies. Producers in both countries have the same set of isoquants, and all isoquants have unitary elasticity of substitution.

Therefore the typical firm in the labor plentiful economy will operate at point A on the figure, and the firm in the capital rich economy at B.

At A, the rate or return (i) on K ($r = rK/K$) is higher than it is at B. This can be seen from the identity

$$r = P/K = P/VA \cdot VA/K$$

where P identifies profits. On the isoquant, value added (VA) is the same at all points as are the factor shares, consequent to the assumption of an elasticity of substitution equal to unity at all combinations of capital and labor. Therefore rK/VA is the same at both A and B. The output-capital ratio (VA/K) is however much higher at A than it is at B, therefore the rate of return on capital is much higher by virtue of the identity.

Suppose now that international capital movements suddenly begin to occur. New investment will all take place in Country A until the rates of return are the same in both countries, at which point wage rates must also be equal. So labor productivity in the two countries must be equal, and, unless the labor force/population ratio differs, so too will per capita GDP.[11]

The assumptions that produce this result are, as noted, frequently found in the literature. Even with a production function in which the elasticity of substitution is not unity at all points and the previous argument does not hold exactly, comparable results are obtained. This way of looking at the two basic questions of development economics suggests why it is so appealing to argue that the reason the economies of some countries now contribute so little to the

---

11. In his chapter in Chenery and Srinivasan (1988), Joseph Stiglitz shows that the difference in rates of return between the two types of countries can be enormous.

well-being of their people is due simply to their following the "wrong" policies. With "right" policies, the above process would begin to be effective and all countries would soon be equally rich or equally poor.

There are two additional generalizations that are especially relevant to our story. In many of the countries presently classified as less developed there have been significant technological developments in earlier periods. In some sense one may say that Britain and Western Europe were latecomers as of the twelfth century. Arnold Pacey (1990, 44) writes that as of 1150 A.D. Europe was the equal of the Islamic and Chinese civilizations in terms of nonhuman energy sources that were used, but "in terms of the sophistication of individual machines, however, notably for textile processing, and in terms of the broad scope of its technology, Europe was still a backward region, which stood to benefit much from its contacts with Islam."

Not only were there textile machines of considerable sophistication and ingenuity, there were also gunpowder, guns, and cannon; printing, irrigation, and other water control works; clocks; ships; and doubtless many other instruments designed to make resources more productive available in the earliest centuries. Such technologies were found in many societies in many parts of the world, especially after about 900 A.D. or so. This generalization is relevant to our analysis because it drives home the importance of the notion of an economic system whose *routine* functioning results in the productivity of resources of an economy increasing in such a way that well-being is constantly enhanced. Although these technological developments were impressive and demonstrated great insight and imagination, they did not produce any sort of indigenous, economy-wide dynamic that led to continuous movement and productivity growth.

The second generalization is even less precise. It does not seem that much of the growth that has taken place, especially in recent decades, has brought the kind of satisfaction that is often attributed to growth of output. There is continuing political and social instability, many varieties of conflict, disappointments that lead to wars and strife of all kinds. The main reasons for this will be explored later. The point here is to call attention to the evidence that growth and change are likely to produce various forms of unrest and instability, which can often defeat the contributions to well-being that greater output could make possible. This argument suggests that the form and content of growth might have some bearing on the extent to which it creates dissension and instability. The argument also has important implications for the role of the government and for the kind of governance that contributes to the growth of well-being. Growth creates, but growth also destroys. The search for well-being requires that this dual role be recognized and taken into account.

So we have then a convincing theory on the one hand that leads us to expect all countries to have about the same level of labor productivity and GDP per capita, and on the other hand we have a body of empirical evidence that appears to be inconsistent with this theory. One could simply say that the theory is wrong, but one must seek more than this. The task is to try to pin down firmly what it is that makes the less developed countries different—if they really are.

Why All Countries Do Not Have Equal Labor Productivity: An Argument

There are two main strands of the argument explaining why all countries did not begin to grow in the early part of the nineteenth century. These strands are related, but it is helpful to treat them separately. I summarize them briefly here and build them up at numerous places in later pages.

1. The first refers to human motivation. The notion is this: The main motivation of individuals through most of history has been the achievement of a social system that was harmonious and stable and that served both the material and nonmaterial needs of all members of the society. Such a notion is quite alien to that of the maximization of individual welfare with little or no reference to nonmaterial needs of the community or to social harmony and stability that evolved with classical economics. The terms *organic* and *mechanical* are often used to distinguish between these two notions.

This argument may be found in many places. Perhaps the most unambiguous statement is Karl Polanyi's *The Great Transformation* (1944). Frederick Hayek argues that people had to learn to be selfish and to overcome their innate instincts toward communal sharing before the advantages of the division of labor, entrepreneurial activity, and so on could be realized. The differences between a society held together by a sense of community and common history and one unified by a market is often noted, especially by noneconomists. Adam Smith had numerous observations that reflected his view that human behavior was heavily influenced by many things in addition to the search for economic gain.

The relevance of this point to the present argument is simply that this transformation has not taken place in many less developed countries and certainly had not at the beginnings of per capita growth in the West. This learning to be selfish—to be dominated by maximizing behavior within a narrow range of specific constraints—has not yet taken hold in many of the developing countries of the world.

The following quote from Polanyi makes the point especially clear:

A self-regulating market demands nothing less than the institutional separation of society into an economic and political sphere. Such a dichotomy is, in effect, merely the restatement, from the point of view of society as a whole, of the existence of a self-regulating market. It might be argued that the separateness of the two spheres obtains in every type of society at all times. Such an inference however would be based on a fallacy. True, no society can exist without a system of some kind which ensures order in the production and distribution of goods. But that does not imply the existence of separate economic institutions; normally the economic order is merely a function of the social, in which it is contained. Neither under tribal, nor feudal, nor mercantile conditions was there, as we have shown, a separate economic system in society. Nineteenth century society, in which economic activity was isolated and imputed to a distinctive economic motive, was indeed a singular departure. (Polanyi 1944, 71)

This departure was something that the West learned early on, and other parts of the world, for the most part, did not—and many have not yet. Now Hayek's point comes to bear: if selfishness or determined pursuit of utility and profit by individuals is necessary to achieve freedom and economic rationality and economic progress, then we have a deep-seated reason for why some countries have lagged and still lag.[12]

There is another aspect of this argument that is relevant. In the organic society of Western Europe social relationships were hierarchical in all areas of the society, and the major sources of privilege were land ownership, the church, or government. Economic life was narrowly circumscribed by the guilds, by firmly entrenched customs and routines, and by many kinds of regulations. All these arrangements were quite inimical to growth of output and to the exercise of entrepreneurial activity, but they solved many other problems and offered a stability that had many advantages.[13] The economic arrangements in most of the presently less developed world were similar except that most of the economic activity was of course agricultural and the levels of output much lower.

Now the question is why and how did the Europeans learn to be selfish (in this way), but the rest of the world did not. The second point bears on this question.

2. Note has already been taken of the evidence that China was surely richer than Western Europe in the years around 1100, and by 1500 or so Britain and probably most of Western Europe had passed China in terms of

---

12. This argument is similar in some ways to that of Marx. Thus Marx believed that capitalism was necessary for a country to become economically rich. It was only after a country became rich that the inconsistencies of capitalism began to be strong enough to bring about its demise.

13. Jonathan Hughes (1970) has a good brief discussion of these points.

GDP per capita, the sophistication of technology and economic organizations, and interest in growth of production. Thus something happened in Britain and Europe that did not happen in China over these centuries. The Enlightenment, Renaissance, and Reformation were the most obvious such "things." These great events convinced the population, or a large segment of it, that it was possible to affect the way people lived and that the human race was not simply at the mercy of the natural elements. More specifically, perhaps, people began to understand that economic activity was not a zero sum game.

It was in this long period that the idea that growth of output was possible became established in the West. Then searching and learning became activities that made sense. It became appreciated that situations and characteristics that seemed to constitute bottlenecks to growth of output and other sources of well-being might well be removed or gotten around through specific efforts.[14] This idea of growth not only induced the search-and-learn process that produced more growth, but also the idea that stability and an overly strong communal sense could be inflicting a great cost on the society.

This idea of growth did not travel well to other parts of the world for a great many reasons, the most obvious of which is that there had been no Enlightenment and no Renaissance and no Reformation in other parts of the world. There had been no long centuries of changing attitudes and ways of thinking that, in the West, resulted in this new economic and social environment. And the strongly held ideas of an organic system committed to social harmony and acceptable sharing of meager output remained in place. The basic resource is knowledge and the basic source of the growth of well-being is the growth of knowledge. From this "axiom" it follows that the failure of the idea of searching and learning to travel from the West to the other parts of the world (or to arise indigenously) is indeed a fundamental factor in accounting for the failure of the latter countries to have begun to grow along with the West 150 years ago.

While there were many important changes taking place prior to World War II, it was not until after that war that the low-income countries began to recognize that their economic plight could be changed by explicit effort. The basic approach to overcome their mass poverty however was simply to seek to imitate the West. This, I shall argue, is neither possible nor desirable. They too must create the great desire for knowledge that induces the searching and learning that is the origin of knowledge. There are two reasons why simply wanting a higher income in order to consume more and relying on foreign technology and foreign firms is not enough. In the first place, technical and

---

14. Albert Hirschman (1958) has an argument similar to the one summarized here in that he places great emphasis on social learning, on learning by doing, and on the importance of on-site investigations. He does not link any of his arguments to the early history of Western Europe.

administrative knowledge cannot be completely transferred from one country to another, from one firm to another, because of the importance of tacit knowledge in the functioning of any successful enterprise.[15] In the second place, the search-and-learn mentality must pervade the entire community. It cannot be limited to a handful of people or firms. It is a social, an organic, notion.

The objective of development policy is to seek to put in place an economic and social environment in which the idea of growth becomes accepted and the searching and learning process that it entails is indigenous. This process was accomplished in the West over a period of centuries, but must be accomplished in the presently developing countries in a much briefer interval. The present essay is concerned essentially with how to do this.[16]

These arguments represent the deeper explanations for most countries to fail to grow along with the West. As already noted, the idea, commonly offered, that development is simply a matter of getting the policies "right" is not adequate—even for the post-1950 period.

On the Definition of Economics

I began by asserting that economics is the study of the relationship between the production, distribution, and consumption of goods and services and individual and social well-being. The conventional definition is that first stated by Lionel Robbins (1935, 16): "Economics is the science which studies human behavior as a relationship between ends and scarce means which have alternative uses." This definition has of course found its way into countless texts and treatises over the years since Robbins's book appeared. Such a definition has advantages in some contexts, but it has resulted in directing attention away from the basic question, namely why economics is of interest to us. Economic activity is of interest because, as noted, it is or can be a significant source of well-being. So an explicit recognition of this link is necessary in order to keep the focus of the analysis sharp and clear, and on the fundamental issue. As already emphasized, the idea that economics should be concerned with the contribution of production and distribution to well-being was surely the basis of its interest to Smith and to most economists of the

---

15. The basic notion of the dual-economy models of Arthur Lewis (1954) and Fei and Ranis (1964) illustrate this point. "Tacit" knowledge refers to that knowledge that a firm accumulates and applies through on-the-job learning. It generally cannot be incorporated into blueprints or formulas, or even articulated. In many cases individuals employing such knowledge are not aware that they are. It plays a major role in the discussions to follow.

16. Those non-Western countries that have succeeded—Japan and the Republic of Korea, and the Province of Taiwan—are, of course, of particular interest and I will argue later that they illustrate the arguments of the text quite well.

nineteenth and early twentieth centuries.[17] That Alfred Marshall viewed economics and ethics (and history) as closely interwined is clear enough if one reads all of *Principles,* not just Book V. (See Shove 1942 and Foster 1993.) Foster (981) writes that Marshall "assumed that any competent economist would have a good understanding of the economic and social history of any period under consideration." A similar notion pervades much of Keynes's writings. Increasingly, one finds, even among economic theorists, recognition that the conventionally made sharp distinction between "positive" and "normative" is open to grave doubt. (See, for example, the fine discussion in Davis 1994.)

The notion that economic activity could be fruitfully considered as constrained maximization exercises seems to have originated with the marginal analysis. Marginal utility was introduced in the late nineteenth century when the economics of Smith through Mill was modified to include demand. The argument was first carried out in the context of a pure exchange (no production) economy in which all households had unambiguously given and known preferences. "Efficiency" had, in such a context, a fairly clear meaning. When the marginal analysis was applied to production, difficulties appeared as the assumptions necessary to make it work—"perfect knowledge," profit maximization, and so on—were obviously extremely strong. Also, the very purpose of production was to change the general environment, not hold it constant. Still the neatness and ease of manipulating led to the continued and expanded use even though many economists recognized that the illuminating power of such an approach was sorely limited. As one probes deeper and tries to think in very long terms, then it becomes even clearer that the idea of economic activity seen as a constrained maximization problem is inadequate.[18] The "givens" disappear, including, particularly, given preferences.

---

17. The determination to stick to the Robbins definition has, I think, robbed economists of the opportunity to push into richer and more fundamental areas of inquiry. George Shackle (1988, 126) writes as follows: "The concern of economics with practical matters has led it to neglect or repudiate a need to envisage the ultimate enigmas, the question of determinism or creative freedom, and that of existence, or not, of a world outside the individual mind."

Charles E. Lindblom (1988, 265) makes an even more severe criticism: " . . . while in the twentieth century the brightest, best educated, and most thoughtful minds are finding new discoveries about the natural world, man, and society in physics, biochemistry, biology, anthropology, psychology, sociology, and political science, there has emerged from economics almost nothing to engage these minds. Who reads economics for a new view of the world?"

I suggest that one important explanation for Lindblom's lament is our determination to stick to the Robbins definition.

18. Two of the most powerful and influential statements of economics as a constrained maximization exercise are Samuelson (1947) and Koopmans (1957). Samuelson's book may be considered as the first full statement of economics as a constrained maximization problem, and he restated it in his Nobel Memorial Lecture. For a short, clear review of the evolution of the notion and its limitations see Pasinetti (1981, Introduction); for a more complete discussion, Nelson and Winter (1982, part III) and Boland (1992, passim).

The Rest of the Book

The next chapter studies the many aspects of well-being and seeks to give it some precise content. It also shows how and why social choice is such a fundamental and difficult notion. Chapter 3 summarizes briefly prevailing theories of the growth of output and some stylized facts and ideas of growth. Chapter 4 introduces a different way to think about growth, a way that takes into account its contribution to well-being and that emphasizes searching and learning in the presence of ignorance. Chapter 5 examines the demand for labor and how work itself can contribute to well-being. In Chapter 6 entrepreneurship, a notion of great relevance in an economy where ignorance is omnipresent, is discussed. All of this discussion will emphasize that too much "openness" to international transactions can damage efforts to enhance well-being, and therefore some form of general protection is in order. Chapter 7 is about international transactions in general and in chapter 8 a form of protection is suggested and defended. Finally, in the last chapter, I discuss the role of government and the making of policy, and again confront the social choice issue.

CHAPTER 2

The Search for Well-Being

Growth economics is the study of the relationship between increasing GDP per capita and enhancing well-being, and development economics studies why some countries have been able to achieve economic growth over the past 150 years and others have not. Therefore we must know what we mean by well-being. I struggle with this concept in this chapter.

Well-Being: Its Definition and Content

Well-being is many-sided and complex, and like all such notions cannot be defined in a final and definitive way. It can however, be discussed, its contents probed, and its measurement contemplated. We study human beings and human life in order to learn what it means to live well, to flourish, to grow. From such study, one may be allowed to believe, an understanding and feel for the concept of well-being can evolve in a way that makes it relevant to the understanding of how well an economy functions, how the economic actors respond to various opportunities and dangers, and, so, how policies can be designed that contribute to the achievement of the objective. In broad terms well-being refers to a well-lived life, a life rich in meaning and personal growth, a life that reflects the fact of one's humanness and one's membership in a community, and, finally, a life built from some sort of conscious thought and reflection as to its content and purpose. The term *well-being* is chosen rather than the more familiar utility or welfare in order to suggest a more searching notion, a notion that seeks to build from a more general idea of the motivations that act, and that should act, on most of the people in most communities.[1]

---

1. The term *well-being* seems increasingly widely used, especially among philosophers but also among economists. See James Griffin (1986), Partha Dasgupta (1990), and Bernard Williams (1985). One also finds the term *meaning* used in contexts where utility or welfare or happiness has been used. Williams (1985, 34) uses the term as he believes Aristotle used *eudaimonia*. This latter term, usually translated as happiness, more accurately refers to "the shape of one's whole life." Griffin (1986, 322) makes a similar point as do other authors. Donald Gifford (1990, 138/9) states that when Thomas Jefferson (in the Declaration of Independence of the United States) asserted that the "pursuit of happiness" is an inalienable right, he (Jefferson)

I review quickly some prevailing criteria of the notion and then try to develop a more comprehensive argument that, I believe, is especially illuminating in the development context.

The Development Objective

Development economics came into being in the late 1940s as a consequence of emerging awareness in Western Europe and northern North America (the North) that a large part of the population in many countries lived in severe poverty. Per capita availabilities of goods and services were well below those prevailing in the North, and, indeed, were so low that malnutrition, inadequate shelter, high death rates, and so on were the common lot of a majority of the population in these countries. Given this origin, it is not surprising that the objective of development was defined simply in terms of increasing GDP per capita at this time. This measure continues far and away as the most common criterion of development. High rates of growth of GDP per capita represent success, and low rates represent failure.

By the 1960s evidence had become available that rates of growth of GDP per capita that seemed acceptable in general were not providing employment opportunities for all members of the labor force. In part because of the failure to resolve the employment problem, but for other reasons as well, the acceptable rates of growth of GDP per capita seemed also to make little contribution to the relief of the widespread poverty. In light of this evidence, employment growth and poverty alleviation came to be generally included as objectives of development on a par with the growth of per capita income.[2] The original idea was that a sufficiently high rate of growth of output would solve the poverty and employment problem. When it became evident that this was not always happening, the argument became that the growth process itself had to be modified in such a manner as to recognize that these objectives were as fundamental as increasing output per capita.

The poverty alleviation objective was sometimes defined in terms of the provision of "basic needs" for everyone in the society.[3] Basic needs, poverty relief, and employment all proved difficult to define in a manner that eliminated ambiguity or that led clearly to specific policies. It was clear at once that any definition of basic needs or poverty must recognize the social and histori-

---

was using happiness as a (lame) translation of *eudaimonia*. Martha Nussbaum (1986) has a thorough discussion of the notion that *eudaimonia* is meant to convey.

2. In many discussions inequality of the distribution of income was emphasized rather than poverty alleviation. I think that, in general, poverty alleviation is now the more commonly cited objective.

3. Paul Streeten was the among the earliest to give attention to the basic needs notion, and, with a number of colleagues, has written on the subject with considerable illumination. See Streeten et al. (1981).

cal context in which they were being considered. Similarly, it was not very clear what level of anything, even food and shelter, could be deemed "basic." A range of questions also arises with respect to any definition of poverty and its alleviation. Drawing a poverty line at some level of income and defining everyone with an income below that line as living in poverty hid a number of issues—the distribution of income within the poverty group, possibilities of family or community support, availability to the poor of public supplies, social mores as to consumption standards, and so on.[4]

Employment also became increasingly ambiguous as a concept and as a guide to policy. The widespread underemployment (especially among the self-employed), the various roles played by women in many countries, the waiting to get a particularly attractive job, the educated unemployed problem, the idea that unemployment is a luxury good that the very poor cannot "afford," and the fact that some economists deny that there is any such thing as involuntary unemployment make it dangerous to think in the customary terms of everyone in a society being employed, unemployed, or outside the labor force. Amartya Sen (1975) added complexity by emphasizing that employment is not only a source of production and income, but also a necessary condition for self-respect and acceptance by the community in almost all societies. Thus it was (and is) far from clear what "full" employment means in a developing country. At the same time most observers agree that there do exist, in the developing countries, major employment problems that raise many issues for understanding how these economies work and for policy.

Amartya Sen has sought to advance our understanding of the development objective by defining the standard of living in terms of functioning and capabilities (1987). Sen defines a functioning as an achievement and a capability as the ability to achieve. Functionings, he adds, "are more directly related to living conditions, since they are different aspects of living conditions. Capabilities, in contrast, are notions of freedom in the positive sense: what real opportunities you have regarding the life you may lead" (1987, 36). Sen seeks, therefore, to establish a base that is not dependent on particular goods and services and is more fundamental than happiness (as conventionally defined) or desire fulfillment. The idea of functioning and capability is intended to bring into the argument more directly the notion of rights and freedoms—members of the society should have the right and the capacity to participate fully and equally in the life of the community. That functioning and capability depend on context seems clear. Sen refers to Adam Smith's example of the man who cannot appear in public without shame unless he has

---

4. A number of studies indicate the poverty income line in the North is set at about one-half the median income of the country, irrespective of the level of the median. See Abramovitz (1989) and Fuchs (1967).

on a linen shirt. Evidently, a linen shirt is not required in an African society of ancient origin where everyone has for centuries worn no or very few clothes. These considerations are similar to basic needs, but offer a more subtle and more fundamental definition of what an economy should be able to provide and what society should seek to ensure is provided to all its members. Also like basic needs, it is a notion that is inherently ambiguous, the full, explicit content of which in a given situation must be worked out by the members of the society. The ambiguities include what capabilities are to be included as required if a person is not to be considered deprived, a more precise statement of exactly what is meant by capability, for example, where do costs enter, and what kind of policy instrument is called for if criteria are to be given practical relevance.[5] The idea is similar to basic needs in another way: they are both partial standards. The question remains, what is the objective after the Sen objectives are met, after the basic needs objectives are met?

In an effort to take these matters into account a number of people have given specific content to the quality of life or well-being by identifying several intuitively appealing characteristics that all members of a society should have and then ascertaining the extent to which they are available in particular societies. Thus life expectancy at birth, infant and child mortality, literacy, and available calories are often used as a measure of the quality of life, and the purpose of development is to enable these variables to reach acceptable levels.[6] All of these characteristics are achieved by allocating investable resources in such a manner as to bring them about. When one uses them as criteria of quality of life or of well-being, one is saying that he/she approves of the allocation of resources and the distribution of output that meets these objectives. There is rarely a discussion in this literature of the extent to which such allocations reflect the genuine choices of the people involved. The assumption, usually tacit, is that these are universally desired objectives that require no explicit justification. Where such an allocation is not achieved, despite rapidly growing incomes, the assumption usually is that the government has acted in an unfortunate manner or that income distribution is at fault. Rarely does anyone mention preferences.

Presumably the assumption is that these objectives would be the same as those that would be chosen by a community where per capita income is rising and its distribution is "right." Then, as incomes rise, people would acquire what is best for themselves, and this would be those things that provided a long life, reduced infant and child mortality, and so on. If this assumption—if

---

5. Bernard Williams raises these and other questions in his contribution in Sen (1987). See also Sen's response to Williams in the same volume.

6. There are many possible references for this approach. See for example Morris (1979), Sen (1981a, 1984), United Nations Development Programme (1991), and Adelman and Morris (1973). Few of these efforts include any role for employment as such.

distribution is "right" as income grows, then people would, in fact, choose to produce and consume these goods and services—is not correct, then those who measure well-being in this way are imposing their criteria rather than those of the community whose incomes are rising. There is no very good argument to support doing this. Thus the choice-making role in the society is fundamental to achieving the development objectives.

The Search for Better Preferences

The Lionel Robbins definition of economics has preferences as given and unchanging and most textbooks repeat this assumption. Earlier economists— Smith, Mill, Marx, Marshall, and Pigou in particular—gave considerable attention to the quality of wants and their origins.[7] The assumption that wants are constant and exogenous (to economic arguments) is of course appropriate in a variety of contexts. When the questions asked of our analyses lead directly to well-being and its growth, then, it is argued, the quality of wants becomes a crucial variable. In more recent decades an increasing number of economists and economists/philosophers have argued that the notion of "better wants" is a viable and fruitful one, and one that lends itself to study with traditional economic tools. (See Knight 1935 and 1956, McPherson 1983, Scitovsky 1986, Taylor 1985 and 1989, Rawls 1971, Sen 1987 and 1987a, and especially Stewart 1995.) In the following few pages, I try to give a brief picture of what is involved in "better wants," how they matter for the achievement of increasing well-being, and so are an essential part of economic development. What then are *better* wants?

The major fundamental source of well-being is the exercise of one's natural and acquired capacities. Such capacities have only a very ambiguous limit, and we can say that they are rarely, if ever, fully realized or their limits even identifiable. Therefore members of the society must continuously press for fuller and fuller realization of their capacities in a never ending effort. As noted earlier, one of the greatest costs to those who live in severe poverty (and have deadly jobs) is that their wants are necessarily so primitive and their opportunities to choose better wants so limited.

This notion is essentially the same as that which John Rawls (1971) designates as the Aristotelian Principle. This principle Rawls defines as the assumption that "other things being equal, human beings enjoy the exercise of their realized capacities (their innate or trained abilities), and this enjoyment increases the more the capacity is realized, or the greater its complexity" (426). He goes on to say that human beings take more pleasure in doing something as they become proficient at it, and of two activities they do equally

---

7. See, for example, the relevant chapters in Blaug (1985).

well, they prefer the one calling on a larger repertoire of more intricate and subtle discriminations. Rawls illustrates his argument by noting that chess is more intricate and complex than checkers and algebra more intricate than elementary arithmetic, so that when one can do both, one opts for chess in one case and algebra in the other.

In the footnote elaboration (426) Rawls makes clear that he (and Aristotle) do not mean by enjoyment, simply fun and pleasure as usually conceived. Rather, the assumption that people choose more demanding tasks and activities rests on the argument that such is natural, is part of being human and part of being alive, and therefore is good. This in turn means, I think, that Aristotle and Rawls attach value to stretching the mind and spirit, and this is quite different from the usual notion of simple enjoyment and pleasure. It means that individuals should have the opportunity to grow in the sense that they become able to undertake increasingly demanding and subtle tasks and activities and reflections. Since any final limit on such capacity is either nonexistent or ill-defined, the growth process goes on indefinitely. This is what growth is for the individual; this is what it means to realize the characteristic of the humanness noted above.

The view of well-being built around the Aristotelian Principle has considerable history. It is clear that John Stuart Mill had something like this in mind when he wrote of "utility in the larger sense" in *On Liberty* and in much of his discussion in *Utilitarianism*. Jonathan Riley (1988) cites many places in which Mill emphasizes that any "autonomous person acquires aesthetic feelings and moral feeling" and has an interest in self-improvement (Riley 1988, 193). Self-development and social harmony, Mill implies, are not means to happiness but are themselves ends. Riley's chapter 9 is especially helpful in making clear what Mill had in mind by his utilitarianism and the role that liberty plays in its realization.

Frederick Hayek in his *Constitution of Liberty* argues that "progress is movement for movement's sake, for it is in the process of learning, and in the effects of having learned something new, that man enjoys the gift of his intelligence." (Hayek 1960, 32). Similar observations can be found in many of the Greeks, in St. Augustine, and modern authors such as Dasgupta (1990). So the idea of search itself as the basic source of well-being is hardly a new notion. It is, however, quite different from most of the contemporary ideas that form the basis of welfare economics and social welfare functions and the criteria of development.[8] The achievement of the Aristotelian Principle is, at

---

8. There are other references that one could mention. See especially Scitovsky (1986) where the notion of "creative consumption" is introduced. On page 60 in this illuminating book, Scitovsky laments that at the same time that income is rising, "creative consumption, . . . the enjoyment of extending or deepening one's experience and knowledge of the world in any of its

its base, a matter of wants: private wants, that is, our wants as individuals, and social wants, that is, our wants for the kind of society in which we wish to live.

There are two specific aspects that emerge from this notion of the ultimate source of well-being that are especially relevant to a country seeking to change from one whose economy has not been growing to one where growth does occur regularly. The first is employment, or, more generally, the allocation of time. Few societies accept the notion that able-bodied adults should not have some form of employment. The most important single means of achieving personal growth and maturity is through working. Note has already been taken of Sen's emphasis on employment as a source of self-respect and community acceptance, as well as of income. Add to this notion—the notion that employment is itself a source of well-being and its enhancement—the argument that it is a major means to implementing the Aristotelian Principle—and employment becomes a particularly strategic part of the well-being story. The idea of working at a job that has little meaning in order to have leisure that is abused or to buy a product or service that contributes nothing to well-being is surely an odd way to think about work, leisure, and income. As just noted, alongside of employment is leisure. There are many ways that the use of leisure affects, or can affect, well-being. Numerous people have noted that the human race can tolerate almost anything except large amounts of leisure.[9] More relevantly perhaps, the use of leisure in a way that contributes significantly to well-being is something that has to be learned. It does not come automatically as a consequence of being alive. At the same time, it is also widely accepted that leisure does provide an opportunity for the achievement of personal growth, not available by working, or from any other source. It also, of course, allows for the relaxation and rest that everyone finds essential. The employment component is the most direct link with macro issues that the notion of well-being has.

The other aspect of well-being of great importance is implied in the previous discussion: the search process must take place within a particular social environment. The search must not violate social norms, or at least not

---

aspects, from taste sensations to literature and intellectual constructs" is decreasing. Arndt (1987) and Penz (1986) are good surveys with numerous references as is Nisbet (1980). A similar notion is that developed by the psychologist Mihaly Csikszentmihalyi (1989), called *flow*. Flow refers to a state that lies between boredom and anxiety. Flow is not fun or happiness, but does involve commitment and requires the pursuit of a goal in the context of rules or constraints. It does not, as I understand it, produce growth of capacity or understanding.

9. Robert Nisbet (1980, 349–51) notes such an observation by numerous writers: Denis Gabor identifies the great trilemma facing mankind today as nuclear warfare, overpopulation, and leisure. Gabor believes, according to Nisbet, that the last is the most dangerous. C. E. Joad is quoted: "Work is the only occupation yet invented which mankind has been able to endure in any but the smallest doses." There are many other similar observations.

violate more than is tolerated by the norms themselves.[10] For most people social acceptance is itself desirable, it adds to one's feeling of security and communalness. Thus well-being includes being part of a community, and severe violations of the behavioral norms of the society therefore have a negative effect on well-being. It may also be noted that social norms—institutions, values, organizations—help determine perspectives, ways of doing and thinking, ideas of achievement and "utility in the larger sense." In this sense, participating in society is part of well-being, and, at the same time, constitutes a constraint on what is deemed feasible and desirable and understandable.

This too is an argument with ancient roots and numerous contemporary adherents. James D. Wallace (1978, chapter 1) emphasizes that a distinctive feature of human life is that activities are possible that do in fact require elaborate conventions and shared goals. A life informed and constrained by convention, says Wallace, is natural for human beings in the same way that nutrition, perception, and growth are natural. Adam Smith and David Hume expressed similar views. Hume, in particular, argued that much of human morality rests on our social needs, needs for human society as real as the physical needs for food and shelter. Herbert Simon speaks of "rule following behavior," rules established by convention and history, reflected in the institutions and practices of the community. Michael Ignatieff (1985) argues that the awareness of our common necessities enables us to understand and to appreciate each other and to trust each other. Indeed much of our activity arises from our acceptance of the needs of others. Aristotle noted that "individual wholeness" requires friendship. To violate all this, to act as if no such conventions (or institutions or rules) existed is to undermine an important aspect of well-being. It is important to emphasize that to be constrained by rules and conventions and norms does not mean simply passively obeying, but rather means that rules are applied or employed as we approach new issues. The idea is that to adapt a practical and existing skill to a new situation is an unusually effective way of learning and changing.[11]

---

10. The term *social norms* is taken from Elster (1989) who explores it at some length. As argued later, included as a norm is the idea that it can be violated to some degree without setting off an upheaval. Wilber and Jameson (1980) have some useful observations on this point.

11. The point is not that people are (or should be) charitable and thoughtful of others. It is rather that such an attitude is part of one's self. Bernard Williams (1985, 51) argues that "other people's welfare, the requirement of justice, and other things, have value. If we take up the other perspective, however, and look at people's dispositions from the outside, we may ask the question 'what has to exist in the world for that ethical point of view to exist?' The answer can only be 'people's disposition.' There is a sense in which they are the ultimate support of ethical value. That has practical as well as metaphysical significance. The preservation of ethical value lies in the reproduction of ethical dispositions." It seems also correct to say that no one has shown that unqualified self-centeredness is either a source of well-being or a particularly "rational" way to

The ambiguity inherent in all these objectives—maybe "definitions" is better—has been emphasized all along. This inherent ambiguity—"inherent" meaning that the ambiguity can never be eliminated completely—creates the great task of individual and social choice, and imposes on everyone the equally great task of search. Both of these tasks occupy strategic roles in the present approach. In the context of this chapter, I add three points to the previous discussion.

This inherent ambiguity means that there is no final resting place, no final definition which determines the ultimate destination sought nor the path to be followed.[12] This means, as just stated, that there is imposed on the society the necessity of constant reevaluation and continued search. The idea is that at any one moment the economy contributes to well-being in a particular way and by a particular "amount." Then we examine the economic performance in terms of basic needs (including basic capabilities and functionings), in terms of equitable command over resources, in terms of the way the performance of the economy affects our deeper values, and the extent to which it is contributing to this fundamental source of well-being. We may conclude, as a consequence of this examination, for example, that the most urgent task is to reduce poverty, and the question is how to go about doing this. Note that this question can be addressed even though a final definition of poverty alleviation is not available.

We may, on the other hand, decide that the present form and content of economic activity is having effects on our deeper values so adverse and so contrary to our wishes that it is necessary to try to change the way the economy performs—even if it means delaying the poverty alleviation effort. Examples are easily found: multinationals are omnipresent and foreigners are undermining the community's sense of what is right and important. Tourism is increasing, providing jobs that help relieve poverty, but also destroying the "webs of significance" (the term is due to Clifford Geertz) that define the society and the sources of its meaning. More generally, we conclude that our economy is too open to the rest of the world, and that well-being would be enhanced if we reduced that openness. The division of labor may have be-

---

live. Indeed, it is not clear what such a notion means. So far as I can determine, economics is the only discipline that makes such an assumption. It is revealing, perhaps, to note that the modern Japanese word for "economy" is *keizai*. In Tokugawa Japan, the same word was an abbreviation of the term *keikoku saimin* which, roughly translated, means "administering the nation and relieving the suffering of the people" (Morris-Suzuki 1989, 13).

12. W. Arthur Lewis (1955, 80) says that backward societies "can grow simply by modelling themselves on the more dynamic features of the more advanced." This position, widely held among economists and politicians, is one that I am strongly disputing. See Bruton (1985) for explicit elaboration. Albert Hirschman (1958) also has a good discussion, in chapter 1, of why Lewis's argument is not acceptable.

come such that many jobs, despite paying well, are degrading and contribute nothing to well-being, other than the paycheck. The spread of the market, though contributing to increasing efficiency and output, is perceived to be teaching people to be greedy and uncaring toward their neighbors, to be a "pig satisfied, rather than Socrates dissatisfied." To modify the economy to correct these deficiencies may raise the economy's contribution to well-being, even though the level of output of goods and services per person remains constant or even declines. Again, it is emphasized that this can be the case even though any sort of ultimate answer to these issues remains ambiguous. All that is necessary is that the direction of change can be identified in order to guide the search. The search is to continue, and, of course, the task of choosing, both for the individual and the society, is enormously complex.

The provision of basic needs (this is the second point) hardly needs specific justification in general terms. An economy that cannot produce enough to provide the generally recognized minimal levels of food, shelter, and health care and similar capabilities and functionings to all its members is of course not performing acceptably. The immediate objective surely is to reach the point where this is in fact accomplished, not just possible. One can defend this primacy by an appeal to common decency and respect for life, or one can speak of access to basic needs (in the larger sense defined above) as a "positive right" in the sense used by a number of people.[13] It does seem possible in this world now that everyone could have sufficient food. More accurately, perhaps, there is the capacity in the world to produce enough food for everyone to have an adequate amount.[14] Even so, I must add, there may be factors defeating the search for enhanced well-being that take primacy over poverty alleviation and the provision of basic needs at a given time, if this primacy is determined by a legitimate and reflective search and social choice process.

The third point is this: the meeting of food, shelter, and health needs or insuring the absence of severe and continuing poverty may be thought of as an input necessary for achieving employability and, more fundamentally, the status of a thinking, aware individual, capable of reflecting on his/her life's plans and purposes and of pursuing the Aristotelian Principle. (Compare Dasgupta 1990.) Thus certain commodities and services, at this level of life, serve as a physical input into a production process. This production process results in the creation of an individual physically capable of exploiting those attributes and capacities that are uniquely human.

It is tempting to argue, as many have, that at very low levels of per capita

---

13. David Wiggins (1987, chapter 1) has a good discussion. See also Berlin (1969, 1980).

14. Amartya Sen's work on famines is especially convincing on this point. See Sen (1981) and Dreze and Sen (1989).

income, the objective is unambiguous: meet basic needs, and worry about other objectives after per capita GDP is high. The preceding discussion was meant to make clear that such an argument must be qualified. First, the content of basic needs, as extended, is itself not clear, and there must be some sort of hierarchy within this category. The second is that all societies have, at one time or another, recognized that there are deeper values, the protection of which takes precedence even over poverty relief. The third argument—questions about well-being arise at a very low level of per capita income—is more important and requires more attention as we go along. The elimination of a poverty that impedes the exploitation of human attributes may generally be the objective with the highest priority but, the argument is, the question of which human attributes are to be exploited arises almost immediately, and hence must be addressed at very low levels of per capita income. This theme will be developed in various ways in other parts of the present essay.

Learning to choose is therefore of particular importance in currently developing countries where per capita incomes are so much lower than in the North and where, therefore, there have been few opportunities to choose and hence to learn to choose. Ignorance may therefore be more dominating than in the North. The temptation to imitate or to seek to imitate life-styles and consumption patterns of the North is thus strong indeed. To imitate does not result in the emergence of preferences that may be identified as autonomous and indigenous, and that will, if realized, lead to an enhancement of well-being. This point is one of the bases for some form of protection to be discussed in a later chapter.

Social Choice: Its Impossibility and Necessity

It is clear, of course, that the preferences being discussed here include not only those concerned with day to day consumer goods, the apples and potatoes that often appear on the axes of indifference maps in textbooks. Rather the main concern is with matters that determine life-styles and the achievement of those activities that do in fact contribute to well-being. The apples and potatoes problems are part of this, but a minor part. The deeper values that define and govern social norms are also part of the preferences that are of concern to a people seeking to enhance their well-being, and somewhere along the line must be chosen.

Kenneth Arrow (1951, 18 ff) distinguished between *tastes* and *values*. *Tastes* refer to the ordering of the direct consumption of the household, and *values* to those ideas and beliefs that determine tastes and one's views as to the kind of society that contributes most to well-being. Arrow emphasizes that no sharp line can (or should be) drawn between tastes and values as he defines them, and "that we must look at the entire system of values, including values about values, in seeking a general theory of welfare" (Arrow 1951, 18). Amartya Sen (1991) also explores similar issues in more detail and in a different context. Such distinctions help us to appreciate the fundamental and deep-seated role that preferences play, and they drive home the argument that "better" preferences are necessary for sustained increases in well-being.

Social choice is the study of the aggregation of individual judgments and ideas of well-being into some sort of social or national well-being. Within almost any nation different people will hold different views on many of the issues that affect well-being. This is the case even though human beings have much in common with each other. John Gray (1991) describes this state of affairs as a "tension between the idea of a common human nature and the idea of human self-creation and self-transformation." These inevitable conflicts inhere in any society and cannot be removed by any sort of policy based on some claims to identify a once and for all final truth.[15] Nor can the problems created thereby be resolved generally simply by some voting procedure (Arrow 1951). Development—the search for enhanced well-being—necessarily involves loss. As already emphasized, growth creates, but growth also destroys. There is necessarily and permanently a deep and abiding pluralism, and this fact means that society, as well as individuals, must engage in this continuous search for better social well-being, and must do so in the presence of great and widespread ignorance and disagreement.

A current issue that illustrates the complexity of social choice is the role of women in the developing economy. This role varies greatly among societies and rests on deep-seated, long-held ideas and values of both men and women in a given society. From the point of view of many observers, well-being could be greatly enhanced if women had a more substantial role than is now the case in formal economic activity, that is, in the activities that are included in GDP. Other people (not only men) are committed to the view that women contribute a great deal more to their own and society's well-being in their role as full-time mothers and homemakers. To arrive at a position that is increasingly satisfactory will require a great deal of discussion and debate and trial and error. For a country—for example, an African nation or a country whose population is mainly Moslem or a male-dominated society—to seek to imitate the North is to court failure, even disaster. There is no neat solution that can be found and put in place, even by the most high-minded of leaders. The role of outsiders is delicate and is best performed by raising questions and identifying possible ways of thinking about the issue. Thus a long, slow process of learning and searching is necessary. Without such the result will

---

15. Isaiah Berlin in several places (e.g., 1969 and 1980) emphasizes the inevitability of the plurality of values that conflict with one another and that cannot be reduced to a common denominator.

surely be tension and doubts, even conflict, all of which reduce well-being and undermine the learning process. I will refer to the gender issue along the way as an illustration of the role of social choice and of institutions, why institutional change (and change in preferences) is fundamental to development, and why it is so difficult.

Such issues, I think, are a major source of the tension and unrest that one observes in almost all developing countries, including the countries that are usually identified as examples of successful development. The ideas also suggest why rapid growth of output may well bring more problems than it solves. They also suggest that social choice is facilitated if there exist a common history, common traditions, culture and myths, common institutions. It is often noted that Japan and the Republic of Korea have major advantages over many other countries in this respect. There are however other countries where the population seems quite homogeneous—for example, Bangladesh—where policy-making has been much less successful.

At the same time diversity and heterogeneity of many kinds do add greatly to the vitality and creativity of a society, and of a world. It may be noted as well here that several observers have argued that Korea and Japan are handicapped relative to other countries in the creation of new technology and the generation of new ideas because of their homogeneity. So the objective is not to eliminate the diversity, but rather to find ways to capitalize on it in the search for both personal and national well-being. This is a daunting task, and it is not surprising that there are few instances of rapid growth of output and rapid social and structural change taking place in peace and harmony.

Summary

I began this chapter with a brief review of prevailing notions of the content of well-being. Increased GDP per capita is part, but only part, of that content. Employment and poverty relief are of equal importance and these, combined with Amartya Sen's notions of functioning and capabilities, I have referred to as expanded basic needs. I then introduced the argument that we should abandon the idea that preferences are "given" to the economist, rather they emerge from the search and learn process that is part of economic activity. This required the argument that there are such things as better and worse preferences. A necessary condition for development therefore is the emergence of new and better wants over time, because the quality of our wants determine to a significant degree the level and increase in our well-being.

The basic criterion of better wants and of well-being in general is essentially what John Rawls (1971) calls the Aristotelian Principle, a notion that asserts that humans should make full use of the unique qualities of their humanness. Households must then constantly search for ways to make fuller and fuller use of their capacities and talents. So an individual and household has two tasks: the first is to decide on current consumption and activities, and the second is to engage in an active and conscious search for better, more rewarding wants—wants that reflect the application of the Aristotelian Principle. This searching and learning process within the household is an important source of dynamism in an economy, especially one in which incomes are beginning to rise for the first time.

As there is almost sure to be a great diversity of views within a society, social choice—the aggregation of individual choices to reach a national choice—emerges as a paramount issue, especially in a society which is just beginning to change. The pervasiveness and complexity of the social choice task is noted in this chapter and will enter the analysis at numerous points in the following pages, especially in the discussion of governance. While diversity and heterogeneity add to the complexity of the social choice task, they also add to the creativity, richness, and dynamism of the society, and thereby contribute to development. The policy objective is then not to eliminate (or try to eliminate) diversity, but to find ways to use it to enhance well-being. This objective requires much more than a modus vivendi that prevents violence. It requires some sort of social reasoning process underlying or supporting the diversity. As is often noted, a society must have some shared meanings or it is not a society. I do not mean to imply that to achieve such a reasoning process is a likely event, but it does define the issue.

Given then that there is no definable ultimate goal to be sought, there must be continuous efforts at searching for the definition of the good life. The argument also means that change inevitably involves loss somewhere in the system, and to think in terms of any sort of compensation of losers is not appropriate. It was also emphasized that this whole process of demand and preference search is a major source of dynamism in a society.

CHAPTER 3

Growth Theory and Stylized Facts

Three Approaches to Growth Theory: A Reminder

The first theory of growth to become widely discussed in the post World War II years was that attributed to R. F. Harrod and independently arrived at by Evsey Domar.[1] This theory was about a dynamic short-run (as Harrod noted) rather than a long-run growth process. A technologically given capital (K) output (Q) ratio is defined, $k = K/Q$, along with a given saving rate, $s = S/Q$. The economy is assumed closed to any foreign activity. Then for national aggregates, we can write (where Δ refers to increments)

$$Q = K/k$$
$$\Delta Q = \Delta K/k$$
and $\quad \Delta Q/Q = \Delta K/Q \cdot 1/k$
but $\quad \Delta K/Q = S/Q = s$
so $\quad \Delta Q/Q = s/k$ or $r_Q = s/k$.

The rate of growth of output r_Q is given by the saving coefficient divided by the technologically given capital output ratio. To grow, a country need but increase its saving rate, and the growth rate would rise accordingly.

The fixity of k and s (a heritage from Keynes) made for convenience in many ways, but created one vast problem. There is no labor in the Harrod formulation, but one may write the growth of output in terms of labor only. Write n as the rate of growth of the labor force and p as the rate of growth of labor productivity. Therefore a full employment growth rate is $n + p$. Obviously if there is to be full employment growth s/k must equal $n + p$, but there is no mechanism at work in the argument that ensures this equality. So full employment growth is a happenstance, and such a result is surely unacceptable.[2]

---

1. R. F. Harrod (1939, 1949) and Domar (1957).

2. That Harrod made such assumptions is not quite as odd as it might seem. In the depressed state of the 1930s the supply curve of labor was horizontal for a long while. More

The second round of growth theory began with a paper by Robert Solow (Solow 1956). The assumption was made that factor prices moved until there was full employment of labor and full utilization of capital. This meant of course that k adjusted to ensure that all resources were used, so that s/k always equaled $n + p$. The saving rate could also adjust, but the main weight is placed on the capital output ratio adjusting to factor prices rather than being fixed by technology. The familiar Cobb-Douglas production function is used to get the following equally familiar result:

$$Q = fA(K,L) \text{ and further } Q = AK^a L^b$$
then $\ln Q = \text{Ln } A + a \text{ Ln } K + b \text{ Ln } L$
and $dQ/Q = dA/A + a \, dK/K + b \, dL/L$
and $dA/A = dQ/Q - (a \, dK/K + b \, dL/L)$
or $r_A = r_Q - (a \, r_K + b \, r_L)$.

The r_A is usually designated as total factor productivity growth (or the Solow residual) in contrast to the more usual labor productivity growth. The a and b are the elasticities of capital and labor respectively and are almost always equated to the relative shares of the two factors. The latter practice requires the assumption of perfectly competitive markets. This equation allows for adjustment to factor supplies in the textbook way so that no conflict arises that results in either continuing unemployment or in a labor "shortage." If, as expected, the rate of growth of capital exceeds the rate of growth of labor and there are diminishing returns to capital, then in some long, long run increasing capital no longer contributes to the growth of output. Growth of labor productivity becomes completely dependent on r_A, and growth of total output is r_A plus the rate of growth of labor, the same as $n + p$ in the preceding paragraph.

It is evident that this formulation yields a growth of labor productivity, $r_{LP} = r_A + a (r_K - r_L)$. Labor productivity growth exceeds TFPG if capital's share is greater than zero and r_K exceeds r_L. Both conditions are widely met.

Since both n and p (and r_A) were assumed to be exogenous, it is usual to criticize this formulation because it concludes that, in the long run, growth is completely exogenous to the economic system. Such a statement is inappropriate. Rather this formulation obtains an estimate of productivity growth, and then the task becomes to explain what is found. There are many studies that do this by putting r_A on the left-hand side of the regression and any

---

importantly, in the developing countries, the assumption of unlimited supplies of labor in the dual-economy models supported the idea of a constant capital-output ratio. There was full employment, in the modern sector, and the demand for labor rose as capital formation took place, which demand was met by in-migration from the traditional sector. This was essentially the W. A. Lewis model for development.

number of intuitively appealing variables on the right-hand side. Such an approach is often informative, but in general has not produced clear enough results for any sort of received wisdom to emerge as to how a country can affect its productivity growth. As empirical work, beginning with Solow (1957), made clear that r_A was an important source of growth, even over shorter intervals, the explanation of r_A became increasingly urgent.

The third stage of post-1950s growth theory is the so-called endogenous growth theory, originated largely by Robert Lucas (1988) and Paul Romer (1986, 1990), but many others have made important contributions. Howard Pack (1994) and N. G. Mankiw (1995) provide good, brief reviews. The basic equation is written simply as $Q = AK$, with A as in the neoclassical model and K as all forms of capital, including especially human capital. The simplest interpretation of this equation is that resources are explicitly allocated to, for example, R&D or training of labor in some form or other, and this in turn prevents the productivity of K from falling.[3] More generally, the idea is that rates of growth of productivity are essentially due to the allocation of resources for that purpose, and this allocation is part of the profit maximizing process. The $Q = AK$ has constant returns to capital. This is largely due to the multiforms that "capital" can take, the assumption that these numerous forms are highly substitutable for each other, and to strong assumptions about externalities.[4]

The idea that productivity enhancing activities are part of the firm's profiting-making efforts is of course important and is a major part of the story to follow. This formulation however implies that we know a great deal more about the sources of productivity growth than we now do. In a sense, the endogenous formulation is premature and not really different from the original Solow formulation that, as noted, points up the importance of explaining productivity growth. We need to understand more clearly the sources of productivity growth before we can create a formal model that gets us very far, that is, one that explains what in fact has happened with respect to growth of output and, especially, of productivity. In this respect the Solow formulation has major advantages over the endogenous models.

Explanations of the rate of growth of productivity, r_A or some variation,

---

3. In my book (Bruton 1965) I assumed that a society releases resources from the production of consumer goods and services, then has the choice of how to use these resources. It may use them for the production of physical capital, technical and administrative knowledge, or human capital. Decisions on where to allocate would depend on expected rates of return. This is very similar to the idea in $Q = AK$.

4. Robert Solow (1994) emphasizes that constant returns capital has to obtain exactly. Even a hint of diminishing or increasing returns to capital will mean that the model will not function in the prescribed way. That is, as Solow notes, a damaging result.

are, in terms of our present knowledge, quite inadequate. The task now is to seek hypotheses, evidence from here, there, and everywhere, case studies, and whatever to give us a firmer grasp on the possible sources. This calls for a more historical, more inclusive kind of approach. In the language used in the previous chapter, these three formulations are mechanical, and, I am suggesting, that there is much to be learned about productivity by a more organic approach. Put differently: these equations are concerned with how growth takes place, and they say nothing about the conditions that enable this mechanism to become effective. (See the reference to Kuznets in note 3 in chapter 1.) This is the sort of thing that I try to do in the following pages.[5]

What Is to Be Explained: Facts and Semifacts

An examination of the evidence available for those countries in which GDP per capita has increased fairly regularly over the last 100 to 150 years suggests the following "stylized facts and ideas" about that growth. These facts are what a theory of growth should explain, or, at least, seek to explain.

1. Sustained growth of economy-wide or sectoral output requires continuously increasing productivity of the primary inputs, capital and labor, and the appearance of new products. Growth of output per capita cannot be sustained very long simply by more inputs of capital and labor producing the same array of products. This growth in productivity has also taken place without penalizing the growth of employment. This conclusion is perhaps the single most fundamental "stylized fact." It rests on solid theoretical foundations and is supported by a vast amount of empirical evidence.[6] At the same time, it is necessary to emphasize that our knowledge of how to bring about increases in productivity is extremely primitive.

2. There are many questions about the estimates of the productivity growth that are available. These questions concern conceptual, measurement, and data issues. Despite such questions, the following empirical observations

---

5. There are of course many difficulties with these equations that I have passed over. The notion of an aggregate production function is itself open to real doubt, all measures of capital stock can be questioned, the measurement of labor is almost as complex as that of capital, the form of the function is surely much too simple, etc., etc. The widespread use of cross-country regressions to estimate parameters or test hypotheses is surely misguided. There are inevitably simultaneity and multicollinearity problems. These are additional reasons for trying to formulate the arguments in a somewhat different way.

6. There are several formulations that give less of a role to productivity growth than is given here. See especially Scott (1989) and Jorgenson (1995). Several people have also argued that productivity growth has been modest in the East Asian high-growth countries. These are exceptions, however, to a vastly larger body of evidence supporting the position in the text.

seem to hold in most countries and most sectors for which data are available. The observations refer both to total factor productivity growth and to labor productivity, except where it is explicitly noted that they refer only to one or the other.

    a. The rates of growth of productivity for GDP among countries vary widely. In general the rate of growth of total factor productivity and of labor productivity is higher in the countries of the North than in the developing countries, and, more clearly, the proportion of the growth rate of output accounted for by total factor productivity is higher in the North. More on this below.

    b. Similarly, these rates vary widely within a country over different intervals of time.

    c. Rates vary among sectors and among firms within an industry, even among units within a firm for a given time interval.

    d. Of great importance to the present story is the evidence that the variance in productivity growth among sectors and firms within a country over a given interval of time is less than the variance among countries for that same interval. This means that there is a "country effect," a point that matters greatly.[7] I review some more detailed aspects of productivity growth in the following section.

    3. The capital/labor ratios rise over time in an economy that is growing, and for most of the sectors that are expanding over any significant period of time.

    4. The reproducible capital-output ratio for economy and sector is not a technological constant, but it does not seem to show evidence of a long-run trend in either direction. Variations in the capital-output ratio are usually much less than variation in other ratios, especially so in the few instances where corrections for underutilization can be made. One must say *reproducible* capital because over a long period of time the capital-output ratio may fall because land becomes less and less important in production.

    5. Real wages rise rather steadily, even in the presence of some unemployment or underemployment. Where open unemployment is severe and prolonged, real wages do level off or even fall, but in these periods growth of GDP usually stops completely or declines.

    6. The wage bill as a proportion of value added drifts upward over extended periods for the growing economy as a whole. There is considerable variance among countries and among sectors in a given country of labor's share, but in a given growing sector or economy over time it changes slowly.

---

7. Evidence to support this position is ample. See, for example, Helliwell (1992, 1992a), Dosi et al. (1990, chapter 3), Arrow et al. (1961), and Chenery et al. (1986).

There are several instances where the rising tendency has been stopped or even reversed.

7. Estimates of rates of return on reproducible capital are the most unreliable and the fewest in number of those measures that play a role in the growth story. The estimates of profit rates that are available show no clear-cut long-run tendency to fall, but they are quite volatile. If capital's share of value added (P/VA) and the K/VA (the capital-output ratio) are both constant over time, then P/K, the profit rate, is constant from the identity $P/K = P/VA \cdot VA/K$. The capital/labor ratio is rising (per 3 above), and this alone would be expected to result in the rate of return on capital falling over time. Since this fall has not happened, the productivity growth that has taken place must have been such that it prevents a rising K/L from resulting in a falling P/K on the average for all surviving firms. An increase in productivity that has the same effect on output as an increase in the labor force will produce this result. This is usually identified as a labor augmenting form of productivity increase. Labor augmenting productivity growth was introduced by Harrod (1939, 1949). In Joan Robinson's language it is "an all round increase" in the productivity of labor. In some sort of long-run growth process, the K/L with L measured in nominal units rises, while K/L_e with L_e measured in efficiency units is about constant. So P/K is constant and if equal proportionate rates of growth of capital and L_e result in an equal rise in output, then the K/VA remains constant as do relative shares. So another stylized fact is that the productivity that takes place is of this labor augmenting form.

If the share of wages drifts upward so that P/VA falls, then VA/K must rise (the capital-output ratio falls) if the rate of return is to remain constant. Available series are not complete enough to enable one to conclude very confidently that this latter process takes place as a matter of routine in growing economies.

8. Net investment rates of growing economies are rarely below 10 percent and more usually in the neighborhood of 12 to 15 percent or even higher. In many of the studies that report regression results of the rate of growth of GDP on various possible explanatory variables, the investment rate appears particularly important. (See, for example, Fischer 1991; Levine and Renelt 1991, 1991a.) Other regressions however show rather clearly that investment does not play a fundamental role. (See, for example, Helliwell 1992.) Thus it is important to recognize the stylized idea that the role of investment in the growth mechanism remains ambiguous. The one unambiguous aspect of investment is that it is not a sufficient condition for continued growth, but yet sustained growth seems always to be accompanied by investment rates of at least 10–15 percent.

Another aspect of the investment issue is evidence that saving and investment rates in countries are closely related. In spite of an international capital market of considerable extent and sophistication, domestic saving is the main source of investable resources. Saving rates matter.[8]

9. In the currently rich countries, rates of growth of GDP have been fairly regular and, for decade comparisons, remarkably stable. The years 1950 to 1975 are the major exception; growth rates during this period were markedly higher than in the years before or after (Kuznets 1971; Maddison 1991). On the other hand, growth rates for the less-developed countries move around a great deal. One observes short periods of rapid growth, periods of negative growth, and periods of stagnation. These observations are, of course, another way of making the basic point of this essay: the reason that the GDP per capita is very low in most of the countries of Asia, Africa, and Latin America is that no sustained growth process has been put in place.

10. History teaches us unequivocally that growth is a long-term process. A corollary of this observation is that the achievement of a fundamental change in the long-term growth rate of an economy is itself a long-term task. There can be a quick improvement in the terms of trade, an easy phase of import substitution, an easy phase in which the removal of severe distortions produce abrupt increases in the growth rate, an episodic technical innovation, etc. After the effects of these sorts of things have worn off and we are down to the real economy, then changing *that* is a time-consuming process. Taiwan and the Republic of Korea are not exceptions to this statement because it seems clear that the process of creating an economy in these countries whose routine functioning produced growth began at least a century before the 1950–60 decade.

11. There are two other "semifacts" to which attention may be drawn, but for which the available data are much less convincing. The first refers to exports. There is some evidence that suggests that exports must grow if GDP is to grow. This is doubtless the case for most very small countries, but it is much less clear for larger countries. In the post-1950 years it does seem that exports and growth went along very nearly hand in hand. Regressions however, in general, show that imports do as well as an explanatory variable of the growth of GDP as do exports. In regressions where it is possible to control for the investment rate and other variables, there does not appear to be any robust independent relationship between any trade variable and the growth of GDP (Fischer 1991). Other regression studies, of which there are many, also give mixed results on the role of exports.

---

8. The evidence of this was first noted by Feldstein and Horioka (1980). There are problems and doubts of course. Taylor (1994) is a good review of the arguments and doubts and the evidence.

Large scale exports of a major staple—oil, diamonds, and so on—do not appear to play the same role that manufactured exports play—whatever that may be. Thus exports, like capital formation, seem to play a key role, but exactly what that role is, is far from clear. I shall be concerned with the role of exports in later sections of this essay.

12. The second semifact that is not very well documented, but is worth noting, refers to the birth and death of enterprises in a growing economy. A growing economy is almost necessarily characterized by the appearance of new firms and the death of some of the existing ones. The data for the United States (Birch 1987, and OECD 1990) show that over the century and half before 1990, the percentage rates of birth of new firms and death of old were remarkably stable. The rates are rather high, in the area of 10 percent per year. These high rates are of course concentrated among small firms. Data for the United Kingdom suggest a similar picture. Data for Western European countries are less readily available. Data for Korea, although not very extensive, also show high birth and death rates for firms, again almost always small ones (Jones and Il Sakong 1980). This semifact suggests an important part of growth: namely that new blood, new ideas, new approaches, new products, are necessary to keep it going, and, since they are necessary to keep it going, existing firms will find it difficult to keep the pace unless they can find ways to adjust continually.

This latter point leads to another that greatly complicates the analysis. These stylized facts refer mainly to aggregates, to macro variables. Growth however is basically an enterprise phenomenon. Firms do not produce GDP. They produce bicycles, shirts, rice, spinach, automobiles, plows, and so on. If an economy is growing it is because firms are growing in number or size or both. So any study of why and how growth occurs must begin with the activities of the individual firm. There is a role for macro analysis, of course, but that role must be studied in terms of its effects on firms.

These "stylized facts and ideas," or, at least some of them, have been used to justify the notion of a "steady-state growth." It is important to recognize that, in the approach examined in this essay, the idea of a steady-state growth is a barrier to understanding, not a help. In particular it is important to appreciate that these growth characteristics imply, indeed require, continuous adjustments of a wide, very wide, range. A major part of a growth story involves identifying these adjustments, how they occur, and how their failure to occur affects growth. The notion of a steady state is, indeed, a way to sneak static-ness back into an analysis that was headed toward being genuinely dynamic. This point is especially important in understanding how an economy that has long not grown can be converted to one that is in fact growing, and growing in a way that contributes to increasing well-being.

More on Productivity Growth

There are several additional facts about productivity growth to which explicit reference is useful. I rely mainly on the valuable collections of Angus Maddison.

1. Perhaps the most unambiguous fact about productivity growth and growth of output is that the 1950–73 period was a towering exception to the decades before and after. Several aspects of this exception may be noted.

   a. Tables 1 and 2, reproduced from Maddison (1991), show growth of per capita GDP and of GDP per man hour, that is, labor productivity, for the North (including Australia) from 1820 to 1989 for the former series and 1870 to 1987 for labor productivity. These data show unambiguously and without exception that rates of growth of both variables were markedly higher in the quarter (almost) century after 1950 than at any time before or after. Rates of growth of real GDP (table 3), also from Maddison (1991), show essentially the same story although there is an exception or two. The rate of growth of GDP of the United States was higher from 1820–1913 than from 1950–73. In Australia GDP grew faster from 1820 to 1870 than in the post-1950 years.

TABLE 1.   Average Annual Growth Rates of Real GDP per capita 1820–1989

	1820–70	1870–1913	1913–50	1950–73	1973–89	1820–1989	1870–1989
Australia	1.9	0.9	0.7	2.4	1.7	1.4	1.2
Austria	0.6	1.5	0.2	4.9	2.4	1.5	1.8
Belgium	1.4	1.0	0.7	3.5	2.0	1.5	1.5
Canada	n.a.	2.3	1.5	2.9	2.5	n.a.	2.2
Denmark	0.9	1.6	1.5	3.1	1.6	1.6	1.8
Finland	0.8	1.4	1.9	4.3	2.7	1.8	2.3
France	0.8	1.3	1.1	4.0	1.8	1.5	1.8
Germany	0.7	1.6	0.7	4.9	2.1	1.6	2.0
Italy	0.4	1.3	0.8	5.0	2.6	1.5	2.0
Japan	0.1	1.4	0.9	8.0	3.1	1.9	2.7
Netherlands	0.9	1.0	1.1	3.4	1.4	1.4	1.5
Norway	0.7	1.3	2.1	3.2	3.6	1.8	2.2
Sweden	0.7	1.5	2.1	3.3	1.8	1.6	2.1
Switzerland	n.a.	1.2	2.1	3.1	1.0	n.a.	1.8
UK	1.2	1.0	0.8	2.5	1.8	1.3	1.4
USA	1.5	1.8	1.6	2.2	1.6	1.7	1.8
Arithmetic average	0.9	1.4	1.2	3.8	2.1	1.6	1.9

Source: Maddison (1991, 49). These figures are adjusted to exclude the impact of boundary changes.

TABLE 2. Annual Growth Rates of Labor Productivity

	1870–1913	1913–50	1950–73	1973–87	1870–1987
Australia	1.1	1.5	2.7	1.8	1.6
Austria	1.8	0.9	5.9	2.7	2.4
Belgium	1.2	1.4	4.4	3.0	2.1
Canada	2.3	2.4	2.9	1.8	2.4
Denmark	1.9	1.6	4.1	1.6	2.2
Finland	1.8	2.3	5.2	2.2	2.7
France	1.6	1.9	5.0	3.2	2.6
Germany	1.9	1.0	5.9	2.6	2.5
Italy	1.7	2.0	5.8	2.6	2.7
Japan	1.9	1.8	7.6	3.5	3.2
Netherlands	1.3	1.3	4.8	2.4	2.1
Norway	1.6	2.5	4.2	3.5	2.6
Sweden	1.7	2.8	4.4	1.6	2.6
Switzerland	1.5	2.7	3.3	1.2	2.2
UK	1.2	1.6	3.2	2.3	1.9
USA	1.9	2.4	2.5	1.0	2.1
Arithmetic average	1.7	1.9	4.5	2.3	2.4

Source: Maddison (1991, 51).

b. Rates of growth of TFP show a similar picture for the few countries for which estimates are available both before and after 1950. Table 4, reproduced from Maddison (1987), provides a summary. Only the United States experienced lower TFPG in 1950–73 than in the 1913–50 interval. (Even this result is qualified a bit with the more detailed estimates presented in a page or two.) For the other five countries TFPG rates were markedly higher in 1950–73 compared to the periods before and after.

The United States differs in several ways from the other countries. With respect to all three series in tables 1, 2, and 3, the U.S. growth rates were lower during the 1950–73 period than the average for the group of countries shown. In earlier intervals the U.S. growth rates were always higher than the average. The U.S. growth rates for all series were more nearly stable over the period up to 1950 than was the case for the other countries shown. There is some suggestion that after 1973, growth rates seemed to return to their pre-1950 levels. This is clearer for the TFPG estimates for countries other than the United States, where the post-1973 rate falls sharply compared to the pre-1950 periods and compared to the other countries. It was not until the 1950–73 interval that, in general, other countries of the North

TABLE 3.   Average Annual Rates of Growth of Real GDP

	1820–70	1870–1913	1913–50	1950–73	1973–89	1820–1989	1870–1989
Australia	10.1	3.5	2.2	4.7	3.1	5.2	3.3
Austria	1.4	2.4	0.2	5.3	2.4	2.0	2.3
Belgium	2.2	2.0	1.0	4.1	2.1	2.2	2.1
Canada	n.a.	4.1	3.1	5.1	3.6	n.a.	3.9
Denmark	1.9	2.7	2.5	3.8	1.7	2.5	2.7
Finland	1.6	2.7	2.7	4.9	3.1	2.7	3.2
France	1.2	1.5	1.1	5.0	2.3	1.9	2.2
Germany	1.6	2.8	1.3	5.9	2.1	2.5	2.8
Italy	1.2	1.9	1.5	5.6	2.9	2.2	2.6
Japan	0.3	2.3	2.2	9.3	3.9	2.8	3.8
Netherlands	1.8	2.3	2.4	4.7	2.0	2.5	2.8
Norway	1.8	2.1	2.9	4.1	4.0	2.7	3.0
Sweden	1.6	2.2	2.7	4.0	2.0	2.4	2.7
Switzerland	n.a.	2.1	2.6	4.5	1.3	n.a.	2.6
UK	2.0	1.9	1.3	3.0	2.0	2.0	1.9
USA	4.5	3.9	2.8	3.6	2.7	3.7	3.4
Arithmetic average	2.4	2.5	2.0	4.9	2.6	2.7	2.8

Source: Maddison (1991, 50). These figures are adjusted to exclude the impact of boundary changes.

achieved higher growth rates in all the series than did the United States.

Table 5 shows additional estimates of TFPG and GDP per man-hour for the United Kingdom and the United States that add further evidence. The main point to note about table 5 is that from 1938 to 1950 in the United States both labor productivity and TFP grew faster than

TABLE 4.   Average Annual Rate of Growth of Total Factor Productivity

	1913–50	1950–73	1973–84
France	1.42	4.02	1.84
Germany	.86	4.32	1.55
Japan	1.10	5.79	1.21
Netherlands	1.25	3.35	.81
UK	1.15	2.14	1.22
USA	1.99	1.85	.52
Average	1.30	3.58	1.19

Source: Maddison (1987, 665), Table 11a.

TABLE 5.   Annual Average Growth Rates

	GDP per capita	TFPG
United Kingdom		
1700–1780	.3	—
1780–1820	.4	.4
1820–90	1.2	.9
United States		
1890–1913	2.2	1.1
1913–29	2.4	1.7
1929–50	2.4	1.9
1929–38	1.4	.3
1938–50	3.2	3.2

Source: Maddison (1991, 38, 71).

at any other period for which estimates are available. This bit of evidence is used in later arguments that seek to explain TFPG. It may also be noted that the TFPG rate for the United States seems to hover around 2.00 until after 1973. Attention may also be called to the fact that in the 1938–50 interval, labor productivity growth and TFPG are the same. In terms of the formula used previously to measure labor productivity, this equality means that the rate of growth of capital and labor were equal. For the war years this equality seems reasonable and will be relevant in later arguments as well.

It may also be noted that Matthews et al. (1982, 213) conclude from incomplete data for the United Kingdom "that there was no substantial phase in the nineteenth century during which the trend in the rate of growth of TFP was upward."

c. Table 6 shows rates of growth of per capita GDP for some Latin American and Asian countries for which estimates are available as early as 1900. The Latin American countries follow the preceding script exactly, except that Chile's growth is somewhat lower in the 1950–73 interval than in 1913–50. In 1973–89 all the growth rates of the Latin American countries fell sharply. The Asian picture is quite different. All of the countries shown in table 6, except Bangladesh, have much higher growth rates in 1950–73 than in the earlier period. The main point however is that all six countries show higher growth rates in the 1973–89 years than in the earlier intervals. These data are for GDP per capita, and our interest is in labor productivity and TFP growth. At the same time, it does seem appropriate to conclude from table 6 that something was going on in these Asian countries that was not present in Latin America.

TABLE 6. Rates of Growth of GDP per capita Developing Countries

	1900–1913	1913–50	1950–73	1973–89	1900–1989
Argentina	2.5	.7	2.0	−1.6	.9
Brazil	1.4	1.9	3.7	1.0	2.2
Chile	2.1	1.7	1.5	1.1	1.6
Mexico	1.8	.9	3.0	.7	1.6
Latin American average	2.1	1.2	2.4	.4	1.6
Bangladesh	.5	−.3	−.7	1.8	.1
China	.3	−.5	3.6	5.3	1.7
India	.4	−.3	1.5	2.7	.8
Indonesia	.4	−.2	2.1	3.3	1.1
South Korea	.8	.2	5.1	6.4	2.5
Taiwan	.3	.4	6.0	6.1	2.9
Asian average	.5	−.2	3.9	5.4	1.5

Source: Calculated from data in Maddison (1991, 24–25).

2. For the years after 1950 there are of course many more estimates of r_A and r_{LP}.[9] These data suggest that the following generalizations are legitimate starting points for an analysis of the 1950–73 period. The observations apply mainly to TFPG calculated for GDP growth. Some observations on sectoral rates of growth are made here and there and are specifically noted.

a. Both r_A and r_{LP} are generally higher in the North than in the South. There are exceptions, important exceptions, but still the generalization is applicable. This result is not the same thing as asserting that r_A is positively related to r_Q.

b. Even clearer is the evidence that the proportion of growth of output accounted for by TFPG, r_A/r_Q, is higher in the North than it is in the South over this period.

c. Within the countries of the North, variation in r_A over a particular time interval is less than that among the countries of the South. Table 7 illustrates these last three points.

d. The rate of growth of capital, r_K, in both groups of countries is similar, while the rate of growth of labor, r_L, is much higher in the South. Thus $r_K - r_L$ is in general higher in the North, so that, over the post-1950 decades, production in the North has become increasingly

9. Readily available sources include Chenery, Robinson, and Syrquin (1986), Elias (1990), The World Bank (1993), and Fischer (1991). There are many other estimates as well. Elias (1990) is the most complete that I have seen and I make use of it in the following. World Bank (1993) compares Elias with their own estimates and with others. All estimates are in no sense identical, but they seem similar enough to proceed.

TABLE 7. Average Annual Rates of Growth of Total Factor Productivity Growth, 1961–88

Region	Number of Countries	Regional Mean	Maximum		Minimum	
			Country	Rate	Country	Rate
EMENA	7	0.55	Malta	1.72	Iraq	−1.70
LACAR	21	−0.24	Brazil	1.90	Haiti	−4.81
AFRICA	21	−1.51	Tanzania	1.64	Madagascar	−4.64
SASIA	5	−0.72	Burma	1.47	Bangladesh	−3.63
EASIA	8	0.22	Taiwan	1.69	Singapore	−2.82
OECD	24	0.68	Greece	1.63	New Zealand	−1.01

Source: Fischer (1991, 36). Calculations based on Summers-Heston income data. EMENA: Europe, Middle East and North Africa; LACAR: Latin America and Caribbean; SASIA: South East Asia; EASIA, East Asia.

capital intensive relative to that in the South. In almost all countries, r_K/r_L has exceeded unity fairly regularly, although there are exceptions. While capital's share—a in the equations above—is generally lower in the North, often much lower, than in the South, $a\,(r_K - r_L)$ is generally higher because of the much larger difference between r_K and r_L in the North compared to the South. The rate of growth of labor productivity ($r_{LP} = r_A + a\,(r_K - r_L)$) is higher in the North than it is in the South (again with a few exceptions), because r_A is so much higher there than in the South. As both total factor productivity and labor productivity were higher in the North than in the South in 1950, the differences between the two regions with respect to these two measures has in general increased with respect to both measures.

e. There are fewer negative values of r_A and r_{LP} in the North than in the South. This appears especially evident over shorter periods of time, but is present in the data from Elias (1990), an almost 40 year span.

f. The relationship between the rate of growth of TFPG and of physical capital growth or between the rate of growth of capital and of labor productivity is different in the North from that in the South. In the North there appears a clear-cut positive relationship between capital and productivity growth. (See Baumol et al. 1989, 335, and Chenery et al. 1986, 23.) For the countries of the South there is essentially no relationship, although for a country or two there may be some relationship over certain periods. There is indeed some evidence that a negative relationship between TFPG and capital formation exists in some countries.

g. Data on relative shares are not regularly available for countries of

TABLE 8. Total Factor Productivity Growth by Country and Industry

	USA 1960–79	Japan 1960–79	Argentina 1956–73	Chile 1960–81	Korea 1960–77	India 1959–79	Singapore 1970–79
Food	1.31	−1.24	−0.82	0.12	5.26	0.24	0.62
Beverages	1.31	−1.24	−0.82	4.74	5.26	−0.90	1.73
Tobacco	−0.68	−1.24	2.83	2.26	5.26	−0.64	3.22
Textiles	1.92	0.31	−0.27	0.19	4.51	0.30	−3.23
Fabricated textiles	1.09	1.01	−0.27	−1.33	1.62	0.30	−2.11
Leather and footwear	0.25	0.69		−2.07	2.80	0.27	−6.50
Wood and products	0.09	1.88	−1.66		5.62	−0.19	−6.57
Furniture and fixtures	0.26	0.95	−1.66	6.57	4.88	0.96	−2.44
Paper and products	−0.16	0.84		2.91	4.52	0.12	2.18
Printing and publishing	0.58	−0.08		0.08		0.01	−1.36
Rubber	2.59	0.59	1.42	−1.50	5.88	−0.81	−1.57
Chemicals and products	1.21	2.44	3.22	−0.18	4.49	−0.36	2.30
Petroleum and coal	−1.79	−3.16		3.69	0.68	0.26	1.49
Nonmetallic minerals	0.07	1.20	1.52	3.29	4.53	−0.50	1.44
Ferrous metals	−0.59	0.90	0.55	0.35	1.87	−0.55	3.41
Nonferrous metals	−0.59	0.12	0.55		1.87	−0.55	−13.87
Metal products	0.50	1.91		5.04	6.01	−0.55	−3.59
Nonelectrical machinery	0.36	1.29	6.49		5.73	−0.03	−3.28
Electrical machinery	1.58	3.28	3.28	−1.91	7.25	0.24	−0.04
Transport equipment	0.65	1.41	6.49		5.10	−0.27	1.27

Source: Pack in Helleiner (1992, 31). Pack cites Nishimizu and Page (1986) and Tsao (1985) as his sources.

the South. The best estimates are for the manufacturing sector which are included in the World Bank's *World Tables*. These estimates in general show virtually no discernible trend over time. Labor's share does seem to drift upward over time in some countries, especially in the North, but in no sense in all or even most. The size of the share does vary from country to country. If capital and output grow more or less at the same rate and capital's share is about constant, then, as already noted, the rate of return will remain about constant.

h. Table 8 illustrates the earlier argument as to the great diversity of TFPGs among countries and sectors within countries.

The arguments of the preceding chapter and the above lists of stylized facts and semifacts suggest labor productivity to be a more revealing general guide to economic performance and economic well-being than is GDP per capita. The two measures of course move closely together, but they do not reflect exactly the same notion. For example rising labor productivity may lead to more time be given to leisure. If leisure time is well used, such an allocation of one's time can "produce" more well-being than can more GDP. Rising labor productivity can be used to achieve more interesting jobs, to pursue a more convincing environmental protection policy, more esthetically satisfying buildings, higher quality product and services etc. I will therefore be concerned primarily with labor productivity, but GDP per capita and total factor productivity are neither scorned nor completely ignored.

The objective of a theory of growth then is to provide an apparatus, a way of thinking, that accounts for the body of "facts and ideas" just summarized. It should do this in a manner that facilitates our efforts to understand how well-being is enhanced and should have explicit policy implications. It is perhaps unnecessary to point out that the three approaches to growth theory summarized above do not accomplish these tasks.

CHAPTER 4

A Way to Think about Growth

In this chapter I describe a growth process that can account for the characteristics listed in the previous chapter and that provides a framework for identifying specific points which are strategic for affecting that process.

The Growth Process

The Beginning State

An economy, at a particular time, can be defined by several variables that also enter the growth story. There exists a great number of firms with an array of physical capital of various kinds, vintages, states of repair, and so on. There is also an array of rates of return on the various capital items, some of which of course may be zero or even negative. There is a labor force, the members of which have a variety of skills, commitment, education, experience, and ambition. The size of the labor force is ambiguous, since who is in the labor market depends very much on the state of the economy. Jobs are of varying quality, interest, and compensation, and they contribute in varying ways to the growth of well-being of the employed. There are also prevailing notions of the role of leisure. There is a body of technical, administrative, and organizational knowledge, some of which is being applied, some known about and not being applied, some not actually known but findable with some search by potential users. There is therefore underutilized knowledge.

The economy is set in a larger, social environment that includes institutions of many kinds, ideas of morality and the good life, memories, and a great many other characteristics that can affect how much weight the community gives to having more goods and services, and that define the boundaries within which production takes place.

The economy, defined in this way, yields a level of output of goods and services at a particular time and a particular distribution of that output. It (the economy) makes some contribution to well-being. There is considerable variance among the capital/labor ratios of the several sectors and firms as well as variation among productivity levels, ranging from very high to very low. Productivity levels vary widely because productivity growth among firms and sectors has proceeded over the past decades at greatly different rates. Some firms and sectors are thus on the brink of extinction and others on the way up.

This is what an economy looks like at a particular moment. Suppose further, for the moment, that this country is closed to the outside world and has long been so.

The Growth Framework

I begin with a simple relationship between capital and output, so that the amount of capital in a given firm is some kind of a function of output, $K = v\,Q$. The interpretation of v is crucial to the story. It helps to begin with what it is *not*.

1. It is not a technologically determined parameter.
2. It is not an "accelerator" coefficient.
3. It is not the "desired" amount of capital, given the rate of output and factor prices.
4. It is not an "equilibrium" or least cost coefficient, given factor prices and output levels.
5. It is not determined by whimsy.

It cannot be any of these mainly because of the assumptions about technical, administrative and organizational knowledge stated above: not all knowledge that is known is being applied and not all knowledge that is available (in some sense) is known by each firm. At the same time it obviously must reflect the knowledge that is and was, in the recent past, available and known.

What v does represent can best be studied by considering the story of the birth and early life of a firm. Most firms start small, and the argument is clearer for a small firm than for a large one. Suppose two people conclude that a market for bicycles exists in their area and decide to start an enterprise to manufacture bicycles at some estimated rate per year. Their objective is to make money. How do they begin?

They surely do a number of things: they visit another bicycle manufacturer some distance away, they look at some publications about bicycle manufacture, they talk to neighboring producers of other products who may know something about supply sources, metal working, tire fitting, and about available labor and wage rates in the area. For financing they may have accumulated some funds from their own saving and obtained some from other members of their family or they may have been able to borrow from a local bank, from which more technological information is available as well. On the basis of information available to them at the given time, they decide on a rate of output at a particular price, and so they commit themselves to a technology

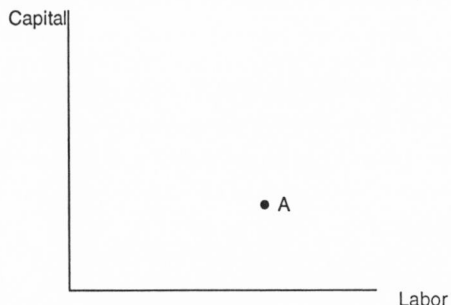

Fig. 2. Choice of capital-labor combinations in a new firm

described by its K/L, K/Q, and Q/L ratios, and expected profit rates. The coefficient v is thus "found."

This technology is shown at A in figure 2. Point A reflects the information that the two entrepreneurs were able to obtain about technology, factor prices and supplies, demand, quality of product, and so on. It is not a matter of whimsy; neither is it a consequence of "perfect" knowledge. It is unilluminating to assume that A is at the tangency of an isoquant and factor price line. Rather it represents the technology that the two entrepreneurs were led to by the information available to them. It is not an equilibrium position; it is not optimal in the usual textbook sense. The entrepreneurs are aware of all this, or soon become aware of it, and so they recognize that they must keep on searching. It is easy to appreciate that another two people who also decided to establish a new bicycle manufacturing plant in the same area would proceed in this same way and wind up at a point other than A in the figure.

The producers are aware explicitly of two things: first, that there is knowledge available that, if it could be found, would enable the firm to lower its costs or increase the quality of its product and so affect its demand, both of which would contribute to higher profits. Similarly, they know that other bicycle producers may come into existence and that existing ones may well find a way to get their costs down. So our two entrepreneurs do not think of A as an equilibrium point, as a point of rest. They accept it as their present production position, and know that it has to be changed. This is true even if profit rates are currently acceptable at A. Another possible inducement to search is that actual demand turns out to exceed the level anticipated when the plant was first constructed, and it does not seem appropriate, as a long-run strategy, to raise prices. So the search effort would be for ways to increase output quickly. The higher-than-anticipated demand is an especially effective inducement to learn more about the factor supply situation in the area where the plant is located.

The v in $K = v \cdot Q$ for an individual producer can now be seen to be a consequence of incomplete and possibly wrong knowledge about technology, factor supplies and prices, the state of the product market, and the engineering proclivities of the original entrepreneurs.[1] Thus, as new knowledge becomes available, as learning takes place, as engineering proclivities clash with economic necessities, v will change. It may be noted that the reason for writing an expression for capital formation rather than writing, say, $L = c \cdot Q$ (where c is the labor-output ratio) is simply the assumption that the initiating decision is a decision to invest. That is what starts the firm. Labor cannot decide to begin to work until this investment begins.

The firm is now in a position similar to that described for the household in chapter 2. There it was argued that the household that sought enhanced well-being did two things: it decided on its current consumption bundle, given its income and product prices and its current preferences, and, in addition, the household sought to achieve "better" preferences. Thus the household is in motion. Here the argument is that the firm does similar things: on the basis of the knowledge available to it, it decides on a current rate of output, a technology, and a product price. At the same time, it engages in (or continues) a search for ways to get costs down, and quality and demand up. As there was the built-in change in the household argument, so now there are built-in sources of change in the enterprise. One may say that in such an arrangement the firm rarely or ever "maximizes" (the meaning of such a term is ambiguous) profits, but rather that it is always searching for more profits.[2] It is this search that constitutes one of the important sources of movement in the economy.

At the given moment when the story begins there are many enterprises (including farms) in existence. They all came into being along the lines described in the preceding paragraphs. Some now are very large, but there are many which continue to be small. So as one looks at an economy at a particular moment, one sees firms of great variety—variety with respect to technology (capital/labor ratios, capital/output ratios, labor productivity, etc.), profit rates, size, and so on. There is no firm equilibrium, where the conventional marginal conditions hold, toward which it is "tending." (See the statement by Schumpeter in footnote 6, chapter 1.) And certainly the econ-

---

1. The role that engineering can play in this sort of situation has been very effectively studied by Louis Wells in Stobaugh and Wells (1984). Wells finds evidence in Indonesia that the appeal of sophisticated technology often outweighs the search for least-cost techniques. Competition and long-run survival tend to push managers toward giving priority to getting costs down.

2. Nelson and Winter (1982) argue in a similar way, although if I understand them properly, they assume primarily that if the firm is achieving a target profit rate, it will not engage in any further search at the moment. This represents a view not compatible with sustained growth. It does seem likely that search will be more committed and more concentrated if profits are threatened. The argument here is also different from those that induce search in response to various specific bottlenecks, change in prices, demand, etc. Such things, I think, affect the direction not the fact of its existence.

omy is not in any sort of general equilibrium. It is, however, an economy that is in motion for the two reasons that have been identified.

The economy visualized in this way cannot be said to be at a Pareto optimal position, that is, it is not one about which it can be said that no one can be better off without resulting in someone else being made worse off. This is true because no market is in the equilibrium defined as "perfect" competition, and there is nothing specified about economies of scale or externalities, conditions necessary for a Pareto optimal to obtain. Indeed, Pareto optimality, like equilibrium and "efficiency," does not really mean much in the kind of picture described in the previous several pages. And Pareto optimality is an efficiency notion, not a welfare notion. The economy has however performed within the social system over some significant period of time, so one is entitled to assume that the economy and the economic performance are compatible with the social system of which it is a part. The social system is of course defined by the institutions, traditions, memories, moral codes, and so on that prevail.

Growth of the output of the bicycle firm and of the productivity of resources that it employs depends on the capacity of the entrepreneurs to find and apply new technical, administrative, and organizational knowledge. Knowledge accumulation and application is the heart of productivity growth, which in turn—to repeat—is the heart of the growth of output and of well-being. In the usual textbook formulations of the theory of the firm, technical and administrative knowledge are viewed as given, and the relationship between inputs and output as simple and direct. Knowledge in a growing economy cannot be of this kind. Rather it (knowledge) must be in constant flux, a flux in which lacunae are omnipresent and relationships (even technical ones) between inputs and output are indirect and exceedingly complex. So then demand is in constant flux and becomes a variable that the firm may seek to affect. Similarly knowledge must somehow evidence an appreciation of the disorderliness of nature. This view of the state of knowledge at a given moment reinforces the basic notion, so often asserted here, that continuous searching and learning must be an essential ingredient of a firm's activity if it is to survive in a growing economy. The notion of underutilized knowledge—that is, knowledge that is findable and usable by a firm committed to growth—is therefore strategic to the present approach. The appreciation of this fact by all economic units is the beginning of a study of the growth of output.

Growth of Output and Productivity

I want now to examine this searching and learning process and its effects on output and productivity growth. To facilitate attention to growth of these two variables a figure different from figure 2 is more helpful.

The axes refer to labor productivity (VA/L) and to labor per unit of capital in the bicycle factory. Suppose, for convenience of exposition, that the amount of capital remains fixed at the level at A, so movements along the L/K axis represent movements of labor only. Point A is the initial position as in figure 2, but now it is possible to identify labor productivity directly. The entrepreneurs are interested in more profits or in protecting their current rate from being reduced by competition from other bicycle producers. This as argued above leads them to continue their searching and learning after they have begun production. A convenient and extra simple way to approach their objective is to make use of the identity, already employed, that defines the profit rate as $P/K = P/VA \cdot VA/K$. Thus any change that increases the share of profits in value added or decreases the capital/output ratio will raise the profit rate and will be, as one says, a move in the right direction. Any possible change from the initial position at A may then be evaluated by trying to establish its effects on P/VA and VA/K.

Learning by Doing

There is little dispute that learning-by-doing or on-the-job learning can take place to such an extent that it matters for the growth of output and productivity. This is true even though there has not been much success in measuring these effects.[3] It is also the case that learning-by-doing cannot continue indefinitely without significant changes in other aspects of the production process. So we can say that learning-by-doing is important, but it cannot provide single-handedly the long-term source of productivity increase.

Suppose, however, to begin, that the only source of change in the firm's activity is due to learning by workers, managers, owners, taking place simply as a consequence of producing bicycles. In figure 3 labor productivity rises from A to B over time due to learning by doing with no change in the capital-labor ratio. So VA/L and VA/K rise, and, if factor and product prices remain unchanged, then P/VA will rise and so too will the profit rate. If the productivity of labor rises due to its learning while the wage rate remains unchanged, then the productivity/wage rate ratio rises. This is the source of the increased profits. Whether the employed workers can push up their wages depends on their bargaining capacity which in turn depends on alternative employment opportunities that people with their kind of experience have and a variety of institutional and political factors. If there are other employment opportunities equally attractive for these workers, then wages of our present bicycle firm workers can be expected to begin to rise. Some of the learning is accomplished by managers and owners. This learning means that new workers hired in the second year will have a higher productivity than did those hired at the

---

3. The most famous example of learning by doing is the story of the Horndal Iron Works, first reported by Erik Lundberg. See Lazonick and Brush (1982) for a discussion and more references.

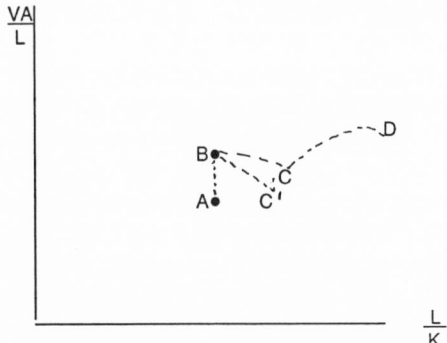

Fig. 3. Labor productivity and learning by doing

beginning of the first year when the firm was just getting under way because management is more informed and aware of ways to use the firm's resources.

These learning effects, in the presence of constant product wages, create an incentive for the firm to increase its employment. If there is no rise in wage rates, the increase in employment depends on the extent to which the capital available at B can be adapted to use more labor.[4] So the managers begin to take advantage of the increased productivity by adding to the work force. The operating point then begins to move southeast from B say toward C. Output per worker falls from B to C due to the conventional variable proportions argument. This process continues as long as productivity is rising (due to learning by workers and managers), wage rates are more or less constant or rising more slowly than productivity, and managers can find ways to use more labor with the same quantity of physical capital. The process then continues along, for example, the route from C toward D.

Learning by doing includes the increasing dexterity and similar sources of increased productivity. Such sources cannot be important very long, and something else must be involved. Thus learning simply by doing requires a capacity to identify new routines, new arrangements, new forms of organization. Such capacity puts an obvious burden on workers and managers to be able to look beyond the existing routine. Total output at C is higher than at B as is the rate of return on capital. The increased employment per unit of capital is however a consequence of the increased productivity (due to learning), and would not—in the present context—have taken place without that learning. In particular it is not due to changing wage rates.

---

4. This point is elaborated at greater length in the following chapter on employment growth. One should note that the increased productivity may simply make the original productivity/wage ratio more acceptable to the firm and therefore elicit no employment or other effect.

Since the rate of output has also risen at B and C compared to A, the entrepreneurs must consider the demand side and product prices.[5] Finally the increase in profit rate may have positive effects on saving and investment rates. More on both of these points later.

So even such a modest source of increased productivity as on-the-job learning can put into effect signals and incentives that have repercussions on important variables of the economy. The story here is an optimistic one. Other stories might have a firm suffering losses at the beginning and the increased productivity then allowing it to become profitable. Other firms may indeed not achieve any learning and so wither away. This is what fermentation among firms means and is part of the growth story.

Active Search and Tinkering

Learning by doing is not enough to keep the firm competitive or to exploit knowledge that explicit searching may uncover, so a more active search effort is required if the firm is to survive in a growing economy over an extended period. The search to be discussed in this section is limited to that accomplished more or less informally (but not casually or episodically) by the several actors of the firm. Formal research and development efforts will be discussed later. Evidently the line between informal search activity and the more identifiable, institutionalized R&D is blurred, but it is convenient to consider the two approaches as distinct. The formal activity does involve some costs, some allocation of resources, while "pure" learning by doing does not.

The entrepreneurs of the bicycle firms and all other firms that survive in a growing economy thus do two things: 1) they produce a rate of output at a specific cost and of a specific quality, and 2) they actively search for ways to reduce costs or improve quality (or both) and so enhance their profit position.

To search actively requires that there be some specific guidelines or clues or signals that suggest directions for search to begin. In the absence of such, the two entrepreneurs would be at a loss as to how to begin and would have to engage in some sort of random process to decide. There would surely be less search if this were the case. The firm has more information and understanding about the technology in the neighborhood of A and B than anywhere else in figure 3. So the search will begin at A. At A there is an awareness that there is underutilized knowledge that might be found and exploited, and there is the awareness of ignorance of exactly what the knowledge is and how it might be

---

5. One of the major advantages of exporting is, in general, that it prevents a demand constraint from appearing and thereby allows activities where productivity is rising to avoid a demand constraint. There is more on this point when an open economy is discussed.

found. The very definition of search implies the presence of ignorance.[6] The operating of their bicycle firm by the two entrepreneurs has created a range of perceptions, hunches, intuitions, beliefs about their ignorance. Such things are incomplete and subjective, of course, and they depend heavily on the environment in which the entrepreneurs have lived as well as on their personalities, training, education, and so on. Evidently the capacity to accumulate the kind of information that helps determine direction and form of search can vary widely from person to person, even from bicycle manufacturer to bicycle manufacturer. Direction of explicit search will then vary from firm to firm—as will success and failure.

The difficulties inherent in such a process may lead the timid or the politically powerful to appeal to the government for protection or for a direct subsidy. One might say that search includes the search for government help of some sort, but this does not seem to be a good way to think about search and, indeed, can well bring growth to a halt.[7]

With the accumulated knowledge that it did not have at the time that it established itself at A, the entrepreneurs know more about bicycle technology, about sources of supply of intermediate goods, about labor quality and availability and wage rates, about markets, and about many other things as well. Since knowledge is, among other things, irreversible, once the firm learns something that was not known when it was first established it cannot unlearn it, point A loses much of its relevance, and the firm may be expected to move away from A, never (except by coincidence) to return. This is another reason why it is unilluminating to think of A as being located on an isoquant.

All this additional knowledge helps determine the direction of search that the firm will take from A. For example, further knowledge about the labor market—availability and cost of labor of varying skills—may lead the firm to seek new knowledge that permits the use of relatively more labor. At the same

---

6. The term *ignorance* seems more suitable than the more frequently encountered *uncertainty*. The latter term implies, I think, that there exists knowledge already out there, but we do not know exactly where to look to find it. The term *ignorance* on the other hand suggests rather that there are voids in which it makes more or less sense to try to create knowledge because of the existing array of other information and insights. This distinction between uncertainty and ignorance is, if I understand it correctly, a fundamental feature of the work of George Shackle. See especially Shackle (1958) and also Loasby (1976).

In his *Principles of Psychology,* William James speaks of "chaotic fermentation." Frederick J. Ruf (1991, 3) writes that to James "the chaotic is fertile, so if we want fermentation—growth, change, and improvement—then we must not only tolerate, but actually encourage the chaotic." Henry Adams in his autobiography also tells us that "chaos often breeds life, when order breeds habit." Growth breeds chaos in the sense that these authors used the term, and to appreciate that chaos, not eliminate it, is one of the tasks of growth theory.

7. This is not to say that government help always defeats growth efforts. I will discuss the role of the government and of rent seeking in the last chapter.

time they (the entrepreneurs) may know or learn quickly as they explore that new technologies do not appear to be findable that will in fact permit the use of more labor per unit of capital. Then a dilemma appears: 1) whether the firm has enough confidence that it could find—in part create—a new technology that uses relatively more labor and so be able to take advantage of the newly acquired information that labor is really cheaper than was thought at the outset; or 2) if the firm should accept the evidence that the possibility of doing so looks pretty barren in terms of technology, and therefore search in another direction even though factor prices are less favorable in that direction. Evidently much depends on the knowledge and ignorance and animal spirits of the entrepreneurs.

There are however many ways to lower costs. For example, to use more capital may enable the firm to develop a technology that permits it to employ labor of less skill and experience and thereby lower labor costs enough to compensate for the added cost of capital. The firm might, for another example, find a way, with different forms of physical capital, to employ women on short work period shifts. This might not only reduce production costs, but also make the new firm more acceptable to the society. Such a change might also, however, violate a truce within the firm or community. "Truce" refers to an understanding as to arrangements and conditions of work that prevail and are understood, ones that have been achieved over time to meet conflicting objectives and interests in the firm. The notion of a truce is explored in some depth in Nelson and Winter (1982). It is an important notion in appreciating the options—the degrees of freedom—open to the firm for the establishment of new arrangements of any kind. Maintenance cost may be a problem that has attracted the attention of the entrepreneurs, the record of current suppliers may be erratic and unreliable as to both quantity and quality, and so forth. The search thus includes a wide variety of targets. Constant tinkering is required. Minor variations day after day after day can change the basic nature of a firm in a surprisingly short time. Tinkering means essentially using what is available to get increasingly effective results. It means identifying and discovering the underutilized knowledge that exists.

Figure 4 may help. In this figure capital and labor are again on the axes, and 4A and 4B each represent a distinct bicycle manufacturer. Production has begun at A and A', and the circle is meant to indicate the space within which technical (or organizational) knowledge has become reasonably well known more or less as a happenstance. Now each firm must decide which direction to begin to probe, to begin to experiment, and to incur the cost of trials and errors. Factor price calculations dictate searching southeast, and this is what Firm A undertakes. Firm B on the other hand believes technological barriers in that direction are too formidable, and so looks northwest. Neither B nor B'

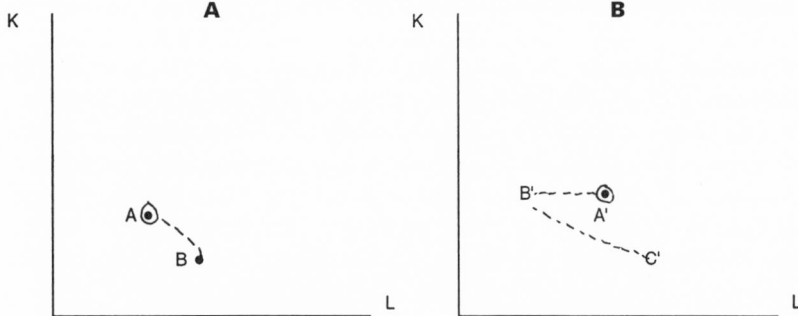

Fig. 4. Different firms search in different directions

is tracing an isoquant, as the level of output may be different from that at *A* and *A'*, as may quality of products, other inputs, and so on.

Another issue is opened up. Suppose that the move from *A* to *B* in figure 4A, *B* is the end of the line. Nothing else is likely to turn up in that area, but at *B'* new learning opportunities are recreated. So that at *B'* further searching leads the firm back down to *C* with higher quality products as well as a more-labor-using productive activity, and Firm 4B begins to grow. Possibly also both will succeed and there will be two very different bicycle firms producing and earning a profit.

The central point at this stage of the argument is that there are numerous ways—numerous directions—that search can proceed that will lead to an increase in productivity and to an enhancement in the extent to which the firm fits and serves the society. Any search may fail. It is the existence of the wide range of possibilities and technologies for reducing costs to which I attach fundamental importance in explaining both the growth of productivity and its variance among sectors and countries. These various issues and examples also point up the importance of the role of the entrepreneur and managers in the development effort.

The Role of Factor Prices and Technological Information

The stylized facts and ideas of long-term growth, noted earlier, imply that there must be some sort of incentives and mechanisms that direct search and learning in those directions that keep the profit rate from long-term decline in the face of rising wage rates and capital-labor ratios, that keep the capital-output ratio from drifting much in one direction or the other, and that allows employment growth to keep pace with labor supply. These facts are about the economy as a whole and are usually discussed in a macro analysis. The search effort, however, is carried out by individual firms.[8] The incentives and inducements that determine the direction of search must therefore bear on firms in some way or another. The stylized facts then represent an aggregation of the activities of many firms, and they in turn create an economic environment in which a firm must function in order to survive. Those firms that cannot maintain an acceptable profit rate in an environment described by the stylized facts will drop out, and the macro growth picture will be given by the average performance of the firms that survive over the period of interest.

Two determinants of the direction of search are of special importance: relative factor prices and the state of technology. I discuss each briefly.

Factor Prices

A simple and appealing argument is that entrepreneurs are induced to search in a direction that they believe will "save" a particularly costly input or one whose price is expected to rise over time or otherwise become increasingly difficult to acquire. This is more or less equivalent to saying that entrepreneurs search in a direction which, if successful, will enable them to use, to an increasing extent, the more plentiful (and hence cheaper) resource or intermediate goods.[9]

Hayami and Ruttan (1985) examine this argument in illuminating detail in their discussion of agriculture in Japan and the United States over the century after 1880. These two countries with vastly different endowments of land and labor were both able to achieve substantial rates of growth of agricultural output. In the United States the abundant supply of land, and hence its low price, combined with high priced and otherwise scarce labor created a strong inducement to find ways to substitute land and machinery for labor. This inducement became especially strong after the railroads made it possible

---

8. One could imagine an economy that was fully planned in which the central planners did all the searching and learning and handed over the new technologies to the firms who then applied them directly. This does not seem to be a route that can be expected to work very well.

9. Wilfred Salter (1966) and others have argued that in a long-run equilibrium, if each factor receives its marginal value product, then all factors are equally expensive. Since firms are interested in reducing costs, entrepreneurs then have no incentive to save a particular input. This of course is a valid argument, but in the context of the approach of this essay it is irrelevant. First of all firms are not in any sort of equilibrium that matters for this argument. Similarly, Salter makes very strong assumptions about the extent to which substitution is possible among all inputs, i.e., he leaves very little room for new knowledge as everything is included in the isoquant. Finally, one may argue that entrepreneurs do, in fact, think in terms of cheaper and more expensive factors and intermediate inputs, and therefore do think about finding ways to replace the dear with the cheap, as they identify them. Salter's book (1966) is extraordinarily stimulating and I make use of other of his arguments later.

to ship grain cheaply from the Midwest of the United States to the East Coast and then on to Europe. In Japan, on the other hand, the high price of land combined with a relatively abundant labor supply provided an inducement to search for ways to substitute labor for land or to "stretch" the land endowment. The result was, in the United States, a major effort to find ways to mechanize all stages of agriculture production, and this was of course broadly successful. In Japan the advantage of a search for fertilizing techniques was apparent, and such search was also reasonably successful. Data in Hayami and Ruttan (180) show the fertilizer-arable land price ratio in Japan to be much lower than in the United States, and the fertilizer use per hectare therefore much greater over the period. Power-labor price ratios were also generally much higher in Japan than in the United States, and therefore (it seems correct to say "therefore") farm draft power per worker in Japan much, much less than in the United States.

Had search in the United States been concerned with "saving" land and using labor as in Japan, then one would expect that wages would have been higher than they in fact were and land development would have proceeded much more slowly, that is, land would have been underutilized or more underutilized than it was. Indeed, it may have been that agriculture would not have been possible in the United States, and the industrialization process got underway much earlier than it did with most food imported. For reasons to be discussed later, however, a slow (or nonexistent) agricultural sector would doubtless have penalized the industrialization process in the United States. Similarly, if Japan had depended entirely on importing agricultural techniques from the United States, their agriculture would have been greatly handicapped compared to its actual development.[10] In particular it could be expected that demand for labor would have been substantially less than it was.

In both these examples it was the direction that search took that mattered, not just the fact and success of search. This direction, as Hayami and Ruttan emphasize, was in significant part a consequence of price signals.

This argument suggests a role for prices quite different from that usually identified in the textbooks. That role is, of course, to direct the entrepreneur to the factor combination which, with existing technology, yields the least-cost package of resources for current production. Now, however, the price signals are intended as well to inform the entrepreneur as to the direction that search should take in order to achieve the largest reduction in costs. Thus prices now

---

10. Obviously many other things could have happened. The point here is not to try to determine what would have happened had search proceeded in other directions, but rather simply to note that there would have been major differences. Since in both countries the new technologies did facilitate the use of all available resources, that fact was a major advantage. As is discussed more below, nonmarket and political factors often have important effects on the content and objectives of research.

have a dual role: to help determine the current factor combinations and to turn the entrepreneur in the appropriate direction to search. It is, of course, evident that short-run aberrations in world markets can provide misleading signals about long-run scarcities of certain intermediate goods. For example, present interest rates around the world or exchange rates may produce misconceptions as to what the future price of commodity imports and the cost of foreign borrowing will be. Evidently all this does not lead to a neat statement about shadow prices. Indeed it leads to a position that there are no neat statements about what shadow prices should be, or even how they are to be defined. It does, I think, show that the spread of information—in addition to that provided by currently prevailing prices—could be especially helpful in the search effort in a country. More on these matters a bit later.

There is, however, a major difficulty with search simply following where factor and intermediate good prices direct. Technological possibilities matter.

The Role of Technology: Inexorableness or Choice

Suppose that price signals are clear and unambiguous as to the direction of profitable search. Suppose further that the entrepreneurs appreciate these signals, and search in the direction indicated—and find nothing. Suppose in the United States in the nineteenth century that it had not been possible to find out how to produce machines that made it possible for relatively few humans to cultivate large amounts of land. Then to have searched in that direction would have yielded nothing. Given the inevitable ignorance surrounding future technological possibilities, is there anything that can be said that is helpful in understanding whether new knowledge can be found in one direction or another or that may be of policy relevance? The answer is, very little. It does, however, seem to be worthwhile to try to identify a few items of relevance.

I noted above that the search must necessarily begin at A and A' in figure 4 because that is where the firms are currently operating. The entrepreneurs know more about knowledge in the vicinity of A than at other places in the figure's space. Thus they may be presumed to know which direction in the immediate area of A search effort is most likely to be technologically successful. If this direction is consistent with price signals all is well. If it is not, then the entrepreneurs have a more complex decision to make; that is, whether to search in a direction where technological success is dim, but where a success would pay off extra well or whether to move in the direction where new technology looks most promising, but where economic fit may be much less appropriate. Evidently only the entrepreneurs with their command of general and specific knowledge, and their intuition and hunches and animal spirits can, or at least should, decide this matter. Some will bet on lucking out on the technology front and win, and others will lose. "Lucking out" is not entirely the right term, because success does depend on what the entrepreneurs know and how firm their tacit knowledge is and how well they are acquainted with the general technological knowledge of the community that might be relevant to their cause. Still, animal spirits also matter.

There may be people other than the entrepreneurs themselves in various occupations in a community who are able to offer or create the kind of knowledge that is helpful in finding the improved technology that better exploits the factor and intermediate goods supply situation. To have access to this sort of source of information is particularly helpful. The following example illustrates this notion in a revealing way.

In several places in Africa one finds extensive "junkyards," usually separated into more or less independent stalls. An individual stall will be a collection of parts, pieces, and things that constitute the "capital" of that junk dealer. The dealers sell physical products, but more important they sell knowledge and technology. They sell ideas and then supply an item that can implement that idea. Some dealers apparently are extraordinarily clever in turning useless things (sometimes obtained from derelict or fruitless aid projects) into useful things in response to a specific request from a client. Clients are usually small-scale domestic enterprises and households. Evidently it makes no sense for such dealers to try to "invent"—to do R&D—independently of the problems that their clients can identify. The face-to-face meetings between the searcher and the potential rescuer are about as precise and continuous as can be imagined. The question raised by the user of the knowledge may be expected to arise either from a scarcity issue, reflected possibly by rising prices, or by the evidence that an intermediate good or category of labor has become more readily available or cheaper or more costly than in the past. A successful result would tend to use available resources more completely.

There are other similar examples that attest to a capacity on the part of certain members of a society to search in a way that yields some considerable success. This sort of thing is exactly what is meant by indigenous knowledge and underutilized knowledge. For the junkyard people to be effective requires that the user of the knowledge be searching and have a rather specific problem to be solved.

The accumulation of knowledge in the neighborhood of A will also help entrepreneurs gain insight about where new technologies are most likely, least unlikely, to be found, and therefore the direction it seems most fruitful to probe. Similarly where there is active search over many sectors of the economy, technological information over this range of activities may provide clues for searchers in many activities. The idea then is to create an environment in which all firms are actively searching, and this in turn will create knowledge that is helpful to each individual producer in creating knowledge specific to her/his activity. The idea of a "network" among entrepreneurs and managers that facilitates conversation and other forms of interaction and thereby spreads new ideas and new practices is helpful. Such networks can spring up without direct outside support or may be induced in a variety of ways.[11] They are a helpful way to create knowledge externalities.

One may also note that indigenous search is likely to recognize and respect social and cultural boundaries the penetration of which society finds defeats well-being. Such boundaries vary sharply among societies over time and often become evident only after some penetration into doubtful territory has occurred. Such socially forbidden areas may include family arrangements (birth control, education, role for the elderly, role of women, etc.), ethnic and religious traditions, certain political matters, certain products, etc. These are grave issues about which understanding is extremely primitive, but the basic notion seems fairly clear: to create a technologically progressive economy that does not violate basic and fundamental sources of meaning.[12]

Later when I introduce international transactions into the argument, this issue will be more evident as other and more alien sources of technical knowledge become available to the community. The possible conflict between domestic scarcity signals and technological possibilities is also more acute when international activities are recognized, and this too will require attention in the later chapter.

Put aside for the moment the role of international transactions. I think the preceding paragraphs describe fairly accurately the way that technical knowledge was accumulated and applied in all countries before the whole process became so highly formal. The role of science was not insignificant, but it played a distinctly subordinate role to the more hit-and-miss, trial-and-error search process (combined with learning by doing) that is present in the process described above. I will argue in the chapter on entrepreneurs that this process, this urge to search and learn, is a consequence of a great many characteristics of a society, and that its emergence is a crucial, perhaps the crucial, condition for the creation of an economy that achieves growth as a consequence of its routine operation. First I want to discuss some other things.

A Time Path through Capital and Productivity Space

If we rule out isoquants as not helpful in the context of growth, we need some sort of instrument to replace them that enables us to picture the life of the firm. Unfortunately there is nothing that appears to work well, but a grope or two

---

11. Literature on networks is now growing rapidly. A paper of direct relevance to the argument here is Barr (1995).

12. Andrew Feenberg (1991) has helpful things to say on these issues.

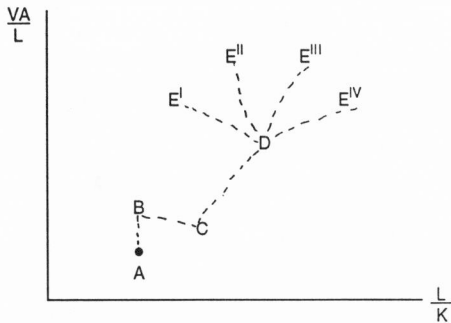

Fig. 5. Capital formation and searching in a growing firm

may be in order. To keep things manageable, I will limit the analysis largely to capital and labor, although it remains crucial to appreciate that costs and cost reductions depend on many other things as well. Consider figure 5.

The bicycle firm began its life at *A* and has moved to *C* in the manner described. Now suppose the firm's explicit searches begin to pay off: The entrepreneurs, after some study, find a way to reorganize the production routine so that productivity rises, the entrepreneurs may recognize that a more cordial atmosphere in the work place results in higher output, and so on. These various activities push *VA/L* up again, say to *D*. The position *D* has been arrived at by the process of internal searching and learning with little contribution from outside the firm.

Suppose at *D* the firm identifies four possible further routes for expansion. How does it choose? The most obvious criterion is the profit rate, and, in our simple way, we examine that by asking what is happening to capital's share and to the capital-output ratio as the route to *E* is followed. A firm may well be able to determine this. The main point at the moment, however, is that whether or not *E* is the profitable choice depends on its route to *D* and the location of *D*. This means that another firm may follow *E'* or *E''* and be equally successful. Again we expect to find a bicycle industry with firms of many different technologies, organizational arrangements, intermediate input composition, and so on. Thus *E'* may "fit" one firm or management better than *E*, and this different fit is due to different histories. If one firm chooses *E'* and another *E'''*, then their future paths are sure to be different. The routes opened to them from these two positions are different. Expected demand also is part of the decision-making package.

Several observers (e.g., Pavitt 1984, Nelson in Dosi et al. 1988) have noted that the technology of almost any firm has a great deal that is, or rapidly becomes, unique to it. A stronger statement is in order: if a firm is to achieve sustained growth of productivity, it must develop its own particular technology and technological evolution. A firm that tries to depend entirely on outside sources of new knowledge or knowledge creation will die off. Search methods and "directions" and identifying and interpreting information will vary among firms, even among bicycle firms, and to a considerable extent one firm cannot really imitate another firm. Giovanni Dosi (225 in Dosi et al. 1988) emphasizes that what a firm can do in the future is constrained by what it has done in the past. Firms will then tend to search in directions that build upon their existing techniques, organization, administration, and tacit knowledge. There is no great pool of knowledge—technical, organizational, administrative—into which each firm can plunge to obtain the most productive technology completely defined. Rather there is a body of ignorance, knowledge, skill, art, intuition specific to each firm and these define the search route and the process of accumulating knowledge.[13]

Recall however the stylized fact noted earlier that the variance of productivity growth among sectors within a country is generally less than the variance of a particular sector among countries. In regressions a dummy variable that represents a specific country in various forms of regressions explaining productivity growth is generally significant in the customary way. This means that there is something about the "country" itself that matters for productivity growth. I suggest there are two general categories of reasons for this. The first reason has to do with ambience, general environment, prevailing ethos, and other equally nebulous notions that I examine in the later chapter on entrepreneurship.

The second reason is that there is general knowledge in the community that all firms have access to and can use in a variety of ways. All bicycle manufacturers do have some things in common. A new technology, or, more accurately, new technical and administrative knowledge that appears in one producer's plant will show up, almost certainly in modified form, in other plants. So in a growing economy, firms learn from each other, even from firms in different activities. The role of firms learning from each other is an important reason why searching and learning throughout the economy is crucial.[14] This is the network notion again. It also helps explain why turnkey projects contribute so little to any sort of indigenous search and learn process. Such

---

13. In the days when automobile manufacturers in the United States dominated the world industry, there were numerous discussions of why General Motors seemed to be so much more productive than the other auto firms. We still cannot say exactly why that was, nor can we say why Japanese firms seem to be able to produce cars so much more cheaply than can United States firms.

14. One reason why, in earlier centuries, the isolated instances of significant new technologies in many countries did not lead to widespread, sustained growth was that the search activity was limited to a very small part of the economy.

projects tend to be isolated from domestic enterprises and ill suited to create the kind of rapport, the kind of learning opportunities that can contribute to the growth of productivity in the community of firms. The process of firms learning from each other is not just a matter of one firm imitating another, but rather that of gaining insight and ideas and understandings that then can be adapted to work in the context of its own operations.

The introduction of continual change, especially of technological change, into the analysis of the firm makes explicit the difficult nature of choice. There is the inexorableness of the flow of new knowledge that seems beyond choice, but yet there must be choice. There is inexorableness and there is choice, that is, freedom, and to appreciate this is basic to seeing a firm through time.

The Role of Capital Formation

To this point all of the increased labor productivity and increased total output has been achieved by the learning by doing and searching while producing. The latter was identified as learning by tinkering. Physical capital formation has been left out of the story. It is of course highly relevant as the survey of stylized facts and ideas showed, and this section is devoted to an examination of its role. There are two issues to which attention is devoted, investment as such and the role of a capital goods sector. That there could be growth of output and of labor productivity without capital formation is quite possible given the sources of the increased productivity, especially organizational and administrative changes and learning by doing. Over a longer period of time however such an argument is less convincing. Rather the argument may be put in terms of no *net* capital formation, but gross investment is positive. Old physical capital is replaced by different forms of new capital as the former wears out or becomes obsolete, but the "quantity" of capital remains constant. In this case new knowledge may be built into the new physical capital, where it acts directly on the productivity of labor. In tinkering with the production process a manager may see that a machine might function better if it were slightly different. As existing machines are replaced, a new machine can reflect this new knowledge. Something like this is necessary to make sense out of the equation $r_Q = r_A + ar_K + br_L$. This equation implies that if $ar_K + br_L$ were zero, output (and labor productivity) would still grow at r_A, but this does not mean, for reasons just stated, that no new capital goods appear in the firm's production process.

The argument of net and gross may work for a given short interval, but over a longer period it is inadequate. Also, one of the firmest stylized facts is that the growth of the capital stock exceeds the growth of the labor force in

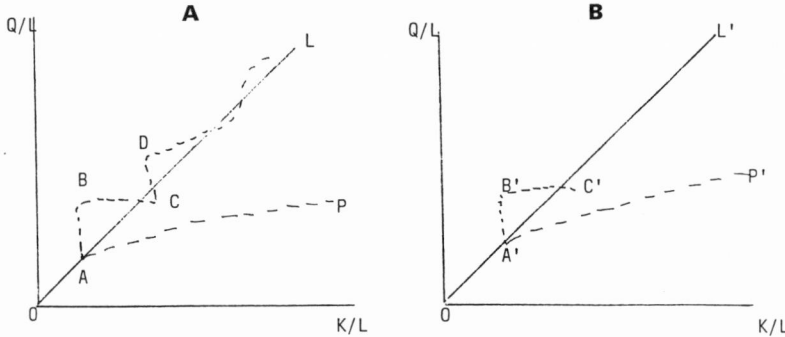

Fig. 6. Successful and unsuccessful searching

a growing economy, even while the exact role that it plays is far from well defined. It is necessary therefore to examine the way capital formation enters the story.

In figure 6A the story begins again at *A* on line *OL,* with the assumption that capital formation is occurring at a rate in excess of employment. The usual formulation has a curve such as *AP* to indicate how labor productivity rises as *K/L* increases with unchanged technical, administrative, organizational, and other knowledge. The curve rises and levels off to reflect the usual assumptions about diminishing returns to capital as *K/L* rises. To draw such a line, however, is not possible in the present formulation of ignorance beyond a modest distance from *A. Any* move from *A* requires some searching and learning, and trial and error, and new knowledge that was not available to the entrepreneurs when they started the bicycle factory at *A.* In figure 6B another bicycle factory starts up at *A',* and the same arguments apply.

In both firms learning by doing and tinkering begin as production begins and produces movement toward the north of the figure. This pushes up the profit rate (subject to what happens to wage rates as before), and this is at least one indicator that additional investment would be profitable. As *Q/L* rises at the unchanged *K/L,* the firm's decision makers face an array of choices: do nothing except enjoy the higher profits, lower prices, proceed as earlier and employ more labor, invest more physical capital to speed up the rate of growth of output and labor productivity. If more investment is decided upon, the further question arises as to what kind of capital and its source of supply. Managers must also appreciate the impact of their decisions on the prevailing truce in their firms, on the community at large and other issues. All of these decisions depend on many considerations and must take place in the presence of a great deal of ignorance. How each firm proceeds depends very much on how their managers interpret the evidence they have, their animal spirits, and their general attitudes toward searching and learning. It is exceedingly unlikely that they will follow the same route.

One or two additional comments may make the process clearer. In 6A from location B, suppose the firm moves toward C. Labor productivity is falling, due (say) to a new machine with which the labor force is unfamiliar. At C the profit rate is below that at A or B, unless capital's share has risen. The firm may now seek to do one of two things: find a way to get capital's share higher or make a major effort to increase labor's capacity to use the new machines. If it is the latter and the firm is successful, production will again move north and Q/L again rises. Indeed, the firm may even have anticipated that Q/L would initially fall with the new capital and then rise as learning and tinkering takes place, and financial arrangements had taken this possibility into account. The temporary fall in profits would then be looked upon as an investment that takes the form of a learning period. This investment pays off in the form of movements in Q/L toward, say, D. One can of course tell a lot of other stories about what happens as the processes unfold.

In 6B suppose the firm moves from B' toward C', and productivity does not rise or rises very little, and at C' nothing further happens. Unless firm 6B is subsidized in some way or other this firm will wither and die. At C' profits are too low to merit a claim on resources for very long, and they then move into other activities. Why did production in 6A move from C toward D, but at C' in 6B not move at all?

Now is it possible to separate the increase in Q/L due to a rising Q/L from that due to an increase in productivity? I have little doubt that someone could find a way to do this, but to do so is surely misleading. There is, I have argued, no such curve as AP or $A'P'$ (in figures 6A and 6B) and ignorance is present, no matter how and in what direction the firms leave A or A'. The whole process of capital formation and search for and application of new knowledge is a unified process that must be seen as a unified process. To take it apart is misleading. The array of choices listed above shows how intermingled the capital and the knowledge accumulation and application process is, and how both depend so heavily on searching and learning in the presence of ignorance.

The Capital Goods Sector

If there is capital formation occurring, there must be the production of capital goods. There are two main domestic sources of new capital goods: the firm (or farm) itself and a separate sector that produces and sells the new goods to the sector that uses them.

That a significant amount of capital is formed within the firm seems clear, but I have found no empirical evidence of how extensive it is. It may be more extensive on farms than in manufacturing. Thus a farmer who works to improve his irrigation ditches or to build a new barn or silo or to clear land is creating physical capital. The saving that makes such investment possible is frequently forgone leisure, but it could be in the form of sacrificing the present output of consumer goods, for example, taking a smaller current output of food products in anticipation of larger outputs later. One can think of similar examples where small manufacturing firms engage in activities that result in more capital stock. The main inducement to do this sort of thing is the prospects of increased yields at acceptable prices. I have more to say on this later.

Physical capital is of course purchased by one firm from another, so we can speak of a capital goods producing firm and sector. In a closed economy, there must be such sectors if the economy is to increase its capital stock at a significant pace. In the present context the capital goods sector is of interest primarily because of its role in the productivity growth story, and I will concentrate attention on that role in the paragraphs to follow.[15]

A domestic capital goods sector has the advantage of proximity with the capital using sectors. Such a sector is, or can be, informed about the content of the searching by the capital using firms. A domestic capital goods sector can have full information about the knowledge currently in use by other firms in the economy, and be concerned directly with building onto that knowledge. It can be aware of the general environment—input supply situation, the state of the labor market, the demand situation, market structure, social and political issues and so forth—that determine the extent to which a new capital good overcomes the barrier against which a firm is currently pressing. Several surveys have found that one of the most successful characteristics of new physical capital (and new ideas) is that their roots are to be found in an understanding of the needs (the search objectives) of capital users. Particularly in labor-plentiful economies, new capital goods emerging from domestic producers may be especially helpful in creating a higher rate of growth of demand for labor than would be the case with imported capital.

Proximity is important for another reason. The full implications of a new capital item, even a relatively simple one, cannot be communicated either verbally or by written directions. They must be learned by extended use. The close observation over time of a new machine by both creator and user can lead to improvements in its contribution to the firm's objectives. Capital items are of course often, indeed usually, modified over time as their use reveals unexpected inadequacies and failures, and correcting these is usually the job of the firm that produced them. Such monitoring is best done—in some cases can *only* be done—if the producer of the capital good is readily at hand.

---

15. I have examined these issues in more detail in my chapter in James and Watanabe (1985). The following paragraphs borrow from this chapter to a considerable extent.

Technological development, and learning in general, is a problem-solving process that enables a firm and a society to create and exploit opportunities with increasing effectiveness in its own environment. A capital goods sector that responds to this situation can become a center of searching and learning in a particular environment. Such a role can, over time, create a group of people who have confidence that technical and economic problems can be overcome. And this attitude in turn can create confidence among clients that it makes sense for them to search out profit opportunities and to ask the capital goods sector to create something that would enable the new opportunities to be exploited. To rely on imported capital goods, even where they are obtainable at lower prices, denies the possibility of creating this capacity.

There are many examples of this argument, but perhaps the cleanest one is that of the creation of agricultural machinery in the United States and Japan. Such machines were not created by farmers in either country, but their producers were closely attuned to the farmers' needs and environmental conditions. In the nineteenth century, firms producing agricultural equipment sprang up everywhere to respond to the opportunities created by demand from farmers, who in turn were responding to opportunities created by a rapidly growing demand for food products. The failure of agriculture in many countries is certainly in part due to pricing and taxing policies, but it also is due to the failure of an effective technological development and learning process to be in place in the relevant sectors.

The labor-augmenting productivity growth that seems to have characterized growing firms and economies applies to the capital goods sectors as well as to the producers of consumer goods. If this were not happening, the K/Q would surely be rising. As productivity increases in the capital goods sector, the real cost of the capital used by the economy declines over time. As this happens the cost of the rising capital-labor ratio declines, and further growth is encouraged.

A last observation. The term *capital goods sector* tends to create an image of a large and complex firm using complex technologies and employing highly skilled workers and managers. There are such firms of course, but capital goods can be produced by small firms employing available labor. The histories of the United States and Japan again show that small firms were strategic in the early periods in producing equipment that was especially suited to the factor endowment and other characteristics of the two societies.[16] Engineering shops can be very small indeed and can thereby exploit new ideas

---

16. Tessa Morris-Suzuki (1994) has a number of examples of the small-scale exceptionally productive capital-goods firms in Japan. The same argument applies to research institutes (which I examine a bit later). Morris-Suzuki is an exceptionally valuable study of technological evolution in Japan. For the United States, Nathan Rosenberg (1982) has many illuminating examples.

quickly and respond to requests from potential clients quickly. A capital goods firm can begin small and grow just as any other firm can.

I have additional comments on the capital goods sector in an open economy in a later chapter.

Some Macro Issues

Full utilization of all resources with price level and balance of payments stability is a frequently employed criterion of aggregate demand management. With sufficient assumptions there is no real issue. If physical capital were a big ball of malleable steel that could be squeezed in such a manner that any composition of output became possible at a moment's notice, if the labor force were uniquely defined and any task for labor could be learned on the job in five minutes, and if all firms used the most productive technology, then aggregate supply would have a precise meaning and would exactly match the composition of demand every minute of the day. If all of the physical capital and all members of the labor force were thrown on the market and accepted the market clearing price, there would also be full utilization of all resources, and that would be the end of the story.

Of course these assumptions are not applicable to any country anywhere, although for some purposes they might possibly help illuminate a phenomenon or two. For developing countries, however, they are a handicap. Physical capital is in no sense perfectly malleable, except in some imaginary long, long run. All jobs cannot be learned in five minutes, and all firms are not always using the most productive technology. All firms do not even know the most productive technology. So aggregate supply is a notion of great ambiguity. Aggregate demand must be thought of, not simply as $C + I + G + X - M$, but as the demand for a huge range of different products and services. Despite all this, the notions of macro economics are of relevance. There are constraints at the macro level that have to be recognized and there are historical patterns of the macro variables whose study is illuminating as to the workings of the economy. It is evident from these statements and from the discussion to this point that the explanation of the macro variables should not require strong assumptions about optimization at the firm and household level. As emphasized, there is no such optimization (in the conventional sense) in a system where ignorance is ubiquitous and institutions have a pervading influence.[17]

There are many macro models of all shapes and sizes. There does not appear to be a conventional model for developing countries that one can plug into the story in a straightforward way.[18] The usual prescription is a more or

---

17. Lance Taylor (1991, chapter 1) has useful things to say on these matters.

18. Stanley Fischer (1991) is a helpful survey of current thinking on this topic. Fischer also

less balanced government budget as the basic means of achieving price level stability. If price level stability is maintained and the exchange rate is "right," there will be no balance of payments problems. This prescription rests on the assumption that price level and balance of payments stability are the basic objectives of macro policy. I proceed in a slightly different way in the following pages.

The Macro Question

The macro question that I wish to explore is this: To what extent and in what way can considerations of aggregate demand and, to a lesser extent, aggregate supply contribute to the development process as that process is defined in this book? In particular, how does aggregate demand bear on the incentives to search and learn by households and firms? It is accepted without debate that severe inflation is harmful, though how much inflation is "severe" will vary from country to country. Chronic balance of payments difficulties are also a major barrier to sustained growth. Both of these difficulties can be avoided by allowing a great deal of idle labor and underutilized physical capital, but the cost of preventing these problems in this fashion is, of course, much too high for any country to accept. So the objective of macro policy should not be stated in terms of price level and balance of payments stability, but in terms of its contribution to the search-and-learn process.

Strong demand for all resources, especially labor, is important for a number of reasons, in addition to the general point that unused resources constitute wasted opportunities and impose unnecessary hardship on a population. The main additional reasons why a strong demand matters seem to be the following.

1. A strong demand for labor is far and away the best way to meet the poverty problem. It is even more evident that the poverty problem, that is, the fact that, in a country where per capita income is generally very low there are people whose income is well below this low average, is virtually intractable in a situation where supply of labor greatly exceeds demand at any sensible wage rate.
2. It may also be expected that the introduction of apparently labor replacing machinery will face fewer obstacles in the presence of ample employment opportunities.
3. Strong demand pressure against all resources constitutes an incentive, in addition to those already identified, to search for ways to increase productivity. Evident profit opportunities from increased output in the

---

reports on some interesting empirical studies. Levine and Renelt (1991, 1991a) also report empirical findings of relevance to the present discussion.

presence of sharply rising marginal costs induce efforts to increase output without additional inputs, that is, to increase productivity. Such a situation requires more or less full utilization of existing resources. More on this point below.

4. Strong demand without "too much" inflation or balance of payments problems may be expected to have favorable effects on entrepreneurs' expectations.

5. A strong aggregate demand helps prevent individual sectors from running into an early demand constraint. It helps, but of course does not prevent, a demand constraint from eventually appearing. As noted earlier, exporting is the most effective means of preventing a demand constraint from appearing for a particular sector.

I conclude then that strong demand pressure, a demand pressure that presses firmly against supply of all resources, especially labor, is a major advantage in achieving the development objective.

Given that aggregate demand is strong relative to resources, there is the further question of whether it matters what the source of that demand is. In most developing countries investment demand will have more favorable effects on growth of output and productivity than will consumption. Even here one must be cautious however as increased consumption of very low income workers can have significant effects on their productivity and well-being generally. A direct increase in government spending—a simple increase in G financed by money creation—is not only likely to have inflationary implications, but does not seem to contribute much to productivity growth although the evidence is far from clear. The most interesting component of aggregate demand in the present context is exports. There are many sides of the role of exports and I want to examine them in some detail later when the argument is opened to include foreign transactions.

The Approach

Even in the very short run, more or less static kind of textbook analysis, there are difficulties, conceptual and empirical, with the notion of full utilization. These difficulties are multiplied many times over in those economies that are just beginning to grow after centuries of nongrowth. To help fix the basic argument of this section, consider figures 7 and 8.

Figure 7 is the conventional production possibility curve as it appears in the textbooks. The curve, RS, defines the maximum amount of bicycles that can be produced given the amount of all other commodities and services that are produced. On RS there is "full utilization" of all factors of production and the knowledge that yields the highest productivity is being utilized. The

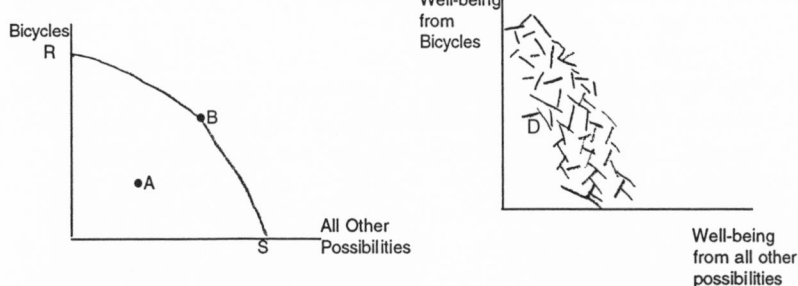

Fig. 7. The production possibility frontier: Old style

Fig. 8. The well-being maze

economy is presumed to be able to reac*h* *RS* without inflation. Figure 8 is different. The hen scratches here replace the production possibility frontier of figure 7, and are used to emphasize the idea that there are many barriers and hurdles to be recognized in any effort to increase output and further that there is no absolute rigid capacity limit. What the hen scratches are depends on the array of institutions, values, history, and policies that characterize the economy at a given moment as well as on conventional economic relationships. The idea is obviously fuzzy, so the line is fuzzy.

At point *A* in figure 7, it is customary to say that all resources are not being utilized, and so more of both bicycles and all other can be produced. Given the way this figure is drawn—no barriers between *A* and *RS*—an increase in aggregate demand should move *A* quickly and without delay to the line, say to point *B,* unless monopolies or other market failures prevent reaching *RS*. Then there would be full utilization of everything, labor, capital, and the most productive knowledge.

At figure 8, the story is different. There is no unique full utilization line, no final barrier, yet it is clear that point *D* does not represent full utilization of much of anything. The role now of aggregate demand in eliminating the underutilization is less clear-cut than in figure 7. Indeed if *D* is lodged against a firmly entrenched barrier of some sort, an increase in aggregate demand with no other change—say simply an increase in *G*—will produce inflation with little effect on resource utilization. The issue is made much more complex when full utilization of knowledge is included in the determination of the production possibility curve.[19] On the other hand, if the barrier against which *D* is currently lodged moves or disintegrates or can be circumvented due to

---

19. The term *full utilization of knowledge* is, as previous discussion has shown, even more ambiguous than the other concepts now being examined.

demand pressure, an increment in aggregate demand may in fact produce increases in output and in resource utilization.

The arguments of figures 7 and 8 may be illuminated in another way. It is generally appreciated that Keynes was a committed neoclassical economist who believed in underemployment equilibrium (and ignorance). He believed that point A could exist with nothing (i.e., no barriers) between it and the production possibility curve, where full employment, full use of physical capital, full use of technical and administrative knowledge barrier prevailed. The reason there were no such barriers was, in Keynes's view, that the workings of the market would eliminate all such bottlenecks and barriers. With simply an increase in aggregate demand, an increase in G, therefore, the economy would move rapidly from A to the full utilization barrier.

Figure 8, on the other hand, tells us that in an economy long stagnant, with no experience in growth or change of any sort, the assumption of no barriers, other than the sharply defined full utilization barrier, is misleading. There will be many incapacities and bottlenecks at the same time that there is evident underutilization. These complications are increased by the recognition that much of existing knowledge is firm, specific, and tacit. Thus there are aggregate demand issues, but these issues must be studied in the context of incomplete markets, misleading price signals, slow response to incentives by firms and households, and a lot of ignorance. At D in figure 8 there is underutilization of resources, but little existing capacity that can be immediately exploited as in Keynes's underemployment equilibrium argument.[20] The axes in figure 8 are labeled "well-being created by bicycles" in order to remind us that some of the barriers reflect values, traditions, cultural characteristics that may constitute important sources of well-being themselves and may change only slowly and painfully. It seems useful to refer to figure 8 as a "well-being possibility maze."

If at D there is no excess demand and the barrier against which the economy is lodged is somehow removed, then demand must increase or else increased utilization will not occur. Similarly, if there already exists excess demand at D, then removing the barrier is an anti-inflation device as well as an employment- and output-increasing device.[21]

So then a major question that must be answered in seeking to identify the role of aggregate demand in a given country at a given time is what the barriers are that appear to be preventing the economy from achieving a fuller use of its resources, especially of labor, and so a higher output, and, no less

---

20. Keynes's argument seemed to apply most neatly to an economy that had been functioning well and had fallen on difficult times. This is in contrast to an economy where growth has never really taken place and there is no capacity that has been created and is now idle.

21. When it is argued (or assumed) that demand must be reduced to control inflation, it must also be assumed that current output is a maximum—which, I am maintaining, is not a convincing position.

important, increasing productivity. Once that is done, it must further be decided whether aggregate demand manipulation is the right instrument with which to meet the problem. Any approach is likely to include aggregate demand, but require other instruments as well. Generalizations are dangerous and can be misleading to the analyst and policymaker alike, and it is essential to examine each economy—to define the hen scratches—in some detail before pronouncing an explanation or policy for a given country.

Some examples may help to illustrate these arguments.[22]

Suppose that at D a simple increase in aggregate demand, brought about say by an increase in G, would result in wage rates being pushed up even though it is evident that there is ample labor readily available. That this could occur could be due to many things—labor unions, political pressure, the practice of multinational corporations seeking to get the "best" labor, and so on. The rising wage rate would produce inflationary pressure, but may well allow for an increase in employment and output. Such a situation suggests that aggregate demand pressure combined with efforts to make the labor market work better may have desirable effects.

Suppose that at D the increase in demand will result in a composition of output and demand that will push up food prices to an unacceptable extent—unacceptable in terms of both political and ethical considerations. Measures to affect the composition of output may then be necessary to accompany the increment in demand.

Suppose that at D it is observed that profit rates are very low because the product wage (wage divided by the price of the product) in many sectors is higher than is common in the same sectors in other countries. Are wages too high or are product prices too low?

Suppose that at D working capital is found to be a major obstacle to firms increasing their output. Then evidently something can be done in this area to accompany the increment in demand.

Suppose that it appears that an improvement in the taxing bureaucracy would make it possible to increase total spending on investment without creating inflation. Attention might then concentrate on improving the taxing bureaucracy.

Suppose that any increase in spending would create an unsustainable current account deficit and the Minister of Finance is convinced that a devaluation would generate inflation and not solve the balance of payments problem in any event.

---

22. Lance Taylor (1988, 68 ff) has a list of issues that are relevant for policy-making in particular. I have borrowed substantially from this list. Taylor is concerned mainly with the consequences of the introduction of a stabilization program.

Can fairly convincing evidence be accumulated on the possibility of increasing exports if domestic absorption is controlled?

Can evidence be accumulated on the extent to which various sectors will respond to additional demand pressure?

Are there specific policies that the government might pursue which would result in the market itself working better? Such policies might include information disseminating, improvement in road and other communicating systems, institutions that modify the stick as opposed to the carrot component of the workings of a market system, and so on. If the price system works reasonably well, there should be fewer barriers within the well-being possibility maze, but, one must emphasize, the barriers will not go away completely even if the market worked "perfectly." Indeed, a perfectly working market may create barriers that impede the process.

The list could be extended, of course. There is danger in this approach in that it may lead to the view that since there are so many barriers, *nothing* can be done and that indeed point D is where the economy must function if unacceptable rates of inflation or balance of payments problems or severe violations of social norms are not to occur. It may also lead to the view that a great many things have to be done, therefore a huge government role is assumed to be necessary, even though such a role cannot be performed remotely adequately. Neither of these extremes is acceptable.

The argument here rests on the assumption, surely quite realistic, that an economy can be understood well enough—the hen scratches can be defined well enough—that only a few things need be undertaken at one time. These things will be those that dissolve the immediate barrier or find a way around it. It is right to argue that it is not possible for a government to do a great range of things because it does not have the capacity to act on a wide range of things. It is therefore essential for the policymakers to learn about their economy along the lines just described, and to act only on those barriers that are immediately relevant and to maintain control of the budget. Then aggregate demand may be enhanced with some confidence. One may well say that it is in this way that the line between macro- and microeconomics becomes blurred to the point where there is no line.

The government fiscal and monetary policy decision makers have a great deal of searching and learning to do, just as the private sector entrepreneurs do. Gustav Ranis (in *African Development*, 1991) states, with respect to Taiwan, that policy there was not made by mandarins sitting around saying what should be done. There was rather "a lot of bumbling and stumbling and going back and forth," and from this an effective policy was hit upon. In order to learn about the management of the macroeconomy and of what can be accomplished with macro tools, there must be trial and error, stumbling and bumbling, that leads to learning. General rules—balance the budget, increase exports, devalue, privatize, and so forth—defeat learning, and without learning there is no hope. This does not mean that to balance the budget is necessarily the wrong policy, but it does mean that such a policy must follow from a picturing of figure 8, rather than from any sort of alleged universal law. I return to these points in the last chapter where the role of the government is examined more systematically.

Inflation

I want now to say a kind word or two about inflation. It is crucial to prevent a rampant inflation and, where such occurs, it is necessary to get rid of it as quickly as possible. It is also crucial to recognize that a zero inflation rate does not make much sense in a developing country. There are two questions: how much price level increase is possible without undermining the development process, and whether the government can maintain a little inflation without it becoming a lot of inflation, that is, can the government maintain control over its budget process. If there is that control, a government can risk inflation much more readily than if that control is lacking.

To examine these questions in specific terms is not appropriate in the present context, but two general points may be emphasized. The first is that strong monetary and fiscal policy capacity (including the capacity to control inflation) is a particularly relevant capacity in the context of getting an economy into a growth routine. To help countries learn to control their budgetary processes is probably more helpful than to berate them for allowing deficits. The second is the appreciation of the notion that inflation can be used as a policy instrument. It is not appropriate therefore to include as a policy objective zero increases in the price level. The success stories—Korea, Botswana, Taiwan, Thailand, and so on—have all managed to have a "little" inflation over extended periods, and it seems reasonable to say that their growth would have been penalized had their governments been determined to have zero inflation. The limited increases in the price level in these countries were a consequence (for the most part) of spending to affect output or output growth. Evidently an increase in spending that has no effect on the output side (wars, boondoggles, etc.) is much more likely to result in damaging continuing price rises. Like everything else that matters, an effective approach to monetary/fiscal policy making must be learned. There are few governments where this learning has been well accomplished.

Saving and the Role of Labor

A brief comment on saving and on labor skills as they affect the macro arguments is relevant, although more complete discussions come later.

Can a saving constraint stop or impede the process that I have described? In general there appears little probability that saving would constitute a significant constraint as long as the growth occurs within the other boundaries of the system. "Other boundaries" here refers to managerial and organizational skills, capacity to identify and carry out projects, to engage in searching and learning, social and cultural mores, and so forth. Within these boundaries the notion that saving is strongly affected by opportunities for profitable investment is more applicable than other arguments about the determinants of saving rates. As growth continues and projects become larger and more complex—and the capacity of all actors also becomes increasingly enhanced—then saving constraints are more likely to appear. At that time the monetary and fiscal apparatus should be able, should have learned how, to have some influence on saving decisions. Even then there is not much likelihood of a saving constraint that severely dampens the process I have described.[23]

The argument above did not refer directly to labor training or to a skill bottleneck. There should not be a skill bottleneck for essentially the same reason that there is not expected to be a saving bottleneck. The activities designed and carried out within the environment will be consistent with the labor that is available. If there is a skill bottleneck, then the composition of investment is wrong, and the composition of investment is not likely to be wrong in the context of the development effort described to this point.[24] At any rate it could be quickly corrected by the searching and learning process described in earlier pages. It may be noted in passing that the growth of output in the West (less so in Japan) proceeded with a largely illiterate labor force. I have more to say on education in chapter 6.

This observation illustrates the point made early in chapter 1 that it is important to distinguish between low productivity and nonrising productivity. The objective is to create a situation where productivity is rising, and a skill bottleneck to that objective should not be important in a situation in which learning is a paramount feature.

The determinants of private investment are discussed in the chapter on entrepreneurs.

---

23. It is giant projects (and wars) that create saving barriers. Such projects—big dams, major highways, huge factories, large-scale housing developments, etc.—are often inappropriate and usually do little to contribute to enhanced well-being. One of the dangers of large-scale loans from international agencies is that they enable a project to be undertaken financially that violates the other boundaries noted in the text. Investments that increase output in identifiable ways are rarely inflationary.

24. One might argue, or even believe, that there may be a situation where literally nothing was possible because of the quality of the labor force, because the productivity of labor was so low. I do not believe that this is the case to the extent that it constitutes a significant problem. Such a situation, if it really was found to prevail, might be one in which multinational firms could play a key role.

The Big Picture: A Summary

One may envision the production part of an economy as made up of thousands of firms whose histories can each be described by figure 5. Investment and learning by doing and by tinkering have taken place over time. Labor productivity has risen, as has the capital-labor ratio. In a growing economy—one in which there are many firms achieving growth—if one particular firm has not accomplished this, it cannot survive. There is a great variety of paths followed, even among firms in the same industry. This diversity is inherent in the search and tinker and learn process because of the ignorance that necessarily prevails.

It is the ignorance that creates genuine choice, and since ignorance and knowledge vary among firms, it is not possible for all decision makers to make the same choices. As a firm creates its history, it then becomes, to some significant degree, constrained by that history. Firms adapt and respond, of course, but in different ways and at different speeds, so we get the great variation in performance, seen in figure 5, that thousands of firms would reveal. Where there is genuine choice and ignorance, rational choice and reasoning give considerable way to animal spirits, intuition, feel, tacit knowledge, precedence, and imitation. So some firms grow rapidly and become large quickly, some struggle along without much change of anything, and some wither and die off.

The welfare maze of figure 8 also identified constraints and barriers in the form of institutions, social and cultural practices, values, and factors that affect the various aspects of the search, tinker, and learn process. These barriers are also seen differently by different entrepreneurs and managers.[25] This consideration will also affect how the various entrepreneurs go about their searching and tinkering.

With this picture of the economy, there is no equilibrium for the firm and the notion of a general equilibrium for the economy as a whole is not a concept that illuminates the growth process. Nor do the notions of equilibrium growth or steady-state growth offer much in the way of illumination. Firms are never in equilibrium because there is ignorance and that fact is appreciated. There is ignorance which defeats rationality and optimization, but at the same time firms do not act whimsically in their search for greater profits. To understand how this process works is the task of growth economics.

As a consequence of all this, firms have different costs and different expectations and different levels of knowledge and therefore product prices may vary among firms in the same market, as does the quality of the product.

---

25. In countries where the population is made up of different ethnic, religious, tribal, or other groups, the welfare maze will vary from group to group. Indeed one group may be willing to ignore completely many constraints that another group gives high priority to honoring.

These considerations suggest that a production function that aggregates over the whole economy or even a major sector cannot really reveal the processes of growth. At best such an aggregate production function simply reports an average outcome without revealing anything about how this average was in fact generated.

There is however an important role for the market and market prices. I have already argued that factor prices can affect the direction of search, as can knowledge of technical possibilities. A firm whose searching and tinkering and learning result in new techniques that take advantage of the way factor prices are moving in their market is more likely to succeed than is one who guesses wrong. It is always possible for a firm to go against the flow and still succeed if its new knowledge is strong enough. The state of the market is itself, in significant part, affected by the outcome of the search and tinkering process. These points have particular implications for policy matters and are examined in more detail in a later chapter.

These market outcomes can be helpfully shown by a series of relationships first explored by W. E. G. Salter (1966, part II).[26] The axes of the charts in figure 9 can best be thought of as measuring the extent of the change of a variable over a specific time period. Salter's data are all index numbers. The main purpose of the exercise here is to examine how productivity growth can affect a number of the measures that contribute more or less directly to well-being. The figures are intended to show how increasing productivity can be transmitted through the economy if it is to make its full contribution to the growth of output and well-being.

a. Growth of wages and labor productivity. Part a of figure 9 shows the relationship between rates of growth of labor productivity and real wages rates by sectors and firms in a smooth functioning labor market. (Salter worked with what he called industries.) In an economy where the labor market works well and all producers hire from the same labor market, all producers will pay essentially the same wage rate. Yet the evidence, as noted above, shows beyond doubt that productivity growth varies markedly among firms and sectors within a country. If all firms pay essentially the same wage rate, but there is great variance in productivity growth, then evidently there can be no statistical relationship between wage rate growth and productivity growth.

b. Unit labor cost and productivity growth. The picture in part b shows the relationship between productivity growth and unit labor costs. This relationship is necessarily negative given the absence of any relationship between

---

26. In developing these relationships, Salter used data for the United Kingdom and, less completely, for the United States for the period 1924 to 1950. He calculated simple regressions for each of the diagrams and placed emphasis on the correlation coefficients. One can raise questions about the econometrics, but the basic message of the argument is extremely useful.

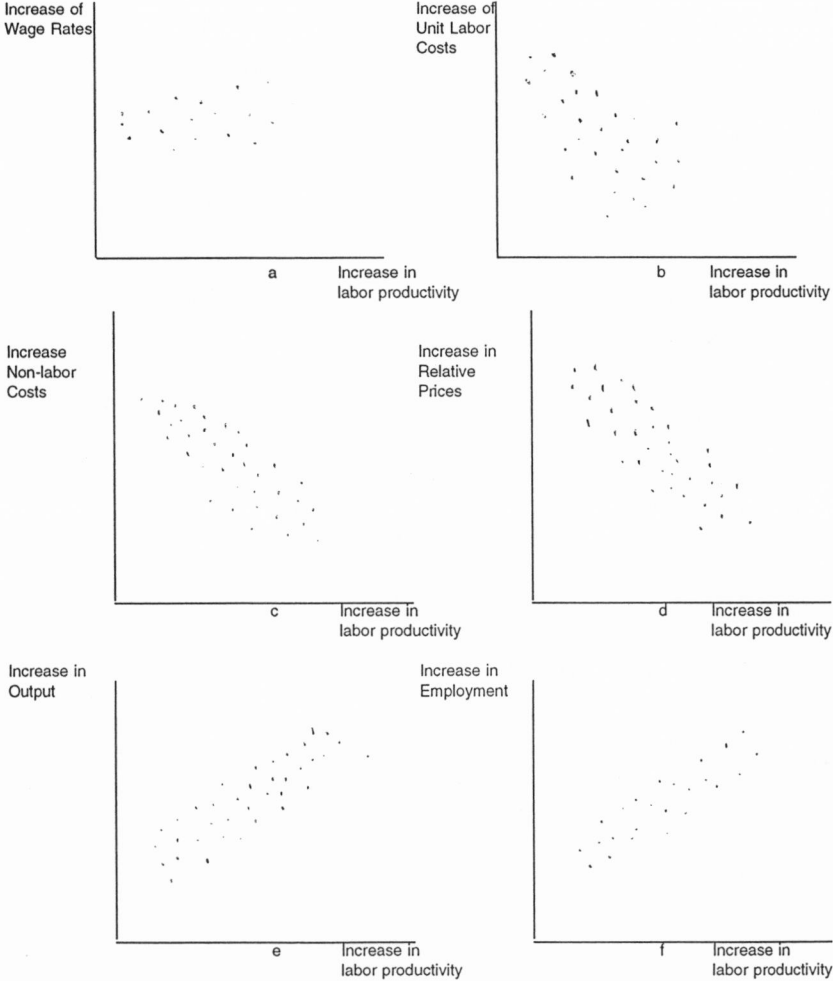

Fig. 9. The effects of productivity growth on wages, output, and employment

wage rate growth and productivity growth. Part b shows that if wage rate changes are unrelated to productivity growth on a sector basis, then the greater the increase in productivity growth, the lower must be the change in unit wage costs. This result follows almost tautologically from the definition of unit labor costs and labor productivity.

c. Nonlabor costs and labor productivity. The relationship shown here is expected to be less clear-cut than were the first two, but it is supported fairly well by available data and by the stylized facts listed above. It is, in effect, an indicator of total factor productivity. The relationship in the figure indicates that, in general, the increases in productivity are not bought by increases in other inputs, mainly capital. We know of course that an increase in the capital-labor ratio will in fact contribute to some increase in labor productivity. The argument recognizes that point, but the more important point is that the sources of continuing productivity growth must act on nonlabor inputs as well as labor; otherwise growth must stop. It must stop fairly quickly (unless the government intervenes in some way or other) because the rate of return on capital will fall. For an economy that has achieved growth decade after decade after decade the relationship shown in part c of figure 9 must hold.

This relationship means that labor productivity may be employed as an indicator of increases in the productivity of all resources.

d. Relative prices and productivity growth. Part d shows a negative relationship between relative price changes and productivity growth. The greater the growth in productivity in a given sector, the greater the expected fall in the relative price of its product. That this occurs must be explained in terms of competitive pressures that keep capitalists from permanently capturing monopoly rents that could arise from the productivity increases. (The functioning of the labor market as shown in part a of the figure prevents labor from capturing those rents.) The fact that relative prices are negatively related to productivity growth is also of importance because it means that the rewards of the increased productivity are passed on to the economy at large. This would not be the case if that negative relationship did not hold.

e. Output and productivity growth. That this relationship holds hardly needs comment. Price behavior as shown in d plus an income effect also created in significant part by productivity growth means that demand for the commodity will rise and will be facilitated by the supply advantages associated with rising productivity.

f. Employment and productivity growth. The last figure shows a positive relationship between employment growth and productivity growth. This happy relationship is explored in detail in the following chapter. The basic reason, however, is obvious: productivity growth encourages output growth which encourages employment growth. Also, the results of parts a and b in figure 9 indicate that employment growth will occur in response to the difference that arises when productivity growth is not matched by increased wage rates at the sector or firm level. How much employment this induces depends on the capacity of entrepreneurs to exploit an emerging difference between wages and productivity. More on this point also in the next chapter.

This set of relationships, though subject to many qualifications and questions, illuminates the vision of a growing economy that I am trying to establish. The increased productivity achieved by the learning-by-doing and searching and learning processes must be transmitted throughout the economy if it is to have its full effect. The figures illustrate how this is done in a market economy. If, for example, wage rates in a given firm or sector rise directly with productivity in that firm or sector then the advantages created by that productivity rise will be limited to the workers directly employed. The impact on relative prices, output, and employment will be greatly dampened. If monopoly power can prevent relative prices from falling as productivity rises, then again the rewards of the growing productivity will be severely limited.

So a further requirement for sustained growth is identified: the economic environment must be such that the consequences of productivity growth are transmitted throughout the system. This could possibly be accomplished through a complete and well-working planning system, but it is much more likely to succeed if most of the activity involved responds to market prices. It is to be emphasized that *this* is the strategic role of prices. This role is vastly more important than their alleged role in bringing about any sort of optimal allocation of a "given" quantity of resources in the context of "given" technology and "given" preferences.

Figure 9 can play an additional role that can be helpful in illuminating the workings of an economy. The six parts of figure 9 may be used to try to find problem areas in an economy. Thus, if one prepares these figures for a particular country and finds that the picture does not look like that shown here, it might be possible to identify problem areas rather neatly. If one found, for example, that productivity was growing well in a country, but other aspects of the economy—employment, price performance, and so on—were not doing so well, then the figures might tell one the source of the difficulties.

Thus, along with a mental image of what figure 8 looks like, the analyst and policymaker needs an actual picture of figure 9. Such would provide a rather effective approach to understanding how the economy is functioning and to prescribing measures to make it function more effectively.

The argument to this point has assumed a closed economy. There have been no international transactions of any kind. I have given considerable attention to a closed economy for one crucial reason: The process of growth that I have outlined has to be built into the system, has to be a genuinely indigenous process, for a country to be able to achieve sustained growth. This process cannot be imported or borrowed, it has to be home grown, it has to emerge from within the society itself. The commitment to searching and tinkering, to learning, is part of the deep-seated characteristics of a society. Where this commitment is not present growth of knowledge cannot take place, and without learning enhanced well-being cannot take place.

Where such a process is not in place and the search for knowledge is not widespread and indigenous, there can be no sustained increase in well-being. It is the search for knowledge that is crucial, and this must be created within the society. In a later chapter when I discuss foreign relationships, I argue that the greatest advantage of such relationships is to be found in the knowledge accumulation process, not in the usual textbook stories of comparative advantage.

CHAPTER 5

Employment

I have emphasized several times in the preceding pages the crucial role that employment plays in the continuing enhancement of well-being, which, as I keep saying, is what development is really all about. I have also asserted that the conventional textbook practice of treating work as a source of disutility is surely misleading and, indeed, empirically inaccurate. Similarly, leisure can easily turn into a disutility, if it is abused or misapplied. In these pages I want to discuss 1) why work itself is, or can be, a source of well-being and its enhancement, as well as (of course) a source of income and production directly, and 2) the basis and means for achieving and maintaining a strong demand for labor.

A Preliminary: The Labor Market

The rates of measured unemployment in almost all developing countries are always quite small, rarely above five percent. Yet there is abundant evidence that all available labor is not fully utilized, that there is considerable mis-allocation of the labor that is fully utilized, and that many jobs are dull and demeaning. Hence there is an opportunity to achieve improved well-being by finding ways to use labor more effectively. There are many reasons why the conventional labor-market categories—employed, unemployed, and outside the labor force—do not work so well in developing countries.

There are many more own-account workers in developing countries than in the North, and to determine if workers classified in this category are fully employed is extra difficult. In some countries it is unclear whether women should be assumed to be in the labor force or outside it. In many countries the unusually large proportion of the 17–25 age group that attend colleges or universities is evidence of unemployment, yet such people are not counted as unemployed. In countries where one sector pays extra-high wages for some reason, there are frequently queues of unemployed people waiting in hopes of a job in that sector even though jobs may be available elsewhere. Often the same argument applies to people who migrate from rural areas to urban areas. In both of these latter cases, the means of support of the "unemployed" becomes a relevant area of inquiry. People without means of support cannot remain unemployed very long, another reason why unemployment is low in developing countries.

The variance of wage rates among workers with similar skills and training is generally much higher than it is in the North, and the gaps between wages of unskilled labor in rural areas and those in urban areas are often very high, double or more.

All of these issues (and others that could be noted) make it especially difficult to determine the extent to which there would be labor available for new employment without an effect on the prevailing level of output, and on the extent to which unemployment as such is a major source of poverty. Also there is virtually no evidence on the extent that available jobs do contribute to learning and to aspects of well-being other than those that income creates. Even in the absence of convincing data that would resolve the kind of issues just reviewed, the general evidence surely enables one to say what was said in the paragraph above, namely, that there is labor that is used much less productively than it might be and that there are opportunities, therefore, to bring about increasing well-being by finding ways to use labor more completely and in more rewarding ways.

At the same time, one must recognize an issue on the supply side of the employment question. Textbooks usually derive a labor supply curve from an indifference map showing the trade-off between income and leisure, a simple choice problem once one has the indifference curve in hand. The issue in most developing countries is a bit different. Where productivity is very low, the opportunity cost of not working is low. Thus a cheap form of leisure—sitting, talking, dancing—may yield much more well-being than unrewarding labor that results only in very modest increases in income.

There is still something more, something a bit deeper. Sitting and talking is not just fun—like tennis and sailing—and cheap. It is something that fits well into the prevailing context, into the way things are. Sitting and talking is then a source of well-being, maybe one that yields the greatest well-being, given the prevailing circumstances as to alternative uses of one's time.[1]

There are two difficulties with this way of thinking that follow from previous arguments. The first is that the community must ask itself whether other uses of time, especially working at a recognized job, would contribute more to well-being than sitting and talking. It seems evident that the answer depends very much and very directly on the kind of jobs that can be made available. One can add that it is also clear that pursuit of "jobs" in order to earn money to buy consumer goods does not necessarily result in greater well-

---

1. I may note in passing that the argument, once quite common, that there is a backward-bending supply of labor in developing countries because of the lack of available consumer goods, is now generally recognized to be not very illuminating.

being or greater increases in well-being than sitting and talking do. The second point follows directly. It does seem fairly clear that certain things that could be acquired with higher incomes—possibly reduced infant mortality, a better diet that results in one feeling better, and so on—are, in fact, recognized as leading to greater well-being than would more sitting and talking.

These two arguments enable one to say that the present sitting and talking probably represents a position of recognized ignorance—ignorance of two things: what does in fact generate the most well-being from the use of one's time and, given this, the further ignorance of how to go about experimenting with ways of learning how to bring about an enhancement of well-being.

Both the supply and demand for labor have direct links with the social and historical environment through several channels, the most obvious perhaps through the gender issue. The argument that the talents of women in many developing countries are not as well utilized as can be imagined was mentioned earlier. Where women are denied access to exciting and productive jobs, the obvious assumption is that the society, not just the women themselves, is paying a price that is "not really necessary." Evidently, to attack this issue simply by aggregate demand or wage policies is futile, and to try to change such an environment may be looked upon as an attack on something truly vital to the community. Many observers would accept the conclusion that greater freedom for women in the labor market would contribute to the growth of GDP as conventionally measured, but would hastily add that to do so would impose other costs that would more than offset any output effect. In such a situation, how should we think of the labor force, its growth over time, and full employment?[2] Similar observations can be made with respect to ethnic groups in some societies.

I conclude then that there is a supply of labor in almost all developing countries that will be available if demand increases in a way compatible with what potential workers deem to be rewarding uses of their time, and that is compatible with their skills and with the conventions of the society.[3]

The Roles of Employment

Amartya Sen (1975) suggests three different aspects of employment:

1. An income aspect
2. A production aspect
3. A recognition aspect

---

2. An idea or two is explored in the last chapter.

3. In some areas of several countries, there can be a "shortage" of labor during the peak seasons for agriculture. In designing specific policies this fact must be recognized.

I want to add a fourth aspect:

4. A learning aspect

All four of these aspects have relevance for the achievement of increasing well-being by a society, although the last two are most directly relevant to the story that I am trying to tell.

Consider first, however, the income and production aspects. Certainly the income aspect is, in language used in chapter 2, essential to "achieving employability and the status of a thinking, aware individual, capable of reflecting on his/her life's plans and purposes." And of course there must be labor in the production of the goods and services that are necessary to achieve this objective. Similarly, the distribution of the goods and services necessary for everyone to obtain the extended basic needs discussed earlier requires that there be jobs for all who wish to work, at wages that enable these goods and services to be obtained. The evidence is fairly clear that ample employment opportunities are far and away the most effective means of ensuring that distribution is such that everyone has access to these goods and services.

Sen's recognition aspect arises from the fact that, in virtually all societies, "working," in one form or another, is expected of all adults, unless illness or physical handicaps prevent it. Even in those where women are not now expected to work outside the home, they are recognized as having a role to play in the society that justifies their claim to a share of resources. So we say that employment is a necessary condition for acceptance, for both social and self-esteem. On the other side, unemployment results in a loss of position. If this is all accepted, then having a job that is recognized by society as legitimate is an important source of well-being because "acceptance" by one's society is, as argued earlier, itself a significant source of well-being.[4] By the same argument, not having a job is a source of dismay for reasons other than the absence of income.

At the same time, there is the complication noted above that sitting and talking when job opportunities are absent, or are not perceived, is part of the allocation of time that is acceptable. It is then unacceptable idleness that results in criticism or rejection by society and, possibly, by oneself.

It is however employment as a source of learning, as a means to pursuing productivity growth and the Aristotelian Principle, that I wish to give specific attention.

---

4. The role of older people, people too old to "work" varies widely among countries, and, within countries, among various groups of the society. In many countries of Asia, Africa, and Latin America old people have a place of considerable prestige and honor which in turn justifies their claim on some resources. This is quite different from the practice in many societies of the North where older people are often looked upon as having little claim on resources.

Work as a Source of Well-Being

The job can teach in a variety of ways.

1. The way most commonly referred to is on-the-job learning, a significant source of increased productivity discussed in the previous chapters.
2. A job should help one gain flexibility, some increased capacity to adapt to changing circumstances, to see and capture opportunities, to achieve transformation capacity.
3. The job should be a source of increased understanding of one's wants, of one's awareness, of one's capacity or the need to "reflect on his/her life's plans and purposes."

At the same time the kind of work that we do should be compatible with prevailing traditions and mores, with the general social conditions that form the boundaries in which we live.

That one's employment should contribute something other than income seems beyond dispute, virtually self-evident. The most obvious reason is that, as already noted, most adults spend a significant part of their time doing what is identified as work. Thus if one spends 40 or more hours per week engaged in an activity that provides only income and production out of all the possible advantages of work, then one is obviously not using one's time very effectively, no matter what the level of income received. Frank Knight (1935, 59) provides a clear statement:

> But when we consider that productive activity takes up the larger part of the waking lives of the great mass of mankind, it is surely not to be assumed without investigation or inquiry that production is a means only, a necessary evil, a sacrifice made for the sake of some good entirely outside the production process. We are impelled to look for ends in the economic process itself, other than the mere consumption of the produce, and to give thoughtful consideration to the possibilities of participation in economic activity as a sphere of self-expression and creative achievement.

John Stuart Mill and Alfred Marshall have expressed similar thoughts, as have numerous philosophers. Marshall, for example, on the first and second pages of the eighth edition of his *Principles*, writes that the "business by which a person earns his livelihood generally fills his thoughts during by far the greater part of those hours in which his mind is at its best; during them his character is being formed by the way in which he uses his faculties in his work, by the thoughts and the feelings which it suggests . . . " (Marshall 1946 [1920], 1,2).

It may be noted, in passing, that the idea is often found that with a job of dull routine that yields adequate income and leisure, appropriate leisure activities can provide the same sources of personal development as does a rewarding job. This is rarely the case. There is no doubt that some leisure activities can be especially fruitful of well-being, but we (we humans) seem to have difficulty finding and following them. People who seem incapable of finding and doing interesting work may also have trouble using their leisure time in a rewarding way.[5]

Our understanding of these three roles of a job as a teacher is quite limited and only a few observations are possible.

On-the-Job Learning

The idea that workers, managers, foremen, owners, can and do learn on the job was emphasized earlier, and only two general points are added in the present context.

The first is that continued repetition is not sufficient to produce continued learning, at least after a routine has been learned. Doing the same thing over and over again day after day, year after year does not result in continued learning and continued increase in productivity.[6] There must be exposure to new ideas, to new routines, to new techniques that induce everyone—indeed force everyone—to rethink what they are doing. At the same time that there must be something new to be experienced, that newness must have some link with existing arrangements. They must not be so new, so different, that the people involved do not know how to profit from the newly available or newly discovered insights.[7]

---

5. William Nordhaus and James Tobin (1973) have estimated the extent to which increased leisure time has contributed to welfare. The estimate is quite high. In the absence of a capacity to use leisure time effectively, one may well doubt that the increased leisure has been as productive of welfare as these authors suggest.

6. Adam Smith felt very strongly on this point. He writes:

The man whose whole life is spent in performing a few simple operations, of which the effects too are, perhaps, always the same, or very nearly the same, has no occasion to exert his understanding, or to exercise his invention in finding out expedients for removing difficulties which never occur. He naturally loses, therefore, the habit of such exertion, and generally becomes as stupid and ignorant as it is possible for a human creature to become. The torpor of his mind renders him, not only incapable of relishing or bearing a part in any rational conversation, but of conceiving any generous, noble, or tender sentiment, and consequently of forming any just judgment concerning many even of the ordinary duties of private life. (1937, 734)

7. Barnett (1953) has a very helpful discussion of the importance of the link of new ideas and processes with existing ones.

It is evident that I am making now essentially the same kind of argument that I made earlier in discussing the new bicycle firm. The bicycle owners were to build on what they knew, and therefore the labor force will be led into new things that are akin to what they have been doing. One of the determinants of the appropriate direction for a firm to search is, in fact, the extent to which the labor force can be expected to learn quickly the new demands placed on it. This seems to be a much more useful way to think about the issue than does asking about the availability of skilled and unskilled labor. The key thing is the capacity and willingness of all levels of the work force to learn to do new things and thereby to increase their productivity.

The second generalization refers to the learning effects that work with a group (e.g., factory work) have compared to those that result when individuals work largely alone (e.g., agriculture). Inkles and Smith (1974) studied work in Argentina, Chile, East Pakistan (now Bangladesh), India, Israel, and Nigeria. They concluded that factory work is more likely to induce discipline, the understanding of initiative and cooperation, the appreciation of on-the-job relationships, greater understanding of productivity in others and in one's self, and a capacity to appreciate the notion of group, as opposed to personal, welfare. All of these characteristics, one may say, contribute to the growth of productivity in a variety of ways. More generally, the evidence suggests that workers (like students) learn from each other.[8] This argument is rarely factored into discussions of the allocation of resources. It does not mean, of course, that a country should push factory work in order to capitalize on these sources of productivity growth. Rather the evidence should help us see a bit more clearly how productivity growth comes about and can be induced.[9]

Development of these characteristics among the work force adds to the capacity of members of the labor force to acquire discipline with respect to time, to follow instructions, to appreciate quality and exactness. All of these add to one's productivity and to one's position of security and ease in a work environment. This more general form of learning also adds to one's capacity to acquire a "productive orientation."[10] Production orientation is to be sharply contrasted with a trading orientation. The latter has been a significant charac-

---

8. Robert E. Lane (1991) is a fine study of many aspects of work and with the idea that work is something more than a necessary evil. I have profited from this work to a great extent and have used many of the arguments that Lane discusses. He has a vast bibliography on the matters related to the role of work in the personal development of an individual and in the evolution of a society.

9. One should note also that farming, and independent work in general, often are deemed more satisfying in themselves, more likely to produce well-being directly, than is wage labor. The latter can easily degenerate into only a means of earning wages.

10. Lane (1991, 255) uses this term to good advantage. He attributes it to Erich Fromm (1947).

teristic in many developing countries for centuries. A production orientation implies that all members of a work force are committed to and involved in a genuinely productive process. Made-up work does more harm than good.[11] It also seems fairly clear that a work force where "production orientation" prevails is much more likely to accept the discipline and the cost involved in searching and learning. Lane (1991) reports the results of a survey in the United States that showed that over one-half of an American national sample "has an inner need to do the best job possible" (255). He adds that people whose jobs allow them some discretion are more likely to express this opinion.

A production orientation is then not the dull, nose-to-the-grindstone sort of idea. It is rather an idea that production itself has some merit, yields rewards in its very doing, and therefore creates a great urge to perform as well as possible. This attitude is frequently lacking in many countries. (It should not be confused with the pressures and tendencies to rush madly around trying to make ever more money.) It is lacking in part because of the nature of the work that is available, and it is lacking in part because we tend to put so much emphasis on output that we ignore the obvious point made above, that work can be a means of self-expression and personal growth, of well-being.

Work and Transformation Capacity

Another aspect of on-the-job learning, closely related to the previous notion, refers to the creation of "transformation" in the worker. Transformation capacity for a worker refers to the worker's capacity to learn a new job quickly at minimum loss of productivity. Such a characteristic is of great relevance in a market where output is growing, technology is changing, and demand is highly volatile. In such an environment the capacity of labor to adjust quickly is necessary in order to maintain productivity growth and high levels of employment. This argument is especially relevant to the idea that the objective is employment security, not job security. Efforts to achieve job security penalize productivity growth and indeed learning in general as well as impose considerable and increasing misallocation of resources on the society. Employment security, on the other hand, requires members of the work force to be able and willing to change jobs in response to the changing composition of the demand for labor.

---

11. The practice, found in many developing (and other) countries, of providing government work for everyone who cannot find other work illustrates the dangers of made-work. In Egypt, for example, a government study some years ago estimated that over 250,000 government employees had nothing at all to do. Sitting all day with no work at all for a year or two will make one incapable of any real work, should it come along.

This capacity to adjust is best learned on the job, or perhaps on jobs. The following example, often the stereotype cited, may help make the basic notion clear.

In Japan many workers are moved from department to department at rather frequent intervals. Such moving may occur at about the time that the worker has achieved greatest productivity at a given task in a given department. At no given time therefore will output of the enterprise, nor the productivity of the individual, be as high as it could be were such movement not to occur. Over a longer period of time however the firm's output and its demand for labor will be able to weather changes in market conditions much better than it would if labor had not experienced a variety of different tasks, and hence became able to adapt to new tasks, technologies, and demand. So, over a period of time, output and employment can be expected to be greater, and to grow more rapidly, than if the firm sought to place labor where its productivity was the highest at each moment. Unexpected changes under this latter approach will tend to result in labor (and other aspects of capacity) being less able to adjust quickly to the new demands, and employment or productivity or both will tend to fall.

The Japanese example applies most obviously to a large company. The notion however is applicable in almost any sized undertaking and to an economy of small firms. Labor's capacity to move quickly from one job to another or from one task to another (e.g., using one kind of machine relative to another) is relevant in any economy where technology and product composition is changing rapidly and continually in all firms, no matter the size.

There are several additional points to make. Evidently, one does not expect certain categories of activities to allow this sort of thing. For example, it is unlikely that a person trained as a medical doctor will stop that activity and become an accountant or a lawyer. Doctors might, however, become farmers or teachers. The fact that all categories of workers or professions cannot achieve such varied experience does not mean that the argument is not of great relevance in thinking about the role of work and learning in creating this capacity in labor.

The transformation capacity notion is applicable to nations as a whole. This aspect of transformation will be examined in the chapter on international activity.

The argument has relevance to the kind of schooling that will best serve the individual and nation. Forms of schooling that concentrate attention on general knowledge about the society and its history, and on training to observe, to ask questions, to appreciate reasoning and logic as well as feeling and art and intuition, are more likely to help the student in the longer run than more specific training in a particular kind of task. This of course is a complicated issue. Schooling in engineering is helpful (but see the later section on education), maybe essential, but even here the main idea is to equip students to think and puzzle and teach themselves, rather than to drill in the details of specific tasks. In general, the argument suggests that it is not the purpose of schooling to provide the student with those exact skills that can be immediately applied in a given activity. This is much more of an on-the-job learning process. It is rather one of the purposes of schooling to equip the student to function effectively in a labor market, and this is quite different from teaching a given skill. This argument is much more clear-cut with respect to elementary and undergraduate education than postgraduate.

The argument also puts great weight on the demand for labor. The most important single aspect of the equipping of labor with transformation capacity is a strong demand for labor. A strong demand for labor is also a means of inducing both the firm and the prospective workers to do a lot of on-the-job learning. I talk about the demand for labor in the following section. Another key notion is that of apprenticeships, also to be discussed.

Work and Increased Understanding

Increased understanding and increased awareness are their own rewards, that is, they contribute directly to well-being. The remarks earlier, especially the quotations of Frank Knight, Alfred Marshall, and Adam Smith (in the note), suggest the kind of argument that applies in the present context. Robert Lane's discussion about this role of work is especially helpful: "Through work, it is said, man realizes his potentials, expresses himself, and partially defines his identity" (1991, chap. 13, 254). This is the basic idea that I seek to explore briefly.

A job or work is itself a source of learning and question generating, and certain attributes acquired in interesting, challenging jobs remain with the individual after the work is completed. Similarly, characteristics of employment that antagonize and alienate also affect our nonwork social life and attitudes in important ways. Jobs that require thought and response to new situations can excite the mind and spirit as much or more than can formal schooling. Such work then forces or induces the worker to think and react and ask him- or herself and others questions about how to proceed—all of which are the stuff from which learning emerges. Work with some independence for the worker, some opportunity for decision making, some substantive complexity, all seem to be especially conducive to generating the kind of understanding and awareness that enhances one's reward from labor. The idea here is different from the increase in productivity measured in the usual way. Productivity may be affected, but that is not the basic objective in the present context. It is rather that in performing these kinds of jobs, in being involved in them in a deep and committed way, our ability to understand and to see is increased. This is what the Aristotelian Principle is all about.

Some evidence is available that suggests that some of the attributes for effective work, especially work that requires cooperation with other people of equal and different levels in the hierarchy, also promote attitudes of tolerance, respect, and trust that carry over beyond the workplace.[12] Again such a spillover effect seems most unambiguous for loosely supervised, nonroutine work. Close supervision in routine work tends to defeat, at least to dampen, self-confidence and independent effort. And this in turn is reflected in the way people approach their life outside the workplace. Especially affected is their confidence and willingness to experiment and to probe beyond specified boundaries. Although work is not the only source of these attributes, it is probably correct to argue that unless work does contribute to their emergence, they will not, possibly cannot, be acquired solely through other means. In particular it seems very unlikely that they can be acquired solely through formal schooling.

An example may help both the reader and the writer to see more clearly what it is that I am trying to understand. In many developing countries there will be one or two very able persons in a key job with many people much less able reporting to him/her. Elementary teaching is such a case in many developing countries. The teachers may well be quite ill prepared, therefore the supervisor provides many detailed guidelines that prescribe exactly how an individual teacher should proceed. The teacher in turn follows the instructions as exactly as possible. One may well believe that given the quality of the teachers this is the best way to proceed. It also seems fairly evident that it is the way to keep teachers ill prepared and ill equipped to develop into independent, imaginative teachers who can respond well and quickly to student needs and capacities. To repeat: it is unlikely that they can acquire those attributes in a teacher's (or other) college and then begin right off in their first teaching assignment to do other than follow directions. In almost all hierarchical situations in developing countries something like this is to be found. Evidently it is a difficult situation to modify. Somehow a way must be found to enable the teachers to learn on the job and gain the confidence and capacity that makes it reasonable to allow them freedom to proceed much more on their own.

These ideas about the quality of work are fundamental in the search for well-being in low-income countries. We also know that in many countries, in rural areas especially, the social and family arrangements are such that the line between work and nonwork is very dim indeed. In these societies, it defeats the search for well-being for people to move abruptly from these very relaxed and personal forms of work organization to sharply defined hierarchical arrangements, with close supervision, strictly enforced hours, and little personal involvement in or attachment to the product. It is important to appreciate

---

12. This is explored further in Lane (1991) and in Kohn and Schooler (1983). This latter book is also discussed by Lane.

that this sort of rapid redeployment of labor into the modern sector, even with higher wages, is not the solution to the employment problem. Here then is another reason for the emphasis on getting the traditional sector itself experiencing growth, rather than seeking to replace it with "modern sector" activities. Employment growth and the well-being that resides in work illustrate this basic point remarkably clearly.

Demand for Labor

The demand for labor of course is an essential part of the employment story and the way that employment and work can contribute to well-being. I concentrate most of the attention on demand for labor generated by the kind of enterprises discussed in earlier pages, and then add a word or two on self-employment.

The Framework

Several years ago my then colleague, Thomas McCoy, and I worked out an equation that gave the growth of demand for labor in the following way.

$$r_L = r_K + r_A - r_B + \frac{\sigma}{K_s}(r_B - r_W).$$

The r's identify the proportionate rates of growth of Labor (L), Capital (K), capital augmenting productivity growth (A), labor augmenting productivity growth (B), and wage rates (W). Sigma (σ) is the elasticity of substitution and K_s is capital's share of value added.[13]

That the growth of employment depends (in part) on the growth of physical capital and on capital augmenting productivity growth needs no elaboration. In the previous chapter I argued that on the average, over extended periods new knowledge must be labor augmenting or growth would eventually cease. So the r_A in the equation can be ignored and attention given to capital formation. Labor augmenting productivity growth itself reduces the rate of growth of demand for labor also in a manner that requires no elaboration. That this is true is the explanation often given for the rising capital-labor ratio.[14] If, as is often the case, one assumes "full" employment so that $r_B = r_W$, this is the end of the story.

---

13. This equation is derived in Bruton in Cairncross and Puri (1976) and, in a slightly different (and better) way, in appendix III of Frank and Webb (1977).

14. As noted earlier labor augmenting productivity growth of a sufficient magnitude will keep the capital-efficiency labor ratio more or less constant and thereby prevent the rate of return on capital from falling despite the rising capital-nominal labor ratio.

In an economy with unemployed, underemployed, and misallocated labor, r_B may exceed r_W, and therefore the last term in the equation becomes relevant. It is this term to which I direct most attention.

The last term of the equation tells us that if the growth of labor productivity exceeds the growth of wage rates, employers will have an incentive to hire more labor. The extent of this inducement depends on the elasticity of substitution between capital and labor and the share of value added accruing to capital. Given σ and K_S, employment growth is greater, the greater is the excess of productivity growth over the wage rate.

Suppose that the labor market functions in such a way that, in the presence of unemployment, underemployment, or misallocated labor, the rate of growth of wages is in fact zero in the face of increasing demand for labor. At the same time labor augmenting productivity growth is taking place, that is, r_B is positive and r_W is zero. The result would be an increase in the demand for labor, the magnitude of which is determined by the extent to which labor can substitute for capital, σ relative to capital's share, and the size of r_B. If labor can easily be substituted for capital (σ is large), diminishing physical returns to labor are modest as employment increases relative to capital, and employment will grow rapidly as productivity increases. To put it a bit differently, given capital's share, the larger σ is, the more slowly does the marginal physical product of labor fall as the capital/labor ratio declines, and so the greater is the growth of employment. Similarly, the smaller is capital's share, given, the larger is the growth of demand for labor. For the net overall effect of r_B on employment to be positive, σ must exceed capital's share of value added.[15]

Evidently if $\sigma = 0$, then the last expression is zero, and r_B can have only a negative effect on employment. Equally evident is the role of wage rates. If $r_B = r_W$ there is no growth in the demand for labor due to rising productivity of labor. So how the labor market functions affects directly the growth in the demand for labor in a fundamental way.

The argument for the growth of the demand for labor may also be put in terms of the growth of output rather than of physical capital. The relevant expression is

$$r_L = r_Q - r_B + \sigma(r_B - r_W).$$

The first two expressions on the right-hand side show the conventional argument that productivity growth may penalize employment. The last expression however recognizes that wage rates matter, and an excess of r_B over r_W, creates an incentive to hire more labor. The elasticity of substitution is

---

15. In manufacturing activities, indeed in most activities as noted earlier, capital's share of value added in less-developed countries is higher than in the more-developed countries. So if the circumstances here described prevailed in a more-developed country, a given value of σ and r_B should produce a higher rate of growth of demand for labor.

again the central concept. Indeed if r_W is zero and σ exceeds unity, the demand for labor will exceed the growth of output, and *observed* labor productivity growth will be negative. This is an illusion, of course, because it is the increase in labor productivity that has induced the increased employment that has, in turn, pushed the observed productivity back down to the unchanged wage rate.

The analysis built around these two equations also shows how it is possible to argue that one cause of unemployment is the low productivity of labor, and that the slow growth of employment may be due to the slow growth of productivity. If, for example, institutional or political or other characteristics tend to keep wage rates "too high," an effective approach to the employment objective may be limited to searching for ways to get labor productivity to higher and rising levels, rather than trying to reduce wage rates.

This argument also shows why almost all estimates of the growth of labor productivity calculated in the usual way *understate* the extent of its increase. In the simplest case, where $r_W = 0$, $r_B > 0$, and $\sigma > K_S$ observed labor productivity will appear unchanged because employment increases in such a way that the marginal physical product of labor is kept equal to the unchanged wage rate by the increase in employment. The equality between wage rates and increased productivity is achieved by increased employment, rather than by rising wage rates. Even if wages rise somewhat, but less than r_B, observed increases in labor productivity will be below that represented by the shift in the productivity curve of labor. This follows from the fact that part of the actual increase in the productivity of labor results in the growth of employment that pushes productivity down.[16]

---

16. A simple diagram makes this point clear.

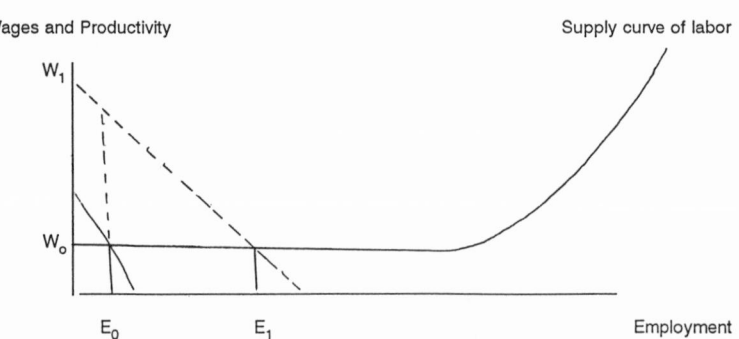

Wages and Productivity   Supply curve of labor

Initially productivity equals the wage at W_0 and employment is E_0. Now labor productivity increases according to the dotted curve. We observe E_0 and E_1 so no productivity change is evident, only an employment increase. Yet productivity has, in a real sense, risen to W_1 and thereby induced the increase in employment that pushed it (productivity) back down to W_0. The usual assumption that wages rise with productivity growth results in this point being often missed.

The growth of output is also greater, the greater is the elasticity of substitution and the smaller is capital's share. The preceding equation can be rewritten with the rate of growth of output on the left-hand side to get:

$$r_Q = r_K + r_A + \frac{L_s \sigma}{K_s}(r_B - r_W).$$

So output grows with employment, and there is no trade-off between the two. This is the consequence of the assumptions that it is possible to substitute, in the production process, labor for capital, and that $r_B > r_W$.

Both of these formulations—the equation for the rate of growth of employment and of output—identify the elasticity of substitution and the labor market as key factors in understanding what happens to employment and to the growth of output. This importance is greatly enhanced by the existence of incompletely utilized labor. I complete this chapter with a brief discussion of the elasticity of substitution and a further paragraph or two on the labor market.

The Elasticity of Substitution

The elasticity of substitution is defined in the textbooks as the elasticity of the conventionally drawn isoquant. In the decade or so before 1985 there were many estimates of its value for individual sectors and for entire economies. The notion itself and the estimates of its value rest on the assumption that it is a technological parameter and indeed defines the shape of the isoquant. I have argued above that, for a number of reasons, the notion of an isoquant does not provide the kind of illumination that we need. So then how can the equations discussed above for the rate of growth of demand for labor be used now?

The idea is simply that σ is not a technological coefficient around which the demand for labor adjusts. It is not a "given" that limits and defines what is possible once factor prices are "right." It is rather something that emerges from search-and-learn efforts of the entrepreneurs who are responding to opportunities to make more money. Its observed (calculated) value is an outcome of that effort, not an ex-ante determinant of the substitution that is possible. Thus the extent to which employment responds to an increase in productivity depends not on some "given" technological coefficient, but on the capacity of the entrepreneurs to find ways to exploit that increase. Some entrepreneurs will do quite well (achieve a large increase in employment and output), others less well, and still others poorly in a specific labor market. Evidently technology is a highly relevant determinant of the outcome of this process, but the principal determinant is the entrepreneur and his/her acquaintance with the opportunities that exist or that can be found or created. I have argued in chapter 4 that the rate of labor augmenting productivity growth, r_B

in the equation, is also a consequence of the search-and-learn process and so will vary widely among enterprises. Here then is another reason to expect diversity among rates of growth of output and employment among activities.[17]

To find ways to substitute labor for capital in a particular activity in a particular country at a particular time requires a great knowledge about the technology already in use and about the availability and cost of different kinds of labor and intermediate inputs. This argument now links up with the bicycle (and general) arguments of the previous chapter. The search for ways to increase productivity is, in effect, a search for ways to take advantage of the resources that the economy offers. Part of this process is the search for ways to use the labor whose productivity has increased. So the search goes on in many fronts.

The Labor Market Again

I began this chapter with a brief discussion of the labor market in developing countries. The main concern was to defend the notion that there was unemployment and underemployed and ill-used labor in almost all developing countries. I want now to discuss some other aspects of the labor market that bear directly on the employment situation as it has been defined in these pages.

The preceding arguments placed emphasis on:

1. Achieving a strong general demand for labor.
2. Recognizing that work itself must contribute directly to well-being through on-the-job learning, improving individual transformation capacity, increasing understanding of one's wants, and deepening one's ideas of the good life.
3. Work providing the income and output that are also important sources of well-being.
4. The role of productivity growth and wage rates in creating demand for labor.
5. The key role of entrepreneurship in the exploitation of opportunities for employment and output growth created by rising productivity, that is, in achieving a "high" elasticity of substitution.

---

17. Evidently the rate of growth of demand for the product is also an important factor in the determination of the growth of output. As I keep noting, one advantage of exporting is that it prevents a demand bottleneck from stopping the growth of output of an activity that has achieved a "high" r_B and has exploited that high r_B further by achieving a "high" elasticity of substitution, and therefore demands increasing amounts of labor.

The task now is to examine the characteristics of the labor market that can affect the extent to which these conditions and objectives are realized.

Labor markets in developing countries do not lend themselves to general characterization. There are numerous legal and institutional and traditional features that affect in one way or another all items in the list above. There are laws and informally enforced practices that affect hiring and firing arrangements, minimum wages, working conditions, nonwage labor costs, job security, government employment, unionization, political power of labor (organized and other), and numerous other dimensions of a great variety of kinds.

In addition there is the argument that wage rates can affect productivity, the efficiency wage hypothesis, and that in some strategic activities conventionally characterized by low wages, higher wages may attract more capable people with major externalities thereby generated. Elementary school teaching and government service are prime examples of this possibility. It is appealing to argue, for example, that government policies would be much better designed and implemented if governments let half? three-quarters? of their personnel go and paid those who were kept on particularly attractive salaries. It is also often noted that corruption of various sorts in public offices might be less tempting if wages were higher.

The empirical and descriptive evidence as to the effects of this great array of market imperfections and interventions on the various objectives of a society is far from conclusive or even generally suggestive. Thus some countries that have a large number of laws and practices that would apparently tend to prevent the labor market from working well have achieved reasonably satisfactory rates of growth of employment and productivity. And there are other countries with fewer violations of free market conditions that have done less well.[18]

At the same time the evidence that there is a market at work is convincing in almost all countries. For example, when the demand for labor is extra weak, legal minimum wage rates are largely ignored in almost all countries by consent of both employer and employee alike. Where there is a tight labor market, working conditions improve and jobs become more interesting along with the increase in wage rates. One concludes therefore that market forces are present and relevant to some, generally unknown, extent in almost all labor markets.

The questions then are these: To what extent are the various forms of interventions necessary—or thought to be necessary—in order to create the conditions and achieve the objectives sought after? More specifically, one

---

18. R. B. Freeman (1993) is an unusually illuminating report on the great diversity that one observes in the labor markets of the world and the danger of making generalizations about the way labor markets function or can be affected by government policies.

might ask to what extent the interventions are necessary to compensate for a weak demand for labor. The latter statement implies that *if* the demand for labor is strong enough, then the market will perform well without any interventions. One must then ask whether the interventions are themselves preventing the market from working in such a way that the stated objectives are achieved or whether they are necessary because the unimpeded market may not do what needs to be done.

There are of course no general answers to these questions. The relevant conditions vary greatly from country to country, and within a country over time. This is indeed what the recognition of institutional, political, and historical considerations force on one in almost all analyses. Recognizing that there are market forces at work does not mean that only market forces are at work or that a society can assume that, if the market can be made to work well, or "perfectly" as some are wont to say, then all problems will be resolved. Eliminating, or seeking to eliminate, all sources of interventions in the labor market may not be the most effective approach. So the need to search and learn and for trial and error is a crucial aspect of arriving at decisions on the appropriate employment policies.[19]

The Role of Education

The arguments of the two preceding sections have direct implications for education. Enormous sums have been spent on formal, especially higher, education in almost all developing countries. Universities have been built in the countries themselves and hundreds of thousands of people have gone to the North to attend more established and more famous institutions. There appears widespread agreement now that there has been "too much" investment in higher education.[20] At the same time few people would argue that formal education has no role to play in the search for regular productivity growth.

The argument that emerges from the discussion to this point is that concentration of effort should be on elementary and secondary education. The reasons for this seem fairly clear. A labor force that is able to read and write easily, do simple arithmetic, follow written and oral instructions, and be able to learn on the job meets the demand for labor more effectively than do

---

19. The problem here, and indeed everywhere, is made more complex because of the inexperience and inadequate training of government officials, the possibilities of rent seeking, and the limited power of governments to affect certain aspects of the society. I confront this issue directly in the last chapter.

20. Mark Blaug (1992) is a good short statement on the arguments and evidence of too much higher education. Weale (1993) is an equally short, clear statement on the difficulties in estimating rates of return on education.

college graduates or people with advanced degrees. Empirical-based innovations and new knowledge of all kinds seem to put greater weight on elementary education than on postsecondary schooling. This type worker is what is required rather than people with college or advanced degrees. Such degrees often tend to make people unable to participate or contribute to the economic activities of the real economy at a given time. The idea again here is to try to create a labor force that *fits in* with the other resources and economic activities. In general it may be said that a labor force with a good elementary and high school education is consistent with the kinds of activities that are likely to come into existence in an economy that is beginning to grow in a systematic way. It may also be noted that higher education does not seem to turn out entrepreneurs in the sense in which this term was used in chapter 3.[21]

The labor force in much of the North, as it began widespread industrialization, was essentially illiterate. (Even today most jobs in manufacturing in the North require only high school education.) Japan, for example, apparently explicitly followed a policy of achieving universal elementary education before pushing secondary and postsecondary education (Blaug 1992). In this instance again one sees compatibility between the quality of labor and other resources and technical and administrative knowledge.

A different, but similar point may be made with an example. The *Economist* (June 25, 1988) noted with concern that continued growth of the electronics sector in Thailand was threatened by a shortage of qualified labor. Such concern represents a misunderstanding. If there is no suitable labor available for a particular activity, then that particular activity is unsuitable. More generally, one frequently reads that industrial development is handicapped by a lack of skilled labor. The rationale of this argument is one that the approach of this entire essay strongly disputes. The very idea is to make use of the resources that the nation has in an effective way and to find ways to get the productivity of *these* resources increasing. It is useful to recall again the distinction made earlier between low productivity and nonrising productivity.

As the economy develops, as demand is created and expanded for labor with the skills and knowledge acquired in higher education, then is the time for further investment in this latter form of education. It is of course recognized that people with higher education can make significant contributions making possible certain new activities that otherwise would not be possible. In general however it does seem possible to say that an economy at a certain time, with a given state of knowledge, will create a demand for a labor force with certain characteristics. To provide a supply of labor with different charac-

---

21. Much more could be said on the role of education. All I seek to do here is to try to make the case that a labor force with an elementary and high school education is surely one that fits the economy as it begins its growth.

teristics from that will mean that labor will be idle (the educated unemployed, e.g.) or that the return on the investment in education will be low, zero, or even negative. Again I am trying to spell out how a sector, in this case the educational system, evolves, or should evolve with the rest of the economy.

This argument means that college attendance now in many countries is (and has been over the past decades) "too" large.[22] We also know that higher education in almost all countries has a strong emotional content, that it is often a screening device, and, given the practice of zero or very low tuition, that private returns for those with higher education vastly exceed the social returns. There is therefore a genuine political and social problem in seeking to curtail college enrollments. This is especially the case when limiting enrollment is accomplished by imposing high tuition. There is however a simple answer to this difficulty: namely the existence of a strong demand for labor with no more than good secondary education. If the opportunity cost of attending college (in the form of forgone earnings in interesting jobs) is high, there can be little doubt that enrollments will fall without much opposition. For this to be possible requires not only that there be a strong demand for labor, but it must be demand for the kind of labor that is available. This is sometimes called unskilled labor, but this is a misleading designation. The demand must be for labor that is literate, has interest in working and learning, and can do what national entrepreneurs and managers direct it to do. One might say that such a labor force is consistent with the other components of an enterprise that depends heavily on domestic entrepreneurship, readily available technology, and other domestic resources.

A Specific Approach

I want to consider briefly an approach to creating a demand for labor that has a good primary and secondary education.

The idea is to create a strong demand for the kind of labor that the economy has—in order to seek to obtain full employment—and to insure that the productivity of this labor grows. Evidently in this kind of approach, much depends on on-the-job learning and tinkering. This topic was examined earlier in some detail, and I wish to add only one point to what has already been said, a point on apprenticeships.

In Germany about one-third (until recently) of the relevant age group attend college, a figure that in general is quite common among European

---

22. Education, of course, makes an excellent consumption good, and I would never say that any society is "consuming" too much education. The argument in the text is concerned with formal education as a source of productivity growth in the economy. Education can directly affect well-being—the capacity to choose, to reflect on life-styles, to use leisure productively, and so on. These too are available at elementary school levels.

countries. In the United States (and Canada) the figure approaches two-thirds. Germany is especially relevant to our story because of its widespread practice of apprenticeships. High school graduates are taken on as apprentices in a wide variety of activities and trained over a period of years to become master plumbers, electricians, carpenters, and so on. Pay is, of course, below that of regular work people, but there is the significant learning effect that such an arrangement offers.[23]

Apprenticeship seems to be an especially hopeful approach in many developing countries where it is so expensive and time consuming—and of doubtful feasibility anywhere—to create a highly trained labor force through formal postsecondary education. It also seems that apprentice arrangements are increasing in many parts of the developing world, especially in Africa.[24] There does not seem to be available evidence of any sort that tells us much about the exact nature and effect of apprenticeships anywhere. At the same time, such an arrangement, as a means of helping to create the strong demand for people with no more than an elementary or, possibly, high school education and thereby to enhance their productivity, does seem very attractive.

Whether private firms will do this on their own depends mainly on the perceived profitability of increasing output and the existing level of unemployment. A labor surplus situation would dampen the pressure on the firm to do this sort of thing at all, and it would certainly dampen the inducement to incur any costs in doing it. Thus it may be necessary in a given environment for the government to subsidize these arrangements. It should not be difficult to design a program that is administratively simple and that has the desired effect, that is, inducing the firms to take on apprentices. In very small firms or in firms in the informal sector apprenticeships are now more common—at least in Africa—than in large firms. In many cases, of course, apprentices are really members of the family who are being taken into the business. It may also be added that the apprenticeship system is especially advantageous in rural areas where, as already argued, it is important to have strong inducements for new nonagricultural activities.

Are *Any* Generalizations Possible?

Despite (or possibly because of) this complex network of objectives and instruments, there is a great need for a place to begin, a point of departure. There are, I believe, several things that can be said very much as a beginning.

---

23. The general way that these arrangements seem to work is along the line worked out in Becker (1962).

24. They apparently are becoming increasingly common in Ghana and Nigeria. I understand also that considerable new research is likely to provide more information on their effectiveness in the near future.

Where one goes after the beginning depends on the particulars of the given country at the given time.[25] The way of thinking that I have studied in the preceding pages provides that sort of beginning. A short list of the aspects that seem most important includes the following:

1. In any economy at any time, there must be a strong demand for labor or it becomes virtually impossible to meet other objectives. The discussion in the previous chapter also made clear the nature and difficulties of achieving such without inflation or balance of payments problems.

2. The literature emphasizes labor-intensive techniques of production as a means of meeting employment and output objectives. This is a limited way to think. The emphases must be on a productivity growth that in turn creates a rising demand for labor and on the way that the labor market works.

3. The role of wages is complex in many ways, but still it seems that the most suitable wage target in the presence of underemployment and unemployment is little or no increase. This is surely the case as a beginning. Thus the case must be made in a given country at a given time that some wages *should* rise even in the presence of unemployment. To accomplish the right wage arrangement will almost surely require specific government action or some sort of compensating action.

4. The role of entrepreneurs in achieving the employment objectives is crucial. There is more on this issue in the next chapter. One major point can be made here. Productivity growth is, as I have often said, the heart of growth. If productivity growth is to be, as well, an instrument to help achieve the employment objectives, there must be considerable capacity to substitute labor for nonlabor input until there is a tight labor situation, and this capacity must reside in entrepreneurs. For this to be at all feasible, the entrepreneur must know the economy—its technology, the quality of labor, its mores and institutions, and so on—in great detail. This means that the whole process must be indigenous.

5. The idea that government employment or make-work programs (or foreign direct investment) can be the primary agents of employment

---

25. R. B. Freeman (1993) concludes his survey with the statement that direct experiences and special case studies are likely to be much more illuminating than are econometric studies of aggregates of one kind or another. This is surely a correct conclusion. It does seem, as I argue in the text, that some generalizations are not only possible, but indeed necessary in order to appreciate the consequences of the specific conditions.

creation is misplaced. It is the domestic economy that must be organized to bring it about.

Is it All Pie in the Sky?

I have put great demands on working and employment. Should we reject this and say simply that where large segments of the population are hungry, poorly housed, and in bad health, the task simply is get jobs that pay a living wage? To claim that giving attention to the quality of work, to the fact that labor can contribute directly to well-being, and so on, is pie in the sky, is academic nonsense. I do not believe this. The countries now beginning their sustained growth have an opportunity to keep all the aspects of work in the forefront of attention. To recognize that all these possibilities reside within employment is as important a part of understanding development as is any other one thing. To pass it over because it is difficult is to pass over development, because it is difficult.

It is tempting to take an even stronger step. A particularly appealing single-valued indicator of well-being is an employment index, normalized in some ingenious way for conventionally measured productivity growth and job interest. Perhaps the most serious failure of the market system as it has evolved in the West is that unemployment in the best of times is rarely below 5 percent and a large proportion of available jobs are so uninspiring and are essentially dead ends. Similarly, one of the greatest costs of underdevelopment is the dreadful dullness (as well as low productivity) of the great majority of available jobs.

CHAPTER 6

Entrepreneurship

There is, necessarily, ubiquitous ignorance, and, if there is knowledge that there is ubiquitous ignorance, searching and learning is set in motion. The searching and learning in turn produce the change that, under specified conditions, leads to enhanced well-being for the population. In the effort to understand how the search for improved preferences enters the story, the household plays a crucial role. On the production side, as has been frequently noted in the preceding pages, the entrepreneur is the crucial agent. In this section I examine this notion as it bears on the story.

It is frequently noted in the textbook theory of the firm that there is no role for the entrepreneur. This is the case largely because of the assumptions of "perfect knowledge" and a "given technology." Once these assumptions are abandoned then the entrepreneur immediately becomes a strategic agent of change. In such a milieu—that is, one in which there is ignorance and awareness of the ignorance—the entrepreneur must play a variety of roles. There are, I think, three that may be identified. I list them and then discuss each in turn.

1. The entrepreneur is one source, perhaps the major source on the production side of the "heroic ethic." The entrepreneur is the person who rises above the "nicely calculated less or more," and sees that "things" must and can be better.[1] More briefly, the entrepreneur is a principal source of the Idea of Progress.
2. The entrepreneur perceives the specific profit opportunity, and is the author of the initial investment decision.
3. The entrepreneur is one—not the only—production worker engaged in searching and learning, and she/he is the author of the decisions to change that emerge from the searching and learning process.

---

1. Kenneth Boulding (1969) uses the term *heroic ethic* in the same fashion as it is used here. In the same article Boulding quotes the sonnet of Wordsworth on a wall in King's College chapel, Cambridge University. The lines of this sonnet most relevant in the present context are:
Give all thou canst: high Heaven rejects the lore
Of nicely-calculated less or more:

The order is from the very general to the increasingly specific, from the institutionally, socially, culturally affected to the activities that can be directly influenced by specific policies. One also expects that the relative supply of category 1 is smallest and that of 3 the largest. All three categories must be present.

The Entrepreneur as the Source of the Idea of Progress

The basic notion is perhaps best communicated by referring to statements and expressions that appear in the literature of development and of ideas in general. Kenneth Boulding (1969, 10) elaborates on his ideas by arguing that "economic man is a clod, heroic man is a fool, but somewhere between the clod and the fool, human man . . . steers his tottering way." Heroism here means, I think, to rise above the mundane calculations of benefit-cost ratios, of internal rates of return, and so on, and to act from some Olympian view that life need not be dull, routinized, and uninspired.

Schumpeter (1934, 93) writes of his notion of the entrepreneur in an especially eloquent way:

> First of all, there is the dream and the will to found a private kingdom, usually, though not necessarily, also a dynasty. The modern world really does not know any such positions, but what may be attained by industrial or commercial success is still the nearest approach to medieval lordship possible to modern man . . . Closer analysis would lead to discovering an endless variety . . . of motives, from spiritual ambition down to mere snobbery.
>
> Then there is the will to conquer: the impulse to fight, to prove oneself superior to others, to succeed for the sake, not of the fruits of success, but of success itself. From this aspect, economic action becomes akin to sport . . . The financial result is a secondary consideration, or, at all events, mainly valued as a symptom of victory, the displaying of which very often is more important as a motive of large expenditure than the wish for the consumers' goods themselves . . . And again we are faced with a motivation characteristically different from that of "satisfaction of wants" . . .

Schumpeter's entrepreneur is not going to be limited by mere low internal rates of return, mere foreign exchange constraints, mere limitations on the supply of skilled labor, and so on. Somehow she/he rises above or beyond that, and responds to an Idea of Progress that is deep within him/her. J. M. Keynes (1935, 162) writes in a similar way:

Only a little more than an expedition to the South Pole, is it [enterprise] based on an exact calculation of benefits to income. Thus if animal spirits are dimmed and the spontaneous optimism falters, leaving us to depend on nothing but a mathematical expectation, enterprise will fade and die; though fears of loss may have a basis no more reasonable than hopes of profit had before.

Keynes adds that

Individual initiative will only be adequate when reasonable calculation is supplemented and supported by animal spirits, so that the thought of ultimate loss which often overtakes pioneers, as experience undoubtedly tells us and them, is put aside as a healthy man puts aside the expectations of death. (162)

Alexander Gerschenkron (1962, 24) writing on developing countries directly argues that to break through the barriers of poverty and nongrowth, a "stronger medicine is needed than the promise of a better allocation of resources or even of the lower price of bread." He goes on to suggest that what is needed is faith that the golden age lies ahead, not behind. One may add that there needs be some thought given to the content of the golden age.

The attitude these quotations reflect was, I suggest, a significant factor accounting for the weakness and insecurity of Europe around the period 1000–1100 referred to earlier (see chapter 1). David Landes (in Higonnet et al. 1991, 16) writes that Europe, around this time, was "too poor in its production technique to sell more than some occasional minerals and, above all, people—a sure sign that there was not much else to sell." He goes on to say that by 1500 Europe was much stronger than any other civilization in the world. This new strength was not, Landes argues, limited to technical knowledge, but also to such directly related characteristics as "curiosity, adventurousness, and greed." He adds on the same page that the "Europeans of the sixteenth century were ferocious in their appetites."

The change in the relative status of Europe (including Britain) and the rest of the world between 1000 and 1500 is so enormous and so pervasive that it cannot be explained in any formal way. The Reformation, the Renaissance, the Enlightenment all represented changes that contributed to the emergence of the Idea of Progress, the appearance of enough individuals with heroism built in, that change began to be seen as possible, as indeed necessary in some psychological and cultural sense. This Idea of Progress that emerged was not in terms of getting prices right, not in terms of relieving poverty, not in terms of achieving Pareto optimality, not in terms of achieving a number of marginal equalities, but rather in terms of vision and grasp and seeing well beyond any existing horizon, of the realization that "things" could be better, that life did not have to be without hope. By the fourteenth century, the European milieu was such that individuals in significant numbers had this kind of vision and could respond to it. Evidently much happened between 1000 and 1400 in Europe and Britain, and these happenings began to be seen by the latter date.[2] It was the failure of this Idea of Progress to emerge or to be transported to all countries everywhere that is the basic reason why labor productivity did not begin to grow in all parts of the world.

Of course generalizations of this nature are naively simplistic, but the basic point is, I am suggesting, of fundamental importance in accounting for the failure of growth to take hold in non-European countries at the same time that it did in Western Europe. The entrepreneurial function must include this heroic role, and the extent to which there are people in a society who can perform such a role depends heavily on the general social, cultural, institutional, religious environment. And the idea that things can be better must be widespread, very widespread. The environment changed significantly in Western Europe in the 500 years after 1000 in directions and ways that facilitated the emergence of people who believed change was possible and profitable. Accompanying these changes in attitude and outlook were the evolution of legal frameworks, accounting methods, rather clearly defined nations, and rather extensive international trade. These changes do not seem to have appeared in other parts of the world and were not imported. How an environment changes in this way is of course far from clear, and how it can be induced to change in this way is even less clear. I shall argue later that one role that the government or government leaders might play in a contemporary developing country is to promote these kinds of changes. Governments were rarely the direct sources of such entrepreneurship in any fundamental way in the early periods in Western Europe.

Islam in particular illustrates these ideas. In the ninth and tenth centuries Islam was perhaps the most sophisticated society that then existed. There were elaborate irrigation systems for agriculture, and methods of cultivation were well in advance of those in other known areas. The livestock and orchards were productive with a great variety of products not known elsewhere. Fertilizer and pest controls were used effectively, and Islamic agronomists were able to produce new varieties. Scientists, poets, mystics were without peer in the world. From around the year 1100 on not only were there

---

2. Much happened in Europe before the year 1000. I do not mean to suggest that nothing happened until the Renaissance, and that it suddenly emerged from the darkness. I do wish to suggest that the Idea of Progress did not take hold anywhere until that time and that its hold in Western Europe and Britain was vastly stronger than in other parts of the world.

no further advances, but severe retrogression set in across most of the Moslem Middle East.[3]

The well-known Islamic scholar, Mohammed Arkoun, has used the categories thinkable, unthinkable, and unthought in studying traditional Islamic societies.[4] He then argues that the philosophical issues developed and studied in the West from the 1500s were simply *unthinkable* in the world of Islam. This *unthought* explains why most people in most Islamic societies have so much difficulty in getting outside of the traditional Islamic view of the world and of itself. Watt (1988, 2) summarizes this view by writing, "For Muslims unchangingness is both an ideal for human individuals and societies, and also a perception of the actual nature of humanity and its environment." It was this tradition of Islam that gained supremacy around 1000–1100, and overcame the more dynamic forces that had prevailed in the several centuries prior to that date. It is important to emphasize that this tradition of unchangingness has great appeal from many aspects, and offers a kind of security and comfort that is extra-welcome in many contexts.[5] In many ways it contributed enormously to the well-being for its adherents. At the same time however it defeated the Idea of Progress.

The accomplishments of the Chinese over the centuries are extensive and well known. The 320 years of the Sung Dynasty (960–1280) were especially impressive for developments in literature, philosophy, and art as well as ocean shipping and trading. One of the earliest mechanical clocks was made during this period as well.[6] Most of these accomplishments were internal matters from the beginning.

Boorstin (1983, 192) tells the story of the mighty navy assembled by Cheng Ho in the early fifteenth century. This navy was not used for trade or for the collection of treasures or to gather scientific information or even to conquer and convert. It was used, says Boorstin, to track down a lost nephew of the emperor and to display the riches of the Ming Dynasty. David Landes (1983) in his superb book on clocks, watches, and time has numerous examples and quotations that show the complacency of the Chinese and their full confidence in their own supremacy. As late as 1793, the Chinese emperor

---

3. Frederick B. Artz (1953) has a clear and concise report on the rise and decline of Islam's economic and other strengths. Artz attributes the decline of Islam's capacity to the increasing dominance of the more conservative branches of Islam. But why did this occur?

4. Arkoun's major work is Arkoun (1984). My discussion relies on Watt (1988, chapter 1) and Kuran (1992). See also Rahman (1982).

5. Watt (1988, 8 ff) emphasizes the "self-sufficiency" of Islam. Self-sufficiency is a particularly comforting feeling.

6. Daniel Boorstin (1983, 500) states that the oldest surviving printed book, the *Diamond Sutra*, was produced in China in 868.

Ch'ien-lung noted the gifts sent to him by Britain's George III and then added, "We have never set much store on strange or ingenious objects, nor do we need any more of your country's manufactures" (Landes 1983, 49).

There is abundant evidence that the remarkable achievements in China were episodes, were specific events, in an otherwise stationary, complacent society. They did not set in motion a great process of economy-wide searching and learning. By the middle of the fifteenth century the Chinese governments had eliminated foreign voyages, and severe penalties were placed on those who tried to explore other worlds. China became even more aloof and unwilling to examine its own state and its own sources of well-being. Clearly the West learned much from China, but the Chinese did not find it possible to learn from the West.

In his discussion of Hindu yoga Stanley Jaki (1974) emphasizes the firmly entrenched idea of a universe that was inherently cyclic.[7] Thus any sort of concern with progression and continual change was a quite alien idea. In such an environment it is hardly surprising that people found it difficult to rise above the existing state of things and see any hope of a more rewarding future. Unlike the Islamic story, there does not seem to be a specific period in the history of Hindu societies when there existed much dynamism and exploration. There were of course notable individual events: the first use of decimals (around 600), recognition of the significance of zero (around the year 1000), surgical developments relevant to a variety of physical problems in the seventh century, and so on. Still, life was necessarily a treadmill from which there was no escape.

The reasons why the Idea of Progress did not travel immediately from Western Europe to other parts of the world—even to Southern Europe—can hardly be specified in any sort of completeness and with any sort of precision. Yet the preceding paragraphs do help us to appreciate how difficult it would be for people long committed to nongrowth to accept and act on the possibility of fundamental and continuing change, especially changes due to their own efforts. The vast array of factors that define a society were such that new ideas that violated these traditions could not prevail—until much later when it became evident that such ideas had in fact led to an economic strength that was unmatched in history. The powerful early societies of China, Japan, Korea, some Middle East areas, and to a lesser extent, India, more or less explicitly rejected any Idea of Progress. Life in these societies was as it should be, and outside ideas and "things" were deemed unsuitable and of no value. Even in Japan as late as the Meiji restoration, the government was forced to find ways to recognize traditional values and ideas at the same time that it

---

7. Some components of the cycle were assumed to last billions of years.

was establishing a more dynamic economic system.[8] Rulers as strong as Mohammed Ali in the first half of the nineteenth century and Anwar Sadat in the 1970s were unable to lead Egypt into modernity in the face of strong opposition from traditional Islamic forces. Such forces were, of course, considerably stronger a few centuries earlier.

In the early post–World War II years, the non-North countries began to see that things could be better. They then however tried to imitate the North, without the history, without the search and tinker and learn notions fully in place. The result is the tension, turmoil, and slower productivity growth in most newly developing countries.

The Role of Religion

Religion is a significant component of a society's traditions and historical context. There is no doubt that the religious convictions and religious environment of a community are relevant to the establishment and acceptance of the Idea of Progress and to the emergence of entrepreneurs as carriers of this idea and to people accepting that well-being can be enhanced. There is also no doubt that our understanding of the exact content of this relevance is hardly clear. I note a few points however to try to give a bit more support to the preceding arguments.

The term Islam is the Arabic word for submission or obedience. The Holy Koran has numerous references to people as the servant, even slaves, of Allah. In Sura 51 (of the translation by J. M. Rodwell in Everyman's Library) one reads,

> I have not created Djinn and men, but that they should worship me:
> I require not sustenance from them, neither require I that they feed me:
> Verily, God is the sole sustainer: possessed of might; the unshaken.

Compare this statement from the Holy Koran with verse 28 of the first chapter of Genesis of the Holy Bible.

> And God blessed them, and God said unto them, Be fruitful, and multiply, and replenish the earth, and subdue it: and have dominion over the fish of the sea, and over the fowl of the air, and over every living thing that moveth upon the earth.

A society permeated by the idea expressed by the lines from Sura 51 will surely feel quite differently about the validity, the legitimacy of searching and

---

8. See the paper by Yasusuke Murakami, "Modernization in Terms of Integration: The Case of Japan," in Eisenstadt (1987) for further discussion of these issues.

learning and seeking to dominate nature relative to one permeated by the ideas expressed in the verse from Genesis. Francis Oakley (in O'Connor and Oakley 1969, 80 ff) argues that the very method of the natural sciences depends on the idea of an "omnipotent God from whom the world. . . . was called into being by the autonomous fiat of his will." Thus the idea of an omnipotent creator—God—led in turn to ideas of natural laws that could be identified and understood and used to accomplish certain objectives. This sort of view was rejected by Islamic society early on and was not accepted until much later—and even now, not completely.[9]

Joseph Needham (1956, 543 ff) summarizes his thorough study of the history of scientific thought in China as follows:

> It will be remembered that the Taoist thinkers, profound and inspired though they were, failed, perhaps because of their intense mistrust of the powers of reason and logic, to develop anything resembling the idea of laws of nature. With their appreciation of relativism and the subtlety and immensity of the universe, they were groping after an Einsteinian world picture, without having laid the foundations for a Newtonian one. By that path science could not develop. It was not that Tao, the cosmic order in all things, did not work according to system and rule; but the tendency of the Taoists was to regard it as inscrutable for the theoretical intellect.

Needham's picture of China then conveys a vastly different environment, a different way of thinking about one's world from that described by Oakley (and many others) for that part of the North strongly affected by the Judeo-Christian heritage. In all these other environments, it is easy to appreciate why an Idea of Progress was absent and why now it is so difficult to create and, often, so strongly resisted.

Ideas can be unsuitable for a society just as technology and factor combinations can for an economy. The general view that truth was given by authority and was to be learned by rote, not searched out, was an established position not only of formal education, but also of the family and village, and it prevails in many areas of the world. Such a view, firmly entrenched, contributes to the rejection of any sort of Idea of Progress that requires searching and learning or the explicit recognition of ignorance and doubt in all matters. There could not be conflict with prevailing religious views simply because there was no doubt in anyone's mind that religion (or tradition in general) dominated any ideas or values that may come from any sort of scientific endeavor. Christianity and Judaism became more adaptable and accommodat-

---

9. Schimmel (1994) is a fine study of Islam before its recent confrontation with the North and with the idea that change is possible.

ing in these respects than did Islam, Hinduism, and the Eastern religions and traditions.

The Outcome

In these societies, the heroic entrepreneur was much less likely to come to the surface, except here and there. Indeed the environment of these societies seemed to discourage, even reject any effort to lift eyes up beyond horizons and beyond the present state of life.[10] The Idea of Progress did not take hold because the institutional arrangements established by history and traditions were too strong to allow the importation of the ideas of the Renaissance or the appearance of any sort of indigenous similar event from occurring.[11] The countries then found it impossible to achieve the changes that were occurring in Europe and that, in turn, were laying the basis for the development of an economy in which well-being was growing routinely. Then by the time that it was evident that incomes were in fact growing steadily in the West, Europe and the United States were so strong, especially on the seas, that the rest of the world, rather than experiencing its own Renaissance and Enlightenment, simply succumbed to efforts to imitate the West, and imitation, as I have already suggested, cannot succeed.

The Role of Income

Another argument of a somewhat more concrete, but quite shaky nature, refers to levels of GDP per capita in these early periods. I have noted earlier that Angus Maddison (1991) has estimated levels of per capita GDP for "Western Europe and offshoots" and China for the years 1400 and 1820 in United States dollars at 1985 prices. In 1400 per capita GDP was $500 in

---

10. In the thirteenth century the areas of the world relevant to the story that I seek to tell were Western Europe and the Middle and Far East. Africa was essentially unknown to non-Africans, and the Western Hemisphere equally unknown to Europeans. So the arguments concentrate on the Middle and Far East. Later of course the British and French pushed the American Indians aside and invented Northern North America in their image, and Spanish and Portuguese did the same in Central and South America.

11. The kind of issues discussed here are similar to those identified by Alexis de Tocqueville (1856). Two quotations from this illuminating book will illustrate the similarities. In speaking of the continuity of ideas that dominated the late eighteenth century in Europe compared to earlier periods, Tocqueville writes, "the torch which set Europe on fire in the eighteenth century was easily quenched in the fifteenth. Arguments of this kind can not succeed till certain changes in the conditions, customs, and minds of men have prepared a way for this reception" (27). And then, "it may be said with perfect truth, that the destruction of a part of that system [feudalism] rendered the remainder a hundred-fold more odious than the whole ever appeared" (49). This latter statement does, I believe, describe most of the developing world of recent decades.

China and $430 in Europe and by 1820 the estimates were still $500 for China, but for Europe and offshoots it was $1,034 (Maddison 1991, 10). The $430 and $500 as of 1400 are, of course, significantly higher than the levels for many countries in Asia, Latin America, and Africa in 1950. While these early estimates are open to both statistical and conceptual difficulties, they do suggest that output per person had been growing prior to 1400 and by that date were high enough, at least for some people, that simply maintaining life was no longer a full-time job.

One might then argue that it was the higher incomes in Europe that convinced the society that further increased incomes were possible. Still this did not happen in China where incomes apparently were somewhat higher than they were in Europe in early centuries. Also, as noted earlier, there were significant technological events in many non-European countries prior to 1400, and Europe was behind in 1100 in terms of technological sophistication. Yet nothing in the way of steady growth appeared in any of the former countries. Saving rates, usually cited as a reason why income level matters, could not conceivably have accounted for the explanation. So, to repeat, something else must have occurred in Western Europe that mattered.

To summarize: In some way or other the Western Europeans became able to see that the feudalism under which they lived was not an inevitable condition of their world, that their world could be examined and understood and hence changed. It was possible to examine, to probe, to doubt, to search and learn without so abruptly undermining fundamental beliefs and sources of meaning that the whole process stopped. This then produced a vision, this *was* a vision, that modified views of the world and that provided the strength—mental and moral—to act, to pay the price. While the emergence of this new attitude was a social phenomenon, it meant that the probabilities of individuals appearing with great vision, with animal spirits, with the determination to achieve change, with the capacity to see beyond any sort of benefit-cost calculations, to reject, along with high Heaven, "the lore of nicely-calculated less or more," and to engage in heroic economics had increased significantly. Really heroic economic activity is always limited to a small number of exceptional people. Even more important is that this "ethos" also results in the searching, tinkering, and learning mentality throughout the society. It is this ubiquity of search that is essential to sustained growth, and such ubiquity is, in large measure, a matter of a national ethos. Now most other nations are convinced that sustained growth of labor productivity is possible, but there remain the legacies of the past and twinges of doubt that it is really morally acceptable to seek such objectives. So there are the tension and unease and instability that characterize much of the developing world.

The Idea of Progress thus seems to continue to be a problem in a number of developing countries. The evidence of this is of several kinds. Perhaps the most common and convincing evidence is simply that so many countries seek largely to imitate the North. There is, I think, considerable fear of genuine reliance on one's own resources and on one's own ideas of the good life. There is a reluctance to accept the responsibility of probing into the unknown with the confidence that such an activity is exciting, illuminating, and possibly exceedingly fruitful of enhanced well-being. There is also evident everywhere an eagerness for very concrete answers to a range of sweeping questions. Many people apparently are convinced that it is somehow not possible for their society to find a way to establish an economic process that will result in increasing productivity over the long term. "Things don't work in our country." The willing dependence on foreign investment, on foreign aid, on foreign advisors, and so on, reflects this attitude. Somehow people in many countries believe that there is something about them that does really prevent their achieving progress on their own. This attitude is often facilitated, or contributed to, by Northerners who define "development" as replicating the North, who push the idea that to achieve enhanced well-being, the developing countries must become like the North. Imitation is not a reflection of the acceptance of the Idea of Progress. Searching and learning is.

Joel Mokyr (1993, 36) argues that around the time of the Industrial Revolution a "widespread thirst for knowledge penetrated Britain down to the small towns of the kingdom where itinerant lecturers were in much demand." This thirst for knowledge led merchants and craftsmen to search for and learn to apply elementary scientific principles in their firms' operations. It is the thirst for knowledge that drove the system, and the source of this attribute must surely be found in the deep-seated, long-evolving characteristics of British society at the time. It is the thirst for knowledge that matters, not simply a desire for more goods and services. If only the latter prevails, there can be no sustained enhancement of well-being.

Edward Mason and Mahn Je Kim in their study of Korea (1980, 446) have written (obviously with tongue in cheek) that it is tempting to argue that Korea became rich because so many Koreans live there. Such a statement is, perhaps, not as empty as it may sound. It refers, or can refer, to an argument that Koreans have learned to believe in themselves, believe that they can change their economy in such a way that its functioning will lead to continually growing well-being. That is the Idea of Progress.

Again: Why Some Countries Got GDP-Rich and Others Did Not

At the very beginning I asked the basic question that development economics confronts: Why are not all countries equally rich or equally poor in terms of goods and services? Why did not all countries begin to achieve growing labor productivity and rising per capita GDP no later than the mid–nineteenth century? The explanation, summarized in chapter 1, may now be made clearer. The ideas that emerged in the Renaissance, the Reformation, the Enlightenment in Western Europe did not travel or emerge in other parts of the world. The Enlightenment seemed to replace the superstition and paternalism and oppression of the long past with the view that nature could be affected and fate did not have to be completely beyond modification. In particular the idea that nature and the natural could be understood was crucial and, as noted, this understanding led to the Idea of Progress. The idea did not travel, except to northern North America and Australia/New Zealand. It traveled to these latter countries because the members of the European society that had established themselves in these areas had brought with them those ideas and ways of thinking and optimism that led to a beginning of search and learning. That these ideas did not travel to the world beyond Europe (that was in fact known to the Europeans) is then the basic explanation of why they did not achieve the growth that Europe and northern North America did.[12]

Then in the years from the middle of the twentieth century, the low-income countries became more or less convinced that the North had something of value after all, and they wanted some too. Political independence added to this desire, and it became accepted that political independence required economic independence. By then the North was so much richer in terms of labor productivity that the temptation for the South simply to imitate the North was all-powerful. The ideas of reason and rationality that were born with the Enlightenment were not adequate to overcome the obstacles that centuries of nongrowth and acceptance of its impossibility had put in place. The best that could be done then would be to imitate, but, as I have tried to show, imitation will not work, a people cannot borrow, cannot import, development as I have defined it. Development must be indigenous, or it is not development. So the first task is to understand how the Idea of Progress, the idea that indigenously created change is possible, can be instilled in a society where it has never before existed. That is the reason we studied growth in a closed economy as a beginning. The essence of its presence is the searching, tinkering, and learning activity to which I have given primary attention. To create that idea, to get the process under way is the necessary condition for development. I consider direct policies to do this in the next three chapters.

---

12. Suppose that the original occupants of Northern North America had been strong and numerous enough to prevent their being swept aside by the Europeans. There would then have been a society here that may well have rejected the ideas that progress was possible in the same way that other non-European societies rejected them. I should note that Japan did not begin its strong growth until the late nineteenth century and then achieved most of its early growth by a remarkable capacity to borrow and adapt. There is more on Japan in the following chapter.

Something of a Hedge and Confession of Doubt

One may easily question this emphasis on tradition or, more broadly, national ethos, and, more narrowly, religion, as impeding the evolution of the ideas of searching and learning, trial and error, risk taking and so on. Certainly the experience of Japan over the last 100 years or so and the post–World War II experience of Korea and Taiwan do not suggest an absence of this particular role of entrepreneurship. In these countries however the government has often played strategic roles in initiating and nurturing economic activities. Many observers have also argued that the new powerful East Asian economies have been better at borrowing and adapting than they have at pushing back the cutting edge itself. And the basic question remains, why did these countries not begin their growth when the West began to grow? The preceding arguments do not deny that particular situations, particular leaders, forms of colonial power, and so on, matter. They are intended however to argue that the deeper characteristics of a society are fundamental in understanding what has happened in an economy and what kind of policies can be effective in the future. There is of course no doubt that our ignorance in this area is as great as in other areas.

The Entrepreneur as Perceiver and Exploiter of a Specific Profit Opportunity

The two remaining roles for the entrepreneur are more prosaic, but of equal importance in helping to understand how increased output occurs and contributes to the enhancement of well-being. Someone (or possibly a group) must identify any specific profit or investment opportunity. In some sense one expects there to be numerous investment opportunities in an economy where incomes are generally very low and where there are labor and other resources readily available. In such an environment however it may be difficult for members of the community to identify *specific* activities that have a legitimate prospect for survival. It was Albert Hirschman (1958) who convinced many observers that this was indeed the case and that government policy should be concerned exactly with the task of generating evident opportunities.

This role, and the similar one of actually carrying out the investment project, have been studied at considerable length by economists and other social scientists over the years. Hypotheses have been explored to the effect that members of minority or immigrant groups are more likely to have the necessary characteristics than are indigenous groups, that certain religious convictions are more conducive to this role than are others, that certain personality traits are necessary, and so on. I think that all these hypotheses (and others) are probably relevant in certain situations, though the empirical evidence to support them is easy to question. It is indeed difficult to determine exactly what kind of empirical evidence would in fact illuminate these questions. I want to proceed in a slightly different way.

Suppose that we could know in some way or other that the environment was one in which the view was widely held that things could be better, that well-being could in fact be enhanced, and yet no new activities emerged. One might then argue that, in some objective sense, there were no investment opportunities available and therefore the government should carry out new or different policies that would create such opportunities. One might argue, on the other hand, that there were profit opportunities present, but that the aspect of entrepreneurship discussed here was not sufficiently strong to identify them. One might even conclude that such projects were being identified, but there was not present the capacity to implement the investment activity necessary to carry them out or that market distortions or government interventions were the barriers. Which of these interpretations is more nearly applicable is difficult to ascertain in a given case. If the capacity to "see" profit opportunities is great enough, then the general policies have less need to be strong, that is, the profit opportunities have less need to be made explicit. A task of the analyst (and the policymaker) is to seek to understand the economy clearly enough to determine the nature of the immediate bottlenecks. The role of government policy in this context is discussed in a later chapter.

Two quite general points may be made.

A. Most profit opportunities can best be seen in a familiar environment. Given that some Idea of Progress prevails, then the seeing of a specific opportunity is more likely to be within the local area rather than on some national (or international) level. Almost all private firms begin small, some of course as one- or two-person enterprises, and beginning with the identification of a fairly local opportunity is to be expected.[13] There are several advantages of such a beginning:

    i. Small, locally oriented firms are more likely to be compatible with the available quality and form of entrepreneurship, not only with respect to the identification of the opportunity, but also with other

---

13. One of the temptations of the modern developing country is to start a new enterprise at a large scale. This almost necessarily involves either the government or a foreign firm or both in some form or other. I argue later that direct foreign investment is a difficult matter for new, inexperienced governments to manage, and therefore is best kept fairly limited. If this is the case, then most firms should and will begin small. Carl Liedholm, Donald Mead, and their colleagues at Michigan State University have studied small-scale enterprises in developing countries in particularly helpful ways.

aspects of management and the searching and learning processes. Just as a firm and its technology should fit the capital and labor endowment of a country, so too it should fit the entrepreneurial endowment. The local orientation is compatible with firms appearing throughout the economy and thereby providing opportunities for the accumulation of both entrepreneurial and managerial experience for a wide range of people in wide areas of the country. These firms are also much more likely to be able to use available labor, with no problems of skill and so on. Keith Marsden in a survey of locally owned private firms in Africa found that all such firms offered jobs to "unskilled workers and devoted considerable time and resources to development and upgrading of skills" (1990, 14). I noted earlier the advantages of avoiding the notion that skilled labor is a bottleneck to employment and growth. The Town and Village Enterprises, now going strong in China, illuminate this same point, as do the Grameen Bank activities in Bangladesh.

ii. As noticed earlier with respect to the bicycle factory beginnings, the idea is not only that small, locally oriented firms are more efficient in the usual textbook sense of this term than are large, nationally oriented firms. The idea is also that they contribute to the emergence of a category of strategic agents of change.

iii. Locally oriented firms can find ways to survive for a while in most developing countries without direct support from the government, if large scale firms, foreign or government supported, are not subsidized in one way or another. This means that any sort of policy to restrict certain activities to small firms or forbid them to large firms is unnecessary, as is any sort of government subsidy.

iv. Transaction costs for small, indigenous firms are likely to be low for a number of reasons. Knowledge of how and whom to trust is present, monitoring of work is simpler, organization and operation of the firm are likely to reflect prevailing ideas of what is acceptable, the nature of the moral commitment of workers and managers and owners is likely to be greater, wage setting and policy doubtless simpler, and so on.

v. Experiencing and learning about a market takes place in a situation in which it is recognized that the harshness of an unqualified market mechanism must be qualified—limited—in some way, if it is not to create an uninhabitable community.[14] Where a market is im-

---

14. Edward C. Banfield (1958) discusses the grave problems that arise when a society goes all out for individual or family self-interest. His economy is essentially a jungle. Banfield (166) quotes Alexis de Tocqueville (from *Democracy in America*): "I do not think, on the whole, that

posed suddenly, or an effort is made to impose it suddenly on a large scale, enlightened or informed culture, limited self interest may well be absent.[15] Learning to use the market in an effective way is a time-consuming process, as is virtually all learning.

vi. The growth of a small firm into a medium- and large-sized firm should proceed as learning allows. One of the questions that the search process must resolve is that of expansion. A firm that expands in this way can be expected to grow only as the understanding and capacity of its owners and managers allow. This is quite different from trying to begin big to exploit alleged economies of scale, or seeking to increase market share, become competitive, and so on. A firm must grow as the firm's managers see it possible and profitable to do so. It is easy to convince oneself that many firms in many countries become larger than can be effectively managed. Whatever economies may exist due to technology can be offset by inadequate management. The evidence does not rule out that an economy can grow easily and regularly with only small-sized firms.

All of these notions suggest that some kind of protection in the presence of some kind of competition is an appropriate environment for the emergence of new, small-scale, truly indigenous firms.[16] The idea that a national (or international) market contributes to increased efficiency and allows firms to exploit potential economies of scale is appealing, but in many instances it is an inappropriate argument. That

---

there is more selfishness among us than in America, the only difference is that there it is enlightened self-interest, here it is not. Each American knows when to sacrifice some of his private interests to save the rest; we want to save everything, and often we lose it all." Some may think that things have changed since Tocqueville studied the United States.

15. The price mechanism was not invented and then imposed on any country. In most countries of the North, it evolved along with other institutions of the society. This fact allowed the community to use the price system as a means of solving problems in a context that also appreciated that its unbridled application creates a jungle. "Homo economicus" can (and should) exist only where members of a society are free to form a variety of associations and institutions. In such a society people are committed to a rule of law, members recognize mutual obligations, and they respect the norms that result from such institutions. Where this is not the case, the market economy degenerates into greed and unbridled economic war. To impose, or try to impose, a market abruptly on a society ill-prepared to prevent its harsh aspects from prevailing will almost inevitably result in reduced well-being for the community.

16. The most difficult problem arises when there are ethnic groups within a country that have different histories, interests, and resources that affect members of each group's capacity to perform their entrepreneurial functions. Then one group gains an initial advantage that the second has trouble overcoming, and the latter then find themselves behind in these activities. This is an issue in several countries in East Africa, in Malaysia, Indonesia, Thailand, and some Latin American countries. I discuss it a bit more in the examination of the role of government in a later chapter.

areas and villages are, to some degree, isolated allows learning time before they confront head-on the established, experienced, large-scale producers. It is this learning time that, I am suggesting, is essential as a means of individuals learning to perform the aspect of entrepreneurship discussed in this section.

B. For most new small firms, initial capital comes from the accumulated liquid assets of the entrepreneurs themselves or from their immediate family and friends.[17] The OECD study (1990) reports that in the United States about 60 percent of the firms financed by "venture capital" were within 50 miles of the investor. Evidence can be disputed, but it does seem fairly safe to say that the lack of finance that a "better" banking system could provide is not in general an immediate obstacle to this category of investment. To put it a bit differently: creating a lending institution of one form or another that is intended to make loans to new, small-scale enterprises is, generally, not likely to break an important bottleneck or to induce the appearance of many new firms in an economy just beginning to grow. Indeed many banks in such situations are essentially limited to lending for trade and imports. As noted in chapter 4, saving in the usual sense does not appear to be a bottleneck with this kind of an approach to development.[18] This situation probably varies from country to country, and as firms get larger and larger, banks do, of course, begin to play important roles.

Satisfactory data on this issue are hard to find. There are many examples of banks established for the specific purpose of lending to small-scale and new firms. There is evidence that these banks have often helped, but also evidence that they often fail to induce new investment in a very significant way. As just asserted, they rarely break the immediately binding constraint that limits the appearance of new firms or the expansion of old ones. In instances where personal and family resources are not adequate and there is a strong demand for investment funds, more traditional kinds of money markets can work well. There is, for example, some evidence in Sri Lanka that farmers will borrow from traditional moneylenders even when a government or private bank is readily available and offers lower lending rates. This is partly a matter of transaction costs—for example, the banks ask a lot of questions that the moneylender already knows the answers to—but also a matter of the traditional sources fitting the overall environment more effectively than a newly established bank can do. This point is not an argument that these traditional sources are doing a good job, but rather that it may well be that the most appropriate

---

17. Cortes et al. 1987, Little et al. 1987, and OECD 1990 have ample data on this point as well as useful discussions of its implications.

18. Saving is a problem as noted with very large-scale investments such as dams, major highways, railroads, big factories, and so on.

policy is one that seeks to find ways to make these arrangements work better, rather than destroying them and putting modern banks in their place.

This latter point may be further illustrated with a reference to the Islamic ban on charging and paying interest. It is often said that such a practice is incompatible with an effective market system and therefore should be abolished and a modern system put in its place. This position is surely unacceptable to millions of Moslems. Western banking arrangements, of course, have a history that is characterized by many examples of failures of all kinds. Islamic banking rests on the idea of a sharing of risks and profits between lender and borrower in an activity that yields an economic return. Lenders are entitled to a share of this return to the extent that it does result in the creation of an economic asset. Indeed Islamic laws of contract in general insist that the risks be shared by all the parties of the contract.

The Islamic approach means that lenders must be more concerned with the profitability of the loans, rather than simply with the creditworthiness of the borrower (*The Economist*, April 4, 1992, 49). This in turn probably makes them more conservative in their lending, and it may be one reason why they have traditionally concentrated on trade, rather than production, loans. As small-scale and local investment opportunities become more common, one might expect banks following Islamic practices to be more willing to engage in lending for productive purposes—and their depositors to be involved in accepting part of the risk that is associated with such lending. A searching and learning process would mean in this case that banks and nations following an Islamic code would find ways to continue to honor that code and, at the same time, find ways to overcome some of the limitations—for example, the way it limits monetary policy—that now seem to be a part of its use.

There are other examples. The bazaar merchants in Iran and other Middle East countries are, and have been for centuries, strategic actors in the economy in a variety of aspects, including providing finance in one way or another. The more recently organized Grameen Trust in Bangladesh (and elsewhere) is another example of a source of funding, beyond family members and friends, that seems to fit, and thereby serve, the economy well. Grameen Banks have had a short but impressive history as lenders to poor people who have shown some evidence of entrepreneurship and had an idea or two for an investment. They began in Bangladesh, but are now worldwide. They are of special interest also because they have been concerned especially with financing projects in which women play important roles. Abu A. N. Wahid (1993) is a good source for the full story.

These arrangements and others like them suggest that there are adequate institutions to prevent any constraint due to saving or finance from being binding, at least for very long. The idea is similar to the other aspects of our story: do not uproot an arrangement that has evolved with the rest of the system through the ages, rather search for ways to make it increasingly effective in facilitating the achievement of increasing output in a way that is compatible with that higher output contributing to enhanced well-being.

The argument on entrepreneurs has reached this point: given an environment where the Idea of Progress exists, or is in the process of emerging, and where government policy (to be discussed) is such that objective profit opportunities are present, is there any reason to believe that the absence of individuals with the capacity to identify and to implement investment opportunities will prevent the appearance of new firms? If one concludes that there are such reasons, then government policy should reflect that fact, that is, it should find ways to facilitate the appearance of this kind of entrepreneurial activity. If one concludes that the society is amply endowed with this category of entrepreneurship, then of course there is no need for government action aimed directly at inducing entrepreneurial activity of the kind discussed in this section.

The Entrepreneur as Searcher, Learner, and Changer

The third aspect of entrepreneurial activity is concerned with the searching, learning, and changing that must take place after the enterprise is in place, if it is to survive and possibly to grow. This function is to be distinguished from that of managing, in the sense of making routine decisions. The same person may do both managing and searching and learning, but it is useful to keep the two roles distinguished. It is also different from the tasks associated with identifying and starting a firm from scratch. I have already argued that continued searching and learning and changing is a necessary part of a firm's activity in a growing economy. If it does not engage in such activity in an effective way it will die away.

Conventional analysis usually places competition or the threat of competition as the basic inducement to search and learn and thereby to increase productivity. This I discussed earlier. Now the question is whether or not there is a supply problem with respect to people who can perform this kind of activity.

Suppose that it is possible to say that the state of the macroeconomy is favorable to investment, that is, there is little excess capacity and the prospects for growth and price level and balance of payments stability appear good. Similarly, the threat of competition is evident to all in one form or another. Finally, there seem to be ample new firms entering into various activities. The present question can now be phrased as follows: Do existing firms achieve increasing productivity and, possibly, though this is not essential, increasing output? Increasing productivity is of course essential. If, under these conditions, increasing productivity does not occur, then we are entitled to conclude that this particular component of entrepreneurial role is lacking.

Data and discussion in Jones and Sakong (1980) illustrate this point with respect to Korea. Their data show that growth in value added in manufacturing in the 1960s and 1970s was due "first to the expansion of existing firms, second to entry of offspring firms, and only to a minor extent to net entrance of new entrepreneurs"[19] (176). There were however many new firms that came into existence, but a very high failure rate. Jones and Sakong conclude that, "on the supply side, expansion [in Korea] has been the result of qualitative, rather than quantitative, changes" (176). I have found no comparable data for other developing countries, but it seems highly probable that most other countries would show a more significant role for small firms.[20]

The general strategy in Korea was to allow small new firms to sink or swim on their own and, once it was evident which could swim, the government would offer support, usually in the form of favored access to funds. There is no evidence (that I have seen) that suggests that the government's support was provided to the firms that had demonstrated their capacity to survive because it (the government) believed that such support was needed to help out a wobbly entrepreneurial capacity. Certainly Korean entrepreneurs responded remarkably well to that support and other incentives. Whether such a strategy would work in other countries can only be ascertained by trial and error. This conclusion is elaborated further in the following chapters.

Conclusions on Entrepreneurship

Several points emerge from this way of thinking about development and about the role of entrepreneurship. The most obvious is simply that the entrepreneur is a key player when the development process is approached the way that I am suggesting it be approached. The presence of ignorance ensures that that is the case. I have also emphasized the ideas of Schumpeter, Keynes, Boulding, Gerschenkron and others that put heavy weight on the role of the Idea of Progress, a notion that goes well beyond the ideas of internal rates of return and benefit-cost analysis and somehow reflects the view that change can occur, things can and must be better. This is largely a matter of society in general, but that fact is reflected in the surfacing of individuals with this heroic vision that movement is an inherent part of the system. In many developing countries, the government may have a key role in the creating of this kind of environment.

---

19. Offspring firms are those founded by previously successful entrepreneurs.

20. Taiwan's economy is dominated by relatively small-scale firms, at least compared to those in Korea. While policies do seem to enter into the explanation, it also seems likely that more fundamental characteristics, including entrepreneurship, are also quite relevant. See, for example, Scitovsky 1985.

Given this environment, or given the emerging of this kind of environment, individuals to perform the direct entrepreneurial functions are not likely to pose a bottleneck *if* the country concentrates on activities—kinds and sizes—that are compatible with the experience and understanding and knowledge of its people. This means in general that some protection from multinationals, from imports, and from government enterprises is needed if this indigenous entrepreneurial talent is to become effective. The basic policy objective is therefore (from the standpoint of the government) to seek to create a widespread Idea of Progress, to establish a general environment in which there is great inducement (i.e., create evident profit opportunities) to new firms to enter and to search for ways to grow. There then are expected to be many small firms testing the waters, making their effort. Some will succeed and grow, some will succeed and remain small, some will fail and drop out. Whether the government should take more action to help successful firms will depend on other circumstances than entrepreneurship and will be examined later.

Entrepreneurship then is not a bottleneck in the presence of the Idea of Progress, continuing and evident profit opportunities, and protection from large, outside firms and large, government-owned firms.

CHAPTER 7

Foreign Transactions

From the very beginning of interest in the status of low-income countries, foreign trade, international capital movements, aid, technology transfer, and foreign training have all occupied a great deal of attention. The initial argument was that the the low-income countries should industrialize, should change their economies from agricultural or mineral based to industry based. The most influential of all early ideas of development—the dual economy models of Arthur Lewis and Fei and Ranis—rested specifically on the idea that the presently low-income countries should expand their modern sector as rapidly as possible and allow their traditional sector to die off. Both Lewis and Fei and Ranis were careful not to equate "modern" with industry, but industrialization soon became widely equated with modern, and traditional often with agriculture. This way of thinking was the origin of the notion that development meant replicating the North. Modern meant "North," and hence great emphasis was placed on the capacity to import physical capital goods and technology from the North. To achieve this, the dominating strategy that evolved was to replace imports—initially of consumer goods only—with their domestic production, a strategy usually identified as import substitution.[1] Import substitution became, during the 1950s and 1960s, the most widely practiced approach to development. Its dominant role continued until the early 1970s when the great success of Korea and Taiwan became increasingly evident to the world. The most evident feature of this success was the remarkable growth of exports of the two countries. A strategy, alternative to import substitution, then emerged, usually identified as an export or outward-looking strategy.

I begin this chapter with a brief review of the import substitution, outward-oriented debate. I want, however, to spend most of the chapter on the way the foreign sector can affect productivity growth. I conclude that some

---

1. The article by Arthur Lewis (1954) and later the book of John Fei and Gustav Ranis (1964) were the earliest statements of the labor-surplus, dual-economy model. Of course there have been numerous books and articles on these topics since the 1950s, but these early works were enormously influential in terms of both policy and theoretical formulations. So far as I can determine John Power (1963) was the first author to study *import substitution* as an approach to development.

kind of protection is likely to be necessary in most countries to put an indigenously grounded growth process in place. An exact form of protection that is most suitable for this purpose is discussed in the following chapter. I end the present chapter with some quick comments on a few other foreign sector issues that are illuminated a bit by the discussion of productivity growth and protection.

The basic notions on which this chapter builds may be stated in the following way: International trade in commodities results in greater availability of goods and services for a country than is possible without such trade. Such trade however cannot provide continuing growth of goods and services for a country. To achieve that, the process that I have examined in the preceding chapters must be in place in each trading country. More precisely, the absence of productivity growth in one country cannot be offset by commodity trade with another country in which productivity is growing. To say the same thing again: Commodity trade is not a substitute for internal productivity growth. In the context of growth of output and of development in general, gains from trade are in the form of contributions to learning and inducements to search. I want now to study how international trade, and international transactions in general, can contribute to the growth of productivity directly and to the growth of well-being.[2]

Development Strategies: Import Substitution and Outward Orientation

The central idea of import substitution[3] was very simple. Production in all low-income countries of the late 1940s was largely agricultural or mineral. Manufactured products, capital and consumer, were imported. The dual-economy models were interpreted to imply that this structure had to be changed. Given this widespread way of thinking, the idea of replacing imports with domestic production seemed obvious. Thus various forms of protection were installed, behind which a wide range of manufacturing activities (producing mainly consumer goods) sprang up in many countries. The presumption, mainly implicit, was that, at some point in the not-too-distant future, these activities would be able to survive without protection. Thus the assumption, also often tacit, that productivity growth would occur was strategic, but little

---

2. Luigi Pasinetti (1981 and, especially 1993) develops this position in considerable detail and with considerable rigor, albeit with rather strong assumptions. Chapter 9 in Pasinetti (1993) is a short, powerful statement of the basic argument.

3. There is a vast literature on both import substitution and outward orientation. Good general discussions can be found in Wade (1990) and Milner (1990). More specific discussion is in the chapters by Bruton and Balassa in Chenery and Srinivasan (1989). All of these sources have extensive bibliographies.

attention was given to exactly how that productivity growth would take place, and even less attention was given to how it (productivity growth) could be induced. The main assumption seemed to have been that, since technology would be imported from the North, productivity would rise quickly as it became understood and generally applied. Also there was very little attention given to the form of protection that seemed to make sense, with the result that most countries employed a great range of forms of protection with little reference to the distortions and other effects on the economy created by the protection package.

The growth process envisioned in the import substitution strategy was essentially that defined by the Harrod model. That model tells us that the rate of growth of output is equal to the saving rate divided by the capital-output ratio. Capital formation was the only identified source of growth, and if the domestic saving rate was not adequate to achieve the target rate of growth (given the capital-output ratio), foreign aid could fill in the difference. Production coefficients were assumed to be more or less fixed because of the dominance of Northern technology. So factor prices did not much matter, at least so far as generating employment was concerned. All problems could be overcome by a high enough rate of capital formation, and aid and foreign loans could make it high enough. Since almost all capital goods were imported, an overvalued exchange rate was a convenient instrument for making capital goods cheap in domestic currency. The overvalued exchange rate added to the need for protection as well as penalized exports. Again the implicit assumption seemed to be that productivity growth would enable the economy to grow into a currently overvalued exchange rate.

That such strategy could not produce sustained growth now seems abundantly clear, but there was little criticism from economists on this basic approach as it got under way.[4] The most convincing evidence of the failure of import substitution came not from analyses of its internal inconsistencies, but rather from the evidence that began to emerge from the great successes in Korea and Taiwan in the early 1970s. The most obvious difference between these two countries and those developing countries more firmly committed to import substitution was the remarkable rates of growth of exports of the former two. These rates of growth of exports were accompanied by equally impressive rates of growth of GDP and employment, combined with fairly stable price levels and a strong balance of payments. Therefore great weight came to be placed on exports as driving growth. It is important to note that the view of exporting as perhaps the strategic factor of growth arose largely as a

---

4. There were of course important dissenters. Gottfried Haberler and Jacob Viner were perhaps the most potent, but in general there was little dissent among economists on this strategy in the 1950s. See Viner (1952) and Haberler (1959).

result of the experiences of Korea and Taiwan, not as a consequence of new theoretical formulations or models. There had been some reference to exporting in the import substitution package, but in general exports were not deemed an essential element of success. Exports were important in import substitution only because they were necessary to pay for the imported capital goods and technology that were assumed to be the real sources of growth.

The apparent success of Taiwan and Korea then led to the general conclusion that an import substitution strategy that inevitably penalized exports was a failure, and for a country to succeed it must abandon import substitution and push hard toward an outward-looking, export-oriented strategy. This evidence persuaded many academicians and international organizations, in spite of the absence of a convincing theoretical framework that would lead to openness.

The emphasis on import substitution and the method of its implementation required a considerable role for the government, and evidence also accumulated that governments were generally not very efficient, often corrupt, and, at best, inexperienced and ill-trained and subject to the pressures of rent seekers from many sources. Hence part of the problem of import substitution was that it called for a large role for the government, a role that very few governments could effectively deliver.

It was easy to conclude from this argument and evidence that government failure was greater and more endemic than market failure. Proponents of the outward orientation strategy, therefore, also pushed the view that the most appropriate development strategy was a market-friendly one. How friendly depended on the advocate, but in all cases the role of the government was to be much more circumscribed than had been the case in the earlier decades of development efforts. Thus by the 1980s, a market-friendly, outward-oriented strategy seemed to be winning the day over an apparently failed import substitution strategy. This combination (market-friendly, outward oriented) would produce, and seemed to be producing, growth with considerable equity, strong demand for labor, and other favorable characteristics for a substantial number of countries.

Then difficulties began to appear. Perhaps the earliest was simply that in both Taiwan and Korea, it became widely understood that the governments played and continue to play important and extensive roles. It was clearly misleading to assume that these governments were "minimal" or that they stood by and watched the market work its own way. There were other specific characteristics of these two countries that were important in explaining their success: widespread literacy, strong work ethic, an accumulation of experience in manufacturing activities during Japanese control, a homogeneous society, strong governments committed to growth, and so on. These characteristics made Korea and Taiwan considerably different from most other developing countries, and made it possible for them to enter world trade quickly and effectively. They were thus much better equipped, much readier, to take advantage of the fact that world trade grew at rates unmatched in history in the quarter century after 1950. Most other countries were much less well prepared to exploit that opportunity.

During the 1980s a great deal of statistical work was carried out that tested, or aimed at testing, the argument that exporting, or some indicator of "openness," was an important explanation of growth of output or of employment. These exercises have, at best, reached ambiguous results and often have shown that exports did not seem to be especially important.[5] The absence of convincing statistical evidence that supports the view of a strong role for exports makes it especially difficult to put great confidence in the argument that they (exports) are the strategic factor in growth.

A particularly striking point with respect to the role of policy is made by Rodrik (1993). He identifies a great range of policies—import quotas and licenses, credit subsidies, tax exemptions, public ownership, and so on—that have apparently worked well in the East Asian countries but have also apparently failed in Latin America, Africa, and the rest of Asia. This powerful point must mean that there are other, deeper forces at work. In the language of the present effort: the institutional environment, the preferences of the population, the search-and-tinker propensity, the capacity to perceive and respond, the historical and political context all matter in fundamental ways in finding ways to create rising well-being.

The main point, however, is that in the successful instances productivity grew. In Japan and Korea import substitution was a success because productivity grew, and this in turn made exporting possible and the exporting in turn added to the rate of growth of productivity. So the question is, how do trade and productivity growth interact?[6]

The state of play as of 1996 therefore seems to be something like the following: It is generally accepted that the import substitution approach as practiced in the 1950s and 1960s offers very little hope of success. An outward-oriented, market-friendly strategy remains widely accepted, but, increasingly, difficulties with the approach are appreciated, and the limited

---

5. A useful survey of statistical results is that of Levine and Renelt (1991, 1991a) referred to earlier. See also Fischer (1991) and Harrison (1991). Chapter 1 of Robert Wade (1990) is an excellent review of the evidence on the role of exports in growth. *The World Development Report* for 1987 (World Bank, 1987) has the most determined effort to show that exports or some more general measure of openness is of fundamental importance in accounting for growth of output and employment and other favorable aspects of growth. Several writers have expressed doubts about the arguments of this publication. See, for example, Stern (1989).

6. As noted earlier some analysts now dispute the evidence on total factor productivity growth in East Asian success stories. This evidence of course is not all in, but it is difficult to appreciate how that success could occur without productivity growth. There is no doubt that labor productivity grew rapidly.

extent to which the Korea/Taiwan story can be explained in these terms is also becoming more widely understood. Similarly, the idea that the appropriate role of government can be adequately described by "minimal" is now often questioned.[7]

Somehow, therefore, developing countries must be able to learn from each other, and, especially, from the rich countries. Somehow again the governments in the new countries must find their role, a role that they can perform effectively. How the people and governments of the developing countries can learn from the North without losing their identity, without becoming clones of the North or (worse) hopelessly poverty-stricken places is the basic question of this part of my story.

The Foreign Sector and Productivity Growth

In the discussion of growth, great emphasis was placed on the existence of currently underutilized technical and administrative knowledge that could be found by search-and-tinker efforts that were essentially part of the production process. There was no independent formal R&D activity. There was however the recognition that for a firm to survive it must continuously search and learn and find new ways to produce and new products to offer the market. It was also asserted that such an effort would in many cases bear fruit, but also in many cases fail. The growing economy therefore is one with a great variety of firms, some experiencing rapidly increasing productivity and thereby thriving, others holding more or less steady, and others slowly or rapidly dying off. The small-scale sectors especially are always in a state of turmoil, of births, thrivings, failings, holdings on, dyings. The new technical knowledge in the North, until around the 1920s and 1930s, was accumulated in this manner, that is, without much of any formal R&D activity.

An economy where this is in fact the case is crucial because it means that the idea of searching and learning, the Idea of Progress, is present, has evolved, and has, in a real sense, become indigenous to the community. That such a state prevail is necessary before more formal approaches to knowledge accumulation and knowledge acquisition can be effective. The early efforts to export the technology of the North directly to the South for immediate application and the efforts to establish R&D institutes in many of the developing countries have largely failed, in my view, because this idea of searching and learning and applying was not indigenous to most communities.[8]

---

7. The term *privatization* is equally inadequate as a guide to policy in the developing world. Wade (1990) discusses the role of government in development, and the difficulty of defining in a general way what that role ought to be.

8. One of the earliest statements that reflected the optimism of knowledge transfer was

At some point, however, it becomes necessary to have access to more formal sources of knowledge accumulation and acquisition than is possible with informal searching and learning if growth is to continue. At this point the foreign sector must be introduced directly. I now explore the various issues involved in doing this.

The Knowledge-Accumulating Process
in an International Context

Figure 10 is the familiar textbook picture of the production possibility curve with the modifications introduced in figure 8 in chapter 4, the idea of a production maze. There is now a further modification. The usual formulations of production possibility frontiers do not identify firms, but since it is firms that produce, not the economy, it is illuminating to introduce them in the present context.

The maze AB refers to a country of the North, a rich country. Suppose initially there is only one firm, Firm C, operating at C in the figure, and producing OY_1 of Y and OX_1 of X. This position reflects the quantity of physical resources available to Firm C and to the productivity with which it employs them. The earlier arguments have shown that C is not a hard maximum, that is, the barrier against which it is lodged can possibly be circumvented or eliminated by active search or learning by doing. Now suppose that Firm C stops producing X and the physical resources that it has used for this purpose are made available to Firm D so that it now produces X. The productivity of these resources for Firm D, flowing from its tacit and firm-specific knowledge, is higher than it was for Firm C. Therefore more X is produced than was possible, given the amount of Y, when Firm C produced both Y and X. Firm D has been more successful in its searching and learning efforts than Firm C, at least as far as the production of X is concerned. That productivity (and productivity growth) varies among firms has been noted in earlier chapters.

The production possibility barriers, RS, refer to a country of the South with about the same quantity of physical resources as in the North. Two firms are also shown here, and arguments similar to those in the previous paragraph apply. Two points may be noticed. The most obvious is that the output of Y and X anywhere along AB is larger than along RS even though, by assump-

---

that of President Harry S. Truman in his inaugural address of January 1949. In this address President Truman had four points, the last of which was the commitment of the United States to share its technical and other knowledge relevant to production with the low-income countries of the world. The United States foreign aid program was known as Point Four for many years. Events have shown that these ideas could not be realized in the simple way that Truman's (and many others') remarks implied.

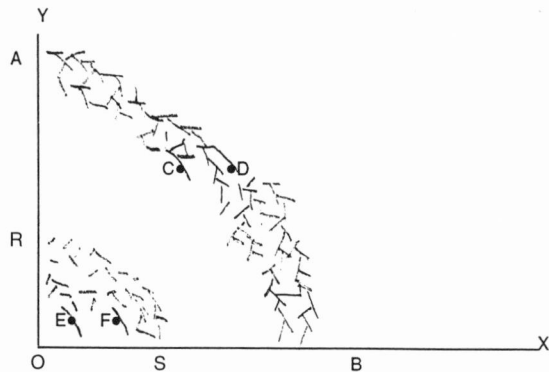

Fig. 10. International differences in labor productivity

tion, the quantity of physical resources is about the same. The second point is that the firms in the South country are at the lower edge of their maze, while those in the North are nearer the outer edge. The former firms would be able to gain more from learning by doing and tinkering than appears likely for those in the North.

In chapter 4 the production possibility maze was introduced to help illuminate the discussion of aggregate demand. In that context, attention was focused on the role that government spending could play, and individual firms played less of a role. Here however firms are the premier agent, and it is useful, if cumbersome, to introduce them explicitly. In particular the fact that productivity and its growth vary widely among firms is a crucial aspect of growth, and this is recognized in the present discussion. At the same time the productivity of firms generally is higher in the rich than in the poor nations.

The distance between the firms along *RS* and those along *AB* indicates the difference between the productivity of resources in the North and the South. This distance and the figure illustrate the general theme of the present chapter: the basic question that development economics asks of international transactions is how learning by the indigenous firms of the South can be increasingly effective by foreign transactions of all kinds.

Research, Technology, and Productivity Growth

The link between research, especially "basic" research, and increased productivity is at best indirect and vague. The approach that I want to describe now is helpful, not because it is "right," *because in fact it is "wrong,"* but because to explain why it is wrong illuminates the knowledge-accumulating process in a particularly revealing way.[9]

Suppose a linear route from basic research at the start through applied research through the development of the applied knowledge to the point that it can be incorporated in blueprints that define a technology so completely that it can be applied directly in the production process by any- and everybody. With such a spectrum, the idea is that the first step in the creation of new and more productive technologies emerges from what is usually called basic research. Then this "pure knowledge" is used as the basis of further research that draws from it the ideas and insights and relationships and characteristics that have relevance for production. This process in turn results in "applicable" knowledge. In these two early stages the people involved are generally classified as scientists, somewhat divorced from the design of knowledge directly usable in production. In the final stage then are the engineers who, employing the pure and applicable knowledge created upstream, develop the blueprints and other details that permit the knowledge to be used directly in the production of goods and services. Whether the new blueprint is employed depends on the extent to which costs are reduced by the new knowledge. The usual statement for the application of cost-reducing knowledge is that the average total costs with the new knowledge must be less than the variable costs for the existing knowledge. The final result is increased productivity of existing resources that moves AB in figure 10 outward, an improved product, or a new product. The research and development then represents an investment, the return on which is the increased profits arising from the reduced costs or from the sale of the new or improved products. In some ideal economy resources would be allocated to R&D until the expected return would be equal to that in other available investment opportunities.

The great uncertainty inherent in this process is to be emphasized as is its probable capital intensity, the latter due to the possible need for physical capital in laboratories, testing grounds, and so on, and the human capital embodied in the scientists and engineers. For these reasons this formal research activity appears to be more suitable to the factor endowment of GDP-rich countries than to that in the developing countries. The countries of the North would then produce knowledge and export it to the South. The South would pay for it with exports of its own output just as it pays for imports of commodities or services or with foreign aid. The developing country would then import the knowledge required to put their firms in the area of AB, and their productivity would more or less jump to the levels in the North. We know that has not happened.

---

9. Nathan Rosenberg (in Evenson and Ranis 1990) has a similar discussion.

A further issue arises due to market failure. It is essentially impossible for the new knowledge to be fully proprietorial, and hence all profits due to the new knowledge can rarely be captured by the originator. So there will be underinvestment in R&D. More fundamental is the public goods nature of knowledge. Once knowledge is created, its marginal cost is essentially zero, and so, by conventional argument, should be "sold" at zero price. If this were in fact the case, then of course, no profit-seeking firm would undertake any R&D unless subsidized by the government. In either event the government must somehow intervene or simply do all the R&D itself, financing the cost from tax revenues, and then make all knowledge free to anyone who wants to use it. This sort of idea seems to be implicit in most textbook theories of the long-run competitive equilibrium of an industry.

The clearest example of this vision of knowledge accumulation is probably the story of the high-yielding varieties of wheat, maize, and rice seeds, their "invention," their development and their application. The possibility of seeds that respond extra well to water and fertilizer was worked out in Mexico and the Philippines. This basic idea was then further developed into specific means for actually manufacturing such seeds. Finally further testing and adapting and modifying was accomplished in order to make the seeds work in various localities. This last step was necessary because type of soil, temperature, pests, and so on have direct effects on the capacity of the seeds to produce their higher yields. The Green Revolution is, however, the only clear-cut example of this way of thinking, and there are in general major difficulties with the vision of a linear development of knowledge from pure science to blueprints that greatly reduce its capacity to illuminate.

This way of thinking about the accumulation of knowledge makes it essentially impossible to explain why the firms of the less-developed countries (E and F in fig. 10) are not up in the vicinity of the firms of the North, C and $D,$ along AB. The above argument as to a sequence of knowledge-accumulating activities is, however, inadequate mainly because it rests on a misunderstanding of the role of science in technological development. There are several obvious points to make and then some which, perhaps, are not so obvious.

The route cannot be one way, from basic research on to the engineering activity that builds from the basic research. This is so because many issues appear at all stages in the spectrum that raise problems that are "basic" and "applied." Indeed, many theoretical problems emerge only as efforts are made to employ the knowledge in the production process. In some instances engineers find practical solutions before the theory is completely established.[10] Similarly, it is often the engineering efforts that identify "needs" that can be

---

10. Gustav Ranis (1978) has several examples of what he calls "reverse" causal origin.

resolved, and therefore set in motion the basic research efforts.[11] If knowledge accumulation cannot be a one-way process, but rather is a process where a great deal of experimenting and searching are taking place at all stages, and results must flow each way, the idea of the spectrum becomes an obstacle, rather than an aid to understanding. This, in turn, tells us a bit more about the kind of society and economy that can generate new, applicable technical knowledge and apply it regularly.

This argument illustrates again the strategic role in the knowledge-accumulating process that the firm must play. It is not only that the firm must be able to use the new knowledge, it must also be able to identify areas where further research should be concentrated. The idea of textbook economics that technology is "given" to the firm by upstream research output is therefore doubly misleading: the firm must in fact "find" its technology by its own search efforts, and it must be appreciated that *it* (the firm) is an integral part of the knowledge-accumulation process.[12] There must then be explicit and continuing contact between knowledge users and knowledge creators. The line between them is indeed hardly a line at all.

These arguments are especially pertinent to relatively small firms in economies just beginning to grow. Such firms face numerous difficulties in relying on simply purchasing "knowledge" in the open market. The most obvious difficulty is for the indigenous firm to know enough to appreciate what knowledge it needs.[13] The problem is even more complex when the knowledge is to be purchased from foreign sellers. The same holds true for heavy reliance on foreign experts, who come in and essentially perform the tasks themselves. Required at this level of activity is the ability to isolate and solve specific problems, not push back some imaginary frontier of little relevance to production. The difficulties of primary reliance on the purchase of knowledge become even more severe when the arguments about the importance of a firm fitting into the social and historical environment are recalled.

There is a final point in this context. As noted above the variance in productivity growth among sectors within a particular country is less than the

---

11. Andrew Jamison (in Wad 1988, 29) quotes a letter from Friedrich Engels as follows: "if, as you say, technique largely depends on the state of science, science depends far more still on the state and requirements of technique. If society has a technical need, that helps science forward more than ten universities." Of course Engels was writing a century ago.

12. The evidence on Great Britain and India suggests that they have been fairly successful in the production of basic research, while firms in these countries have been much less successful in the performance of their roles. Rosenberg (in Evenson and Ranis 1990, 149, 154) notes that in India over recent years the government has funded and performed over 80% of R&D, while in South Korea and Japan the percentages are 7.7 and 24 respectively. The firm does appear to be the bottleneck in India.

13. The sale of knowledge is a prime example of asymmetric information, as the seller necessarily knows more than the buyer—otherwise the buyer would not have to buy.

variance in productivity growth across countries within a particular sector. Such evidence implies that there is a flow of new general knowledge in a country that can be captured and applied by firms within the country irrespective of their productive sector, while knowledge specific to a sector has greater difficulties traveling internationally. Why should this be? It is, I think, because of the key role of the firm and of the environment in which it operates. A firm in an economy in which searching is a part of the ethos will not only be more inclined to engage in such activity itself, but will learn from the efforts of other firms and organizations which are also searching. In an economy where such an ethos is not in place, a firm will have a hard time—an impossible time—borrowing directly from foreign firms in the same activity. What some form of international contact does is to enable a firm in one country to profit from the environment, the searching and learning ethos, of many other countries.

On Importing Knowledge

Exporting as a Searching Process

Begin as in the previous discussion. Assume that existing firms deem it profitable to increase output, but that additional inputs, other than unskilled labor, are becoming increasingly expensive. So the firm, now at E or F in figure 10, has a major incentive to increase productivity. In earlier chapters it sought to do this by searching domestically for underutilized knowledge, but now it can also look abroad.

How exactly can it learn from abroad? There are several obvious methods that are frequently advocated: formal training abroad of workers at all levels in a variety of forms, the hiring of foreign experts who will advise on what new technology is available, creating a joint venture with a foreign firm that can bring new knowledge, purchasing blueprints and patents abroad, and possibly hiring foreigners directly to work in the firm. In many instances any one or all of these methods can be very productive and serve to move E or F toward the AB area. Such procedures however have two difficulties. First they almost invariably, almost necessarily, bring knowledge that will be less productive in the developing country than it is in the country of origin.[14] Secondly, primary reliance on such an approach can rarely contribute much to the basic objective, that is, creating an economy in which searching and learning become thoroughly indigenous. A brief paragraph on each point may help.

---

14. "More productive" refers not only to input/output measures, but also to other sources of well-being recognized by the community, for example, effects on employment or income distribution or geographic location, and so on.

Technology imported into labor-rich, capital-poor countries from capital-rich, labor-poor countries has the obvious handicap of not fitting the factor supply of the importing country very neatly. This point is always recognized, of course, but does not probe deep enough. One must ask whether the imported knowledge is such that the importers can learn from it and build on it in such a way that the knowledge accumulation and productivity growth continues. For this to happen there has to exist some sort of indigenous knowledge base with which the imported knowledge links.[15]

Equally fundamental is the fact that much knowledge is tacit, can be communicated orally only inadequately and incompletely, and simply cannot be incorporated into any actual blueprint.[16] It is thus essentially impossible to supply "knowledge" that can be applied completely and productively by individuals who have not, in some important ways, grown up with that knowledge or with knowledge similar to it. The knowledge, to be fully productive, must then be homegrown in some fundamental sense. This argument is, indeed, one of the basic reasons why all countries are not equally rich or equally poor.

The association with the North must be in a form that recognizes and contributes to this homegrown requirement. This is the reason that the firm establishment of searching and learning process is so fundamental to sustained productivity growth. To bring the technology of the North into the South (except here and there) is not an alternative to having some basic indigenous process of learning in hand. It is a supplement to it, an important supplement. Still there is the question then, how to bring about this supplementing?

Suppose the firms E and F are eager to increase output via increased productivity and have achieved the search-and-learn ethos. In their seeking they generate specific questions for which they need specific answers. They look at home and look abroad. Now add an additional assumption, namely that the creation of the strong incentive to increase output has been created in significant part by a strong demand for exports of products other than the country's traditional exports, which, if met, would be especially profitable.[17] The firms then have an incentive to export and an opportunity to ask foreign

---

15. I think that the indigenous knowledge base did exist in Taiwan and Korea by 1950. Both of these countries had had long periods of growth before 1950 and had thereby created a strong foundation of indigenous technical and administrative knowledge. They then were able to choose the foreign knowledge that they could not only use immediately within their own economy, but also could build on further and further. The various writings of Nathan Rosenberg put great emphasis on the necessity of an indigenous technology in order to profit from imported knowledge. See especially Rosenberg (1982) and below for further elaboration.

16. A good illustration of this idea is cooking. There are an unlimited number of cookbooks with detailed, very detailed, recipes. A half-dozen people using the same recipe will turn out a product whose taste and other characteristics are sure to vary widely among the six cooks. A recipe cannot be complete enough to produce exactly the same result among users.

17. An exact way that such may be accomplished is described later.

importers and other foreign sources specific questions that they (the domestic producers) have identified as they sought to increase output without relying unduly on increased inputs. It is the recognition of a specific production bottleneck that leads to a search for a specific, usable piece of knowledge. Knowledge is thereby imported which is directly applicable, which is understood because it fills an identified need within a prevailing milieu. Thus one basic advantage of exporting is that it provides an effective means of importing the kind of knowledge that contributes directly to increasing output and productivity, and that fits in with the production process employed by the exporting firm.

The preceding argument may be contrasted with an argument that puts the basic emphasis on replication of the North as the basic development objective. There the major purpose of exporting is to earn foreign exchange with which to import capital goods from the North. With the imported capital goods, productivity would, it was expected, *rise*. Something like this has happened here and there in the developing world, but in most instances the problems identified in the preceding pages have dominated, and the increased productivity has been modest and rarely has it achieved the level of the countries in which the capital goods originated. The main point however is simply that such a procedure has not contributed to the creating of an economy in which productivity growth occurs simply as a matter of its routine functioning, and *that,* to repeat again and again and again, is the objective that developing countries must pursue. What exporting helps accomplish is not mainly the importing of physical capital, but rather the importing of the kind of knowledge, technical and administrative, that breaks bottlenecks and, in turn, leads to further development and application.

The origin of this process is again the inducement to increase production which induces a search from a technologically understood position. The searchers, the entrepreneurs, know what kind of thing or idea or technique they need in order to achieve their immediate objective. They (the entrepreneurs) are then able to appraise knowledge that is found or is offered to them. The appraisal extends not only to matters of direct production activity, but also to matters of more general relevance—for example, the way it commits the firm to timing and regularity, the extent of its contribution to transformation capacity, the way it affects labor and the inherent interest of work, the way it might affect the existing truce within the firm, the quality of the product, and so forth. The knowledge importing initiated in this way seems much more likely to serve the basic development objective than if it began in a vacuum or in an effort to engage in "modern" enterprise. Learning from abroad by exporting may well be the most important instrument for learning from the rest of the world.

In some instances the exporting firm may have to pay for the knowledge, but in many it will not. To repeat, earning foreign exchange is not the basic aim of the export activity, although it is not suggested that the exports be given away. The fact that earning foreign exchange is not the basic objective of exporting does have a significant effect on the kind of protection that seems best suited to produce the desired results. I emphasized earlier the strategic role of new small firms. It is probably right to argue that small firms have a more difficult time exporting. Part of an export policy may then include export marketing arrangements by the government. Something of this sort is part of the explanation of Taiwan's success.

The evidence to support this argument is by no means beyond dispute, although a number of people have suggested it and have found bits and pieces of evidence to support it.[18] I have emphasized in a preceding paragraph that the statistical evidence on the relationship between exports and growth is at best ambiguous and, in general, does not support the widespread existence of a causal link between exports and growth. The evidence in Nishimizu and Robinson (in Chenery et al. 1986) is consistent with the present argument, but, as the authors emphasize, there are difficulties with the data and techniques used. There is also evidence from specific activities, even specific firms, and interviews and other kinds of unsystematic bits and pieces. Despite this lack of data, the argument is appealing in general a priori terms and does constitute a coherent explanation. Evidently much more study is needed.

On Preventing a Stop/Go Situation

A balance of payments problem is one of the more common problems, along with inflation, that force a country to slow its growth or stop it completely. Periodic balance of payments difficulties can thus force an economy into a stop/go pattern that has adverse effects on productivity growth. A strong export performance combined with ample foreign exchange reserves allows a country to weather balance of payments problems without slowing down or stopping the economy. The basic idea is again not to import capital goods in order to imitate western industries, but to be able to maintain the flow of imports in order to avoid a slowdown in economic activity.[19] Available foreign exchange reserves can also help dampen a modest inflation by permitting

---

18. See especially Larry Westphal (1982, 1990). An interesting and extremely useful study is that of Nishimizu and Robinson in Chenery, Robinson, and Syrquin (1986). This latter study examines exports and productivity growth, which is the most relevant relationship. Rodrik (1993 and in Fishlow et al. 1994) offers reasons why the arguments are not terribly persuasive. Rodrik (1993) is an excellent review of the empirical studies on trade and growth.

19. I should perhaps note that an economy that can respond immediately to changing relative prices—that has unlimited transformation capacity, great entrepreneurs, perfect knowledge, and so on—does not need this role for exporting. I know of no developing economy that is in this category.

a quick surge of imports as inflation pressure mounts. Evidently this role of reserves as an anti-inflation instrument is quite limited.

Foreign Training

In the chapter on growth of output I emphasized the importance of the role of good elementary and secondary education in getting development under way. I now want to say a few things about foreign training, almost always higher education. Foreign training has, without doubt, had many favorable consequences for individuals and, sometimes, for the developing country. At the same time one must add that there is evidence that much of the foreign training that has taken place has constituted a cost without a benefit, private or social. Costs include a range of things: brain drains of one kind or another, irrelevant and misleading "knowledge," impeding the evolution of domestic universities, creating unfortunate and unwanted preferences and expectations, contributing to personal problems of one kind or another, and so on. Foreign training is also a part of the general problem of too much higher education. The idea then that foreign training is a significant source of productivity growth is probably as often false as true.

Still there is a role for foreign training for most developing countries. The aim, of course, should be to use such training to contribute to the internal search-and-learn process within which development resides. I list a few dicta here that are relevant to this role.

1. Foreign training should be brief and concerned with rather specific issues that arise from a demand at home.
2. Technical and not-so-technical workers may learn well from spending a few months working in a company abroad.
3. Formal graduate programs leading to an advanced academic degree should always be viewed with a great deal of doubt and suspicion.
4. The basic idea is not to equip participants to master an academic discipline or to advance that discipline. It is to equip them to learn about learning.
5. Externalities due to living abroad—meeting "new" people, experiencing a new environment, a new ethos, eating new food—are easily exaggerated.

Despite all these doubts, foreign training should not be prohibited. There is however surely too much of it and it is too cheap for the participant and too profitable for the foreign institution.[20]

---

20. One hears of successful economic policies due to policymakers trained abroad, the

Foreign Advisors

Essentially the same thing can be said about foreign advisors as was said about foreign training. Some have been enormously effective, played strategic roles in both the public and private sectors, and many have been harmless and some have done harm. To some degree foreign advisors are not very helpful because their hosts are not equipped to use them well. This point illustrates the argument made earlier that outside advice is more likely to help when there are specific, concrete questions that can be asked. Inability to identify such questions is a failure of hosts. There are, one must note, many foreign advisors who are themselves ill-equipped for their role. So the conclusion: Foreign advisors, like foreign training, is a side effect, a possible strategic intervention here or there. It is not a fundamental part of or contribution to the development objective.

Foreign Investment

Foreign direct investment has become enormous in recent years and in many countries exceeds official aid flows by a large margin. The stock of foreign direct investment in the mid-1980s as a percentage of GDP varied widely among countries. In Korea it was 2.3 percent, in Taiwan 8.1, Singapore 53.8, Brazil 9.6, Thailand and Indonesia about 11–12, Kenya 12.0, and India 0.6.[21] In some countries, for example, Malaysia, most of the foreign invest-ment takes place in free trade zones. Variation in the ratio of foreign direct investment to total investment in a given year is also great, ranging from very high in mineral producing countries to quite low in others. There is also a great deal of evidence of some very productive investments, investments that have created employment opportunities of very attractive sorts and some very valuable capital.

Foreign private investment is an excellent carrier of packaged technology from abroad. This means that it brings with it the technology created and developed elsewhere. It is much less successful in contributing to the emer-gence of a searching and learning process in the host country. Foreign entities have in general had little success in establishing links with sources of domes-

---

Berkeley Mafia in Indonesia and the Chicago Mafia in Chile. Policies followed in these countries are of interest and their study is profitable to all observers. The foreign training of the individuals involved was surely relevant, and these examples are to be taken seriously. They do not however constitute a refutation of the text position, but do indicate that generalizations are risky.

21. Data are taken from Sanjaya Lall (in Balasubramanyan and Lall 1991, 147). Lall's work on foreign investment and foreign technology transfer is most illuminating. The cited article refers to additional papers by him on this subject.

tic knowledge creation, although there are some success stories.[22] In some instances the presence of a strong foreign unit will have negative effects on domestic investors' efforts to find ways to utilize more fully the country's available resources and to raise the productivity of *these* resources. There is, for example, evidence for some countries that wage inequality (between skilled and unskilled labor) increases with increasing foreign investment. Foreign firms can also simply usurp the most obvious investment opportunities and make it more difficult for the domestic entrepreneur to identify potentially profitable investment projects. In a country seeking to establish the Idea of Progress and productivity growth firmly over most sectors of the economy, foreign direct investment can be an obstacle rather than an effective instrument.[23]

At the same time, for a government simply to forbid any foreign investment is surely to miss out on an important opportunity. To control and direct the foreign units is often difficult, and it is easy to appreciate how mistakes can be made. It is an area also that lends itself to corruption in many forms. So, as discussed more fully in the policy chapter, a strict general policy that is sure to limit the inflow of direct investment appears most suitable for most countries, but a lot of learning is in order.

A country's position with respect to foreign investment is perhaps the clearest signal of interest in and determination to achieve a firm grounding of a technology that is in an important sense its own and therefore compatible with the other components of the society of which it necessarily is an integral part. When emphasis and privilege are given to foreign firms by a developing country, the latter is implying that it is not up to the task of its own development and must call in outsiders to do the job. Such an attitude is false both ways: the developing country *is* capable of achieving its own development, and it is *not* possible for foreign firms to do the task for them. The story of Japanese technological development and to a slightly lesser extent that of Korea illustrates this point. Foreign investment was virtually nonexistent in pre–World War II Japan and quite small in Korea after 1950. Yet these countries have built an unambiguously indigenous technological base from which sustained increases in labor productivity have been achieved.

Evidently this issue is still another which taxes the social choice procedures of a developing country. It is also an issue on which international lending (and advising) agencies and unilateral donors often have (and express) strong views.

---

22. Rodrik (in Fishlow et al. 1994) cites strong evidence from plant-level data that there is essentially no evidence of spillover of technical knowledge from foreign-owned plants in a number of countries. See also Nadiri (1993).

23. I have followed the Lall piece cited in the previous footnote closely in this paragraph.

Exporting as a Source of Sectoral Demand

In the arguments relating to employment, I noted that a demand constraint could easily appear for individual activities or sectors. This possible constraint is especially relevant for activities in which productivity is growing rapidly over considerable intervals of time. The most suitable way to prevent a demand constraint from appearing is to be able to export. With the capacity to export, a sector can continue to increase its productivity and its employment (in the manner described in the chapter on employment) until the growth of productivity in that sector has exhausted all possibilities. This sectoral demand argument, along with the knowledge importing through exporting, are probably the most important ways that exporting contributes to growth of productivity and output.

This argument is a kind of comparative advantage argument. A country can specialize in those activities in which productivity growth is taking place in the most sustained way. There is, however, no general rationale to account for which activities in a particular country will in fact have the highest productivity growth. More on comparative advantage and productivity growth follows immediately.

Comparative Advantage and Productivity Growth

There is still the question of the sources of knowledge that moves AB in figure 10 outward. *If* the argument about a spectrum of research and development activities were right and *if* it were possible to transport knowledge completely and effectively from anywhere to everywhere, then we could answer this question by simply saying that the rich countries have a comparative advantage in basic and applied research and in drawing up blueprints, and the developing countries in other things. The latter countries produce other things to export and buy the basic and applied knowledge and use it at home. This I have argued is surely not the way that the knowledge that pushes AB rightward comes into existence and is spread around the world.

Modern research laboratories are however, surely relevant, even though the empirical evidence on the relationship between investment in formal R&D activities and productivity growth and product improvement has not been well established.[24] There do exist in many, indeed most, developing countries

---

24. There is an abundance of literature that studies the relationships between R&D outlays and productivity growth. See Griliches (1991) for a good brief summary with many additional references. Robert Evenson with numerous colleagues has studied the role of various forms of R&D on agricultural yields. See for example Evenson (1975). A major problem in these statistical efforts is a spillover effect of R&D in one sector or industry or firm on the productivity of resources in another sector or industry or firm. Simple regression of a sector's productivity growth

formal research institutes of various kinds. It seems clear that most of these institutes have not been effective in the sense that they turned out "knowledge" which was relevant to the production activities of the countries in which they were located. It must also be emphasized that there have been some that have been quite successful in this regard. The Malaysian Rubber Research Institute and the Korean Institute of Science and Technology are examples of successful efforts in this respect. The International Rice Research Institute in the Philippines cannot be described as a Philippine institute, but it too has been effective as has the International Center for the Improvement of Maize and Wheat in Mexico. Morris-Suzuki (in Tokunage 1992) tells us that in the 1930s Japan had dozens of local research laboratories established by prefectural governments. These small side efforts were aimed at encouraging technological change in traditional Japanese activities.

One might put the argument in a slightly different way. The *AB* area moves out in the rich countries, and as it moves out this creates an opportunity for the developing countries to learn more and more by importing knowledge mainly through exporting commodities and services and possibly the other means noted above. And the process continues on and on. The importing country thus is, in some sense, always well behind the countries in which knowledge is in fact being created through R&D, and that, in consequence, are always in the neighborhood of the *AB* region. The country that depends on importing knowledge in these ways is also of course completely dependent on the knowledge-producing countries for its continued growth of productivity. In this kind of process a great deal depends on the kind of knowledge that is made available in the North and on the capacity of the importing country to learn to adapt it to their economic and social environment.[25] Such an argument suggests that it is only in the rich countries that knowledge that can move *AB* out is to be created. This is surely incorrect, as I have already emphasized, and I want to argue now in a very different way.

Indigenous R&D

One important reason why formal R&D institutes have not worked very well in many developing countries is that they are usually so divorced from the

on its R&D is therefore not adequate. Such spillovers help to explain why productivity growth takes place in one activity even if there is no R&D activity in it. This is sometimes reflected in the physical capital or intermediate goods of one sector that are obtained in another. Obviously much of the increase in yields and in labor productivity in agriculture is due to R&D in other sectors.

25. Perhaps something like this has gone on in Japan and Korea, and to some extent still is going on, especially in Korea. Japan's slowdown in recent years may reflect its dependence on R&D in other countries in the North. Several authors have argued that Japan is much better at adapting knowledge than in creating new technical and administrative knowledge and hence will always be dependent in the manner described in the text unless changes are forthcoming.

reality that they are intended to serve, from the environment within which the knowledge they create is meant to be used, that they cannot turn out a process or product that fits the needs of the producing community.[26] The idea then is that producers are induced to keep pushing hard and in so doing identify areas where new knowledge would be especially valuable. Research activity somewhere in the system responds, and their specific questions induce some agency somewhere to find answers. Formal R&D *emerges* then—either as separate institutes or as departments in the producing firm itself—as producers become convinced that such organizations can indeed provide information that will result in greater profits.

Consider an example that refers to the industrialization process now under way in Southeast Asia. I draw heavily on the analysis of Tessa Morris-Suzuki (in Tokunaga 1992). Morris-Suzuki argues that Japan was successful in acquiring technology from abroad that led to a "bottom-up modification of indigenous technology" (138). The Japanese did borrow and adapt, but more fundamentally her entrepreneurs were able to build onto existing indigenous technology, thereby contributing to the emergence of a widespread innovative capacity. That is what adaptation means. This "bottom-up" strategy was achieved largely by small-scale activities, and indeed its most important aspect was that it enabled "small firms in Japan to adapt to technological change, and in many cases to become sources of parts and supplies for the modern industrial sector" (Morris-Suzuki, 140).[27] Therefore an *economy-wide* searching and learning capacity became established that had its genuine base in Japan. A quite similar story applies to Korea. In both countries the turbulence in the small-scale sector was especially crucial.

The story is different in Southeast Asia. The most obvious and most important difference is the heavy dependence on direct foreign investment there relative to the role that it played in Japan (or Korea). The main consequence of this large role of foreign investment is that much of the technology transfer into these countries is within a multinational enterprise. Production in these countries mainly use imported intermediate goods and export a large share of their output to other countries.[28] A substantial part of these exports are some kind of manufactured products designed to meet certain externally determined standards.[29] This strong export orientation, this strong ignoring of

---

26. Recall the story of junkyards in Africa (in chapter 4) and their role in creating knowledge directly relevant. In that example face-to-face meetings between searcher and potential learner are about as complete as possible.

27. For a more complete survey of these issues and evidence see Morris-Suzuki (1994). This is a remarkably illuminating study.

28. Hafiz Mirza (1986) develops this point especially effectively with respect to Singapore, but it applies equally well to Malaysia and Thailand, and to some extent to Indonesia.

29. Morris-Suzuki (in Tokunaga 1992) reports on the growth of the Original Equipment

the domestic market means that the kind of bottom-up process described for Japan cannot occur. Small-scale, indigenous firms are especially likely to be left out of such a process. A grave question can then emerge: what are these countries prepared to do when their labor becomes costly and the international firms seek other locations where labor is still cheap? There has been, in recent years, a large number of relatively small investments in Thailand made by small, family-owned and -managed firms from Taiwan and Hong Kong. Apparently the main motivation for such investment is cheap or at least cheaper labor than is available at home. Foreign investment in search of cheap labor may solve an employment/poverty problem in the short run. It will not create an indigenous growth for the long run. Why does Thailand apparently have to have foreign investment in small-scale activities?[30]

This picture of recent developments in Malaysia and Thailand needs qualification, but the point here is to make clear the basic argument of this part of this section. The earlier junkyard story, the Japanese story, and the Malaysia/Thailand story illuminate particularly important aspects of the vision that I am trying to establish. The junkyard and Japanese story suggest reasonably clearly the route to the establishment of an internally based growth success. The Malaysia/Thailand story suggests the great risks that reside in dependence on foreign investments and how such dependence puts many of deeper values and institutions in great jeopardy.

Where does formal R&D activity fit into all this? The idea is that such activities evolve in order to solve problems to help to remove barriers that have surfaced as firms sought to increase productivity. So then formal R&D comes into existence as a consequence of domestic firms' efforts to increase output. Supplying such activities before then will not do the trick. This argument also means that sending people abroad to study at the MITs of the world will not help much until the community of firms are actively engaged in the effort to increase productivity.[31] Formal research and development activity

---

Manufacturer/Value Added Resaler agreements. These agreements force producers in these countries to make their products under a strictly specified set of conditions. Such (reasonable) arrangements strongly dampen any sort of domestically induced search efforts.

30. One should add also that the rapid growth in both Malaysia and Thailand, and to some extent in Indonesia, is creating tensions in many areas. While growth always creates tensions—because as noted earlier growth always destroys as well as creates—the tensions in these countries are surely more severe and dangerous than would be present with a slower, more indigenously based growth.

31. I am tempted to conclude this argument by saying that MITs are a consequence of high incomes, not a contributor to high incomes. I think that this is a misstatement as the sentences in the text try to make clear. It is correct, as indicated in the text, to say that an MIT or an imitation of an MIT set down in a developing country in which producers are not actively seeking specific advice and information will be a net drain on the economy. The reason is that it will necessarily produce a knowledge that can find no place, no home, in the community, and impede the

cannot be a leading sector until the economy is already in the process of pressing against barriers that it recognizes. And this requires that the searching and learning process be widely established in the community.

The Capital Goods Sector

I discussed the role of a capital goods sector earlier, but it is useful to add a few more comments here in the context of an open economy. In the early days—the 1950s and most of the 1960s—of industrialization efforts, it was generally assumed that physical capital goods should be imported by the developing country because they would be too expensive to produce domestically. As noted above the import substitution approach to industrialization followed in the 1950s and 1960s usually called for protection of consumer durables and other light manufacturing activity, but relatively free importation of capital goods. An overvalued exchange rate provided further subsidy to capital formation. Thus physical capital was to be imported, put in place, and certain industrial products that had been imported were then to be produced domestically. As emphasized, the great failure of this process was that the necessary productivity growth did not take place. One of the reasons that it did not was that the activities that produced the capital goods were thousands of miles away and thereby prevented the back-and-forth learning, adapting, and probing necessary for sustained productivity growth from taking place. A domestic capital goods sector does allow such continuing contact between producer and user.

There are several more ways that a domestic capital goods sector can contribute to the establishment of built-in productivity growth in addition to those mentioned earlier. It is, in many cases, the most effective conduit for importing technical knowledge and for understanding what is necessary in order that such knowledge be made directly usable in the developing country. This is particularly true for economies in which there are many relatively small-scale firms that use capital goods produced by a small number of firms. Through the means listed above these latter firms can have access to foreign technical and other knowledge that affects their capacity to produce capital goods that work well in their economy. Agricultural implements illustrate the point. The importation of foreign-made agricultural machinery has often failed to meet the needs of domestic farmers. Domestic producers of such implements however can find ways to learn much from foreign producers that affects their own productivity as well as the productivity of the farmer who uses the implements.

---

evolution of knowledge and the development of institutions producing knowledge that will be applicable.

The argument is sometimes advanced that a domestic firm may import a piece of physical capital, take it apart, and learn how to make *that* item. The point here is quite different. It is that the domestic producer of a capital good learns from abroad how better to produce *their own* capital product. Some products or components of products may be imported, but the basic notion is that of learning from abroad how better to produce one's own product. This process is best done along the lines suggested in the preceding pages.

Perhaps the best example of a public investment policy that recognizes these arguments is that of Taiwan. The Taiwan government has invested in a number of capital goods industries that clearly violated the dictates of comparative advantage as usually formulated. These activities—petrochemicals, power, heavy metals—were more capital-intensive, riskier, more import-using and skill-demanding than might appear to be appropriate for Taiwan. The evidence seems clear however that their presence in Taiwan has contributed to the growth of productivity in many other sectors of that economy. Similar evidence is available for Korea and here and there elsewhere.[32]

A capital goods sector that can perform these functions effectively contributes directly to the growth of productivity, and its creation may therefore represent a correct allocation of investable resources even though contrary to the usual formulations of comparative advantage. An economy that ignores this role of a capital goods sector may not achieve an investment allocation that contributes most completely to the sustained growth objective. The difficulty and danger that arise are evident: if cost considerations are violated to too great an extent, the economy may be penalized more than it is helped. Also, simply having a capital goods sector does not guarantee productivity growth, and so the violations can possibly be in vain. The upshot is that a country that seeks an investment allocation that contributes most to the sustained-growth objective must weigh these advantages and these costs continually.

Openness and Preference Development

In chapter 2 I argued that 1) it does make sense to think of a hierarchy of preferences, that is, that some preferences are "better" than others, 2) that increasing well-being requires that individual and community preferences go up this hierarchy to ever "better" preferences, and 3) that a convincing crite-

---

32. Further elaboration and evidence on this general argument may be found in Ranis (1990), Ranis in Galenson (1985), and Amsden on China (1977) and on Korea (1989). For more general discussions of the role of the capital goods in facilitating productivity growth see Rosenberg (1982) and Bruton (1985). The literature on the role of a capital goods sector has increased rapidly in the last decade, and now the idea is not as unexpected as it was in the 1970s and earlier.

rion of better could be found in what John Rawls (1971) has designated as the Aristotelian Principle. It was also argued that one of the great costs of severe poverty is that preferences are necessarily so primitive. While taking preferences as given and unchanging is the conventional practice of economists, I cited literature that showed that several earlier and contemporary economists have explored preference development in a number of contexts. I also noted that to discuss this topic is extremely difficult for economists, but not to discuss it is to fail to recognize a crucial part of the story of the enhancement of well-being. I now undertake a few paragraphs on preference development in an open economy.

The basic point is that already discussed with respect to technology: learn about the possibilities of new consumption and how to evaluate these; but blind imitation without reflection on what is observed in other, richer countries is likely to create problems. In a world in which there are so many forms of international communication and transportation and so much contact among all nations, people in virtually every country are exposed either to a huge range of goods and services or to descriptions of such goods and services. The continuing exposure to the lifestyles of the rich abroad by the poor at home makes it extremely difficult for the latter group to reflect carefully and systematically on what the life-style is that will in fact contribute to their well-being as incomes rise.

These considerations about preference development are part of the argument for limiting the role of foreign firms in a developing country and of the argument that there can be "too much" openness. It also provides an alert to the advantages of education, in all of its various forms, as a source of understanding and awareness of addressing the question of one's life-style. Education that helps people find the preferences that do in fact contribute to well-being may over time be more fundamental to development—as conceived here—than education as a source of increased labor productivity.

Conclusion

The basic premise of this chapter is that the most fundamental role of international transactions for countries seeking to develop is that of the transfer of technical and other knowledge that affects production and knowledge that affects the evolution of preferences and of life-styles in general. Emphasis has in all instances been placed on learning from abroad, rather than on seeking to duplicate that which is observed abroad. This argument does not mean that the gains from foreign trade associated with the routine application of comparative advantage are not important, but they surely play a secondary role in the development process. Where the application of comparative advantage results in a sacrifice of learning, it is comparative advantage that is to be sacrificed, not learning.[33]

The arguments are many and varied and iffy and wobbly, and they do not lend themselves to elegant formulations about either foreign trade policy or the mechanisms by which foreign trade acts on economic performance. Certainly the idea of a policy—for example, outward looking, import substitution, export promotion, and so on—that is appropriate for all countries at all times is unacceptable. So we need to probe and learn just as in all areas of development economics.

What does seem surprisingly clear is that some form of protection seems very much in order in many instances, and to that issue I now turn my attention.

---

33. Grossman and Helpman (1991) have treated a number of these issues with elegance and insight.

CHAPTER 8

A Form of Protection

The arguments of the preceding pages have placed emphasis on the importance of some form of protection. Protection was deemed necessary for one basic reason: to provide learning time for all members of the community—labor, managers, entrepreneurs, marketing people, consumers, and people in general as searchers for the good life, searchers for the knowledge to realize their full capacity as humans. It has also been emphasized that a country must learn from other countries, and enterprises in one country can learn from those in another, so links with other countries must not be eliminated. One important means of learning from other countries is to export. So a form of protection should be in place that does not penalize exporting. To learn requires searching, so the form of protection should induce searching in all phases of the economy. In particular, it must not weaken the inducements for producers to search for ways to get costs down, a role that competition or the threat of competition performs extra well. So the form of protection should not eliminate competitive pressure. Similarly, the protection should not so distort the economy that it creates the stop/go situation that is so damaging to productivity growth. In this chapter I want to describe a form of protection that seems to be particularly suitable for the achievement of these objectives.

The Undervalued Exchange Rate Form of Protection

One of the most common policies among developing countries from the 1950s until the 1980s was an overvalued exchange rate. The rationale of this practice rested on the widely held view that capital formation was the major source of the growth of output. The basic policy objective therefore was to achieve a high rate of capital formation. To reach this objective governments sought to keep the price of capital low in domestic currency, and, since most capital goods were imported, the easiest way to do this was to maintain an overvalued exchange rate. The balance of payments would be protected by tariffs and other forms of impediments to imports. That such an approach did not have the expected and desired effects has been amply demonstrated and widely recognized.[1] Protection by means of a haphazard tariff structure and various

---

1. This argument is elaborated in my chapter in Putterman and Rueschemeyer (1992).

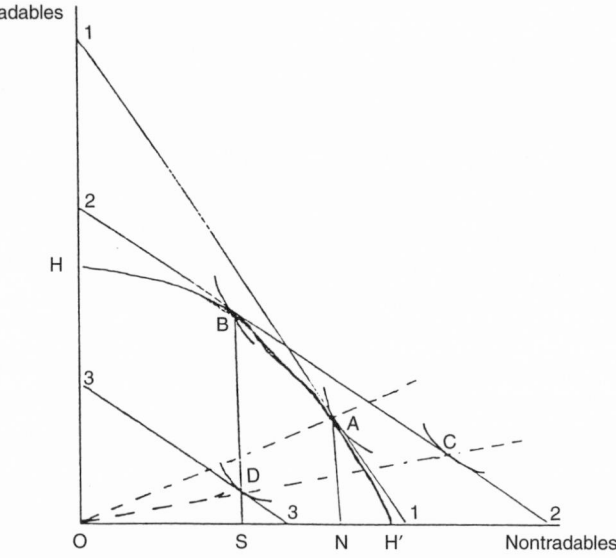

Fig. 11. Protection by an undervalued exchange rate

forms of exchange control, combined with an overvalued exchange rate, clearly has not contributed to the achievement of the set of circumstances outlined in the preceding paragraph.

An *undervalued* exchange rate is itself a form of protection as it obviously increases prices in domestic currency of imported goods and services above those which would prevail with an "equilibrium" exchange rate. It also is a form of export promotion as it makes the country's exports cheaper than they would be with an equilibrium rate. There are other advantages and a number of disadvantages that I discuss later. Now I want to examine the details of the undervalued exchange rate.

Max Corden (1985) is, so far as I can determine, the first person to study exchange rate protection, and I follow him closely in presenting the basic argument. Figure 11 is adapted from the one that he develops (Corden 1985, 273). Corden, in the cited study, was not concerned with the development question.

In the construction of the figure, it is assumed that the nominal price of nontradables is given and that all foreign prices are constant. It is further assumed that exportables and importables may be aggregated into tradables. The production possibility frontier of tradables and nontradables is shown by *HH'* and the initial price ratio between the two by the slope of line 1. This ratio is the exchange rate. The economy is therefore at *A* on *HH'* as given by

the community indifference curve. At *A* there are *ON* of nontradables produced and absorbed, and *AN* of tradables. In this initial position it is further
assumed that trade is balanced and that there are no items in the balance of
payments other than exports and imports. Thus there are *AN* of exports and
AN of imports. The exchange rate represented by the ratio of the two prices
and the slope of line 1 may be said to be the "equilibrium" rate.

Now suppose that the country abruptly devalues. The devaluation raises
the relative price of tradables, and so the price ratio line changes from line 1 to
line 2. The rise in the price of tradables relative to nontradables will induce
resources to move into the former sector from the latter. Production then
moves from *A* to *B* on *HH'*. The increase in the relative price of tradables
however induces the community to seek to increase its consumption of nontradables relative to that of tradables. So the community then seeks to move
its absorption from *A* to *C*. But *C* is not achievable. To resolve the problem,
domestic absorption must be reduced in order to reduce the demand for
nontradables until it is compatible with a level that can be produced. This
reduced level of absorption is given by line 3 which is parallel to line 2, and
the economy winds up at *D*. At *D* the production of tradables is *SB* and their
absorption (imports) is *SD*, so there is an export surplus of *DB*. Absorption of
nontradables is *OS*.

There is an export surplus brought about by the devaluation, so it is
possible to say that the country now has an *undervalued* exchange rate, the
most immediate consequence of which is the accumulation of foreign exchange. The country is thereby lending abroad. At *D* private saving plus taxes
exceed domestic investment plus government spending. The easiest way to
imagine this is to suppose that private saving equals private investment, and
the government achieves a budget surplus with which it buys the foreign
exchange not used for imports. Foreign exchange reserves rise over time as
the situation at *D* continues in place,[2] and they must be so managed that they
do not lead to inflationary pressures that defeat the effort to maintain the
exchange rate at line 3.

The indifference curve at *D* is below that at *A*, so the economy is "worse
off" after the devaluation than when it operated at *A*. The accumulation of
foreign exchange will (as Corden notes) add something to well-being, so it
should not fall by as much as the difference between *A* and *D* indicates. It is
however convenient to speak of the difference between *A* and *D* as the cost of
the exchange rate protection. This arrangement does favor the production of
tradables relative to nontradables, but such a bias seems not merely of little
concern, but in many cases positively advantageous as new productive activ-

---

2. There are ways to maintain the undervalued exchange rate other than accumulating
foreign exchange reserves, but I do not discuss them here.

ities are encouraged. Therefore it is appropriate to say that the undervalued exchange rate does not distort to the extent that additional costs (i.e., additional to that shown by the difference between A and D) are imposed on the economy. So I will continue to speak of the difference between A and D as the cost of this form of protection. Suppose for the moment that all other impediments to trade are either nonexistent or are removed with the devaluation, and that there are no capital movements of any kind.

The cost, defined by the difference between well-being at A and that at D, is an investment, an investment in searching and learning. The return on this investment is the increased productivity that the induced searching and learning is expected to produce. The enhanced searching and learning effort is induced by the new signals and new incentives that are created by the new exchange rate. Consider the following arguments.

New profit opportunities are created by the added incentives to export existing items and to find new products to export, and by the increased capacity of domestic producers to compete with a wider range of imports.

These new and more evident opportunities should help alleviate any entrepreneurial obstacles that may exist.

The more evident profit opportunities should add to the inducement to search and learn in order to increase productivity, and this, in turn, should add to profits. The fact that there are no other impediments to importing means that there is the constant threat of competition from abroad, and this will add to the inducement to find ways to increase productivity.

The range of activities that the country can engage in is increased, and this fact will have a favorable effect on the creation of transformation capacity. As noted previously, an open economy without much transformation capacity is especially vulnerable to changes in demand and technology because it cannot adjust very quickly to such changes without major costs being imposed on the community. The greater transformation capacity will also be reflected in the elasticity of substitution among inputs. As noted in our discussion of employment, the elasticity of substitution is an outcome, not a technological parameter, and is determined by the capacity of the entrepreneurs and managers to adapt production techniques to changing factor supplies and prices.

In the absence of foreign capital, domestic entrepreneurs are very much on their own, and in the face of the favorable profit opportunities they will have an inducement to exploit local resources and local practical knowledge to the maximum extent. The practical knowledge here refers to that which is revealed in the habits and tradition of the work force. It is available mainly in use, and it is difficult to transfer it in usable form. It is the tacit knowledge referred to earlier. This learning-by-doing effort is especially facilitated in the context of new opportunities.

The enhanced opportunities to export also should add to the importation of useful knowledge in the manner described earlier.

One may also mention that the higher prices of imported consumer goods should induce everyone to think more carefully about the quality and availability of domestically produced goods and services, and indeed about their own preferences, their own ideas of the good life.

The undervalued exchange rate (combined with the government budget surplus) will also contribute to the prevention of the kind of balance of payments problems that, as noted in the previous chapter, can force the economy to slow or stop completely to correct. In many instances it is true to say that the main source of a stop/go situation is the emergence of a balance of payments problem. The present strategy obviously will help prevent this from happening.

From a macro standpoint one can also say that it may be possible to tolerate a stronger aggregate demand with an undervalued exchange rate than with an equilibrium rate. I discussed in a previous chapter the difficulties of the aggregate supply notion in a developing country. At the same time it is necessary to push the economy hard in order to induce the kind of search effort that is required and to create the strong demand for labor. If the indigenous sectors do respond quickly along the lines described here, then the economy should be able to tolerate this pressure, and, as argued above, live with a little inflation that is constantly being undermined by increasing productivity and output. Obviously there are great dangers here, and a government must proceed with caution—must learn about how the economic agents do in fact respond—but protection in the form examined here does provide some room to maneuver, some time to learn.

If all these possible consequences do in fact happen, really do happen, then the rate of return on this form of investment will be very high. The assets created by such an investment, in addition to increased foreign exchange reserves, are in the form of human capital and an economy with increasing transformation capacity and sustained contributions toward the emergence of an economy with a built-in ability to achieve increased productivity of factors and greater autonomy in the search for better preferences and for enhanced well-being in general. The consequence of these new and different assets is that the production possibility curve will move outward at a faster rate than it otherwise could do. That of course is the reflection of the higher rate of productivity growth.

In this context the term *undervalued exchange rate* is somewhat misleading. It is the "right" exchange rate given the objectives and arguments. There remains the huge problem of finding (and defining) the exact level of undervaluation that is appropriate. Where tariffs and other trade barriers exist, where capital comes and goes, and so on, the task of definition is even greater. The same observation of course holds if one were speaking of the "equilibrium" exchange rate. I discuss some of these matters in the following chapter. There are some other points that may be made here that will help to illuminate the argument.

1. It is useful to emphasize what the undervalued exchange rate is not intended to do. The objective is not to increase exports in order to solve a balance of payments problem. There is no balance of payments problem at A in figure 11. The economy is on its production possibility frontier, exports and imports are equal, and the exchange rate is under no pressure. Similarly, the objective is not to increase exports in order to increase imports of capital goods to speed up the rate of capital formation and hence the growth of GDP.[3] The objective is not to solve an unemployment problem, because at A, as just noted, all resources (including labor) are fully utilized. So one must not evaluate the undervalued exchange rate argument in terms of the extent to which it does or does not contribute to the achievement of these objectives or does so only with limited efficiency.

2. There are some severe implementation problems of course. Perhaps the main one is the necessity to reduce domestic absorption. I argue in the next paragraph that this problem may not be as severe as the argument built around the figure would seem to indicate. There is a problem here that must be appreciated, however.

3. Figure 11 was drawn with a conventional production possibility frontier and with the economy operating on that frontier at point A. To reach this frontier the assumptions are strong indeed: all resources are employed and the most productive technical and administrative knowledge is utilized by all firms in the economy. At A it is not possible to increase output without adding resources or knowledge. These assumptions are of course never fully realized in any country, and I examined some implications of alternative assumptions in earlier pages. That they are not means that it is almost always possible to increase output given new incentives to search for ways to do so. The incentives created by the undervalued exchange rate can in fact do that, and if they do, and do so with some speed, its cost—the cost of investing in search-

---

3. The "two-gap" model identified domestic saving and foreign exchange as constraints, and it examined conditions under which one or the other constraint would be effective. The role of foreign aid and other sources of foreign exchange was to prevent the economy from slowing down or stopping because of the lack of foreign exchange. Such an analysis rests on strong assumptions about the inflexibility of the economy and the capacity of entrepreneurs and labor to take advantage of opportunities for investment and to create new ways of doing things. Two-gap thinking therefore represents a quite different approach from that studied here. The two-gap model would view the accumulation of foreign exchange with dismay. There are many articles on the two-gap notion. The most comprehensive is Chenery and Strout (1966).

ing and learning—will be greatly reduced. The extent to which a country can respond quickly depends on a number of characteristics. The following seem to be the most relevant things to consider:

a. If existing transformation capacity is already substantial, then a modest undervaluation (and so a low cost) may have the desired effect.

b. If existing transformation capacity is quite low now, but learning capacity is impressive, a sharp, but brief, undervaluation should do the trick.

c. If the country imports very few basic food items, the undervaluation can probably be greater than it could be if it (devaluation) pushed up the prices of basic foods.

d. A high personal saving rate, nonrising unit labor costs, a strong preference for domestically produced goods, do themselves provide considerable protection for domestic producers.[4] So where these circumstances prevail with considerable strength, the protection provided by the exchange rate can be less than in those countries in which the opposite characteristics hold.

e. If there exist a large number of able entrepreneurs of the kind described earlier, the extent of undervaluation and the length of time that it obtains can be less than where entrepreneurs seem to constitute a current bottleneck of importance.

These characteristics vary from country to country, and the policymaker must have some idea of their extent in his/her country in order to gain some insight into how much undervaluation is needed and how long it should last in order to achieve the objectives.

4. There is one further important condition for the success of this sort of approach to development. It will not be possible for all new activities that spring up to export immediately—even with the advantageous exchange rate. Indeed at the outset one would expect that only a small number will be able to export even at the favorable exchange rate. The new activities must therefore have a domestic market, because learning by doing requires doing, requires producing, and producing requires a market. The domestic market must therefore grow. In most developing countries the largest sector is agriculture, and a growing domestic market almost necessarily means that incomes in the agriculture sector are rising. To penalize the agricultural sector in order to subsidize industrial sectors cannot succeed unless exports in a wide range of new activities take off at once, and this, as just noted, is unlikely. A part then of the undervalued exchange strategy is to find a way to ensure that the agricultural sector will expand to create a growing demand for the output of new activities that cannot export right off. One of the most damaging mistakes made in the

---

4. This point is elaborated in Bruton in Chenery and Srinivasan (1989).

1950s and 1960s was the widespread practice of squeezing agriculture, thus dampening a major source of increasing demand for nonagricultural output. Indeed an important advantage of the present argument is that agriculture is protected also, and that the incentives noted above affect it as well as manufacturing.

A strong agricultural sector has other advantages. The most important of these is that rural, nonagricultural activities will be encouraged. If this encouragement is strong enough to have an effect, then migration to large urban areas will be slowed and smaller towns will become more acceptable environments where living and learning are as conducive to the enhancement of well-being as is life in urban areas.

5. For small countries the idea of an expanding agricultural sector does not often make much sense.[5] The most immediate answer to this problem is that almost all firms in the small countries will have to learn to export right off. This may mean that the devaluation will need to be greater and hence the initial cost of protection will have to be higher than in larger countries. Whether that high cost has to be maintained for a long period depends on the various considerations listed above.

There are other possible approaches for countries too small to depend on the growth of domestic demand to supply the necessary expanding markets. A customs union of some sort with adjoining countries is appealing, but these arrangements do not have a very convincing history among small developing countries. More informal arrangements among a number of countries or between a small country and an adjacent large one are probably more likely to work.

6. An undervalued exchange rate will tend to encourage foreign investment. Especially does it make attractive the purchase by foreign firms of existing national firms in the developing country. This latter practice is especially damaging to the achievement of development objectives as they are defined in this essay. Data for around 1970 show that about one-third of the subsidiaries in developing countries of North-based enterprises resulted from the acquisition of the existing national firms (Vernon 1977, 72). There is great variance among the countries of the North and among industries in this respect. Japanese firms seem to be the least likely to establish a subsidiary by acquiring a domestically owned and operated firm in the developing country. The undervalued exchange rate provides protection on the product side, and some similar kind of protection from foreigners taking over on the investment side is also needed.

---

5. There are many small developing countries in the world, but the proportion of world population living in them is relatively small. This latter fact does not mean that they can be neglected, but it does mean that they can be treated in more ad hoc ways.

Tourism is also encouraged by an undervalued exchange rate, and tourism can do—as is being increasingly recognized—as much damage to indigenous development efforts and to national well-being as foreign investors often do. There is abundant evidence that tourists can have painful consequences for culture, religion, economics, politics, and the environment. And tourism is a rapidly growing activity around the globe. A country pursuing a development strategy built around the undervalued exchange rate should levy an exceedingly stiff tax of some sort on all activities and events associated with tourism.[6]

The argument that tourism earns foreign exchange net is frequently employed—more so in the 1950s and 1960s than in the 1990s. It is probably not correct since tourism has usually been a very import-intensive industry.[7] The idea that a country should encourage tourism in order to earn foreign exchange to import capital (or other things) is, as implied earlier, a misplaced argument. The same statement applies to tourism as a source of employment.[8]

Can All Developing Countries Have an Undervalued Exchange Rate?

Evidently every country in the world cannot export more than it imports—unless an awful lot of goods are lost in transport. The present argument however is meant to apply only to developing countries, defined in some conventional way. Then the question can be changed: Can all developing countries have an undervalued exchange rate? Such a rate gives the developing country an advantage in exporting above that which is provided by an equilibrium rate, and, for that reason, it could be rejected or defined as violating GATT or international friendship.

Suppose however that the countries of the North—Western Europe, the United States and Canada, Japan, and Australia and New Zealand—all agreed to allow the developing countries of the world to have an undervalued exchange rate as a form of foreign aid. No other aid would be provided to these countries. Present funds allocated to foreign aid might be used to help solve any dislocations created by the imports from developing countries into the

---

6. The *Economist* for March 23–29, 1991, has a good brief survey of tourism.

7. One way to put a damper on tourism is to reduce its import intensity by inducements or regulations that result in hotels, tours, restaurants catering to tourists, and so on, using domestically produced goods and services. The undervalued exchange rate will of course have some effect in this direction.

8. Tiny countries, for example, islands, where a significant population exists may, it is often said, have only tourism to keep them going. It is difficult to argue that these people should migrate or do something which would greatly reduce the availability of goods and services to them. The number of such places is of course not large, and can be treated independently of the arguments in the text.

rich countries. The latter countries would commit themselves not to impose *any* limitations on imports from the developing countries as long as they were so classified. The rationale of this sort of "foreign aid" follows from the main arguments of this book: the basic source, the deep-down source, of the establishment of an economy in which growing productivity occurs as a consequence of its routine functioning, is learning by doing, by producing, by working. The most productive form that foreign aid can take therefore is that which facilitates producing by domestic firms and the seeking, by entrepreneurs and labor, for ways to increase productivity and to raise the quality of the product that is produced. If such an agreement were in fact possible, it would, I suggest, be much more effective than most—in no sense all— foreign aid now provided in contributing to the achievement of the basic objective of development as defined in this study. There is little evidence of our capacity to institutionalize the aid-providing process, and, even in the multilateral organizations, aid is heavily politicized and often dominated by ideology. It seems unlikely that this situation will change, and this proposal tries to give aid a new twist that could in fact make it very productive.[9]

Aid to meet emergencies and catastrophes of whatever kind is of course very much in order and indeed has usually worked a bit better than aid identified as for development.

The Outcome

Suppose for the moment that the above story did in fact materialize. It will not, of course, but appreciating its content and exploring its implications help one to understand some of the forces at work in the developing economies.

In the best of circumstances we would see emerging an expansion of some existing activities, emergence of a wide range of new activities, increasing demand for labor over wide areas of the economy, agriculture becoming more profitable and responsive, and exports increasing in range and value. Virtually all of the producing units will be small scale because domestic capital markets do not permit the establishment of large-scale units and, more fundamentally, because entrepreneurial and management capacity is such as to limit the size of viable operations. There then should be a great deal of action in the private sector of the economy: new firms appearing, some old firms dying off, some growing rapidly, some slowly, the composition of aggregate output changing, and productivity rising. Since all this will be happening within the context of the nation, it can be expected to be consistent with the existing social, cultural, traditional, and historical characteristics of the society. It can be said therefore to be a truly indigenous process of

---

9. Aid in this form is discussed at greater length in my chapter in Pechman and McPherson (1992).

development, not simply efforts to replicate the North or to modernize. The process will not be conflict-free, but the conflicts should be manageable and containable within the nation. It is this small-scale, indigenous activity that it is the aim to create. There is a great deal of churning and turmoil and heaving and ho-ing of all kinds, and nobody should think in terms of equilibrium or equilibrium growth. It is an atmosphere in which searching and learning dominate and the Idea of Progress begins to take hold throughout the society. Well-being can be enhanced.

Things will not happen this way and have never happened this precise way. In the presently GDP-rich countries something like this did, I think, in fact take place, and as a broad stroke it is not misleading to apply it to Japan, Taiwan, and Korea.

Now suppose that this process does not work in exactly this way in a given country. What is the appropriate approach? With this vision in mind the policymaker looks at the economy and tries to identify specific bottlenecks that seem to be preventing it from working in this ideal way. Perhaps the undervaluation is not strong enough, perhaps the government has not been able to maintain a large enough budget surplus, perhaps agriculture needs extra inducements, perhaps funds to facilitate small-scale private investment appear to be a bottleneck, maybe domestic entrepreneurship is more of a problem than expected, etc. etc. etc. In these cases further attention is required from the policymaker. I want to explore all this in more detail in the following chapter. There is one further point that it is suitable to make now.

The modern developing country must find its way in a world of rich and powerful economies which are not about to relinquish their power in world economic (or other) matters. As I have argued often in preceding pages, this fact has many implications. Here it may be noted in particular that few indigenous firms in developing countries are going to be able to compete immediately with those in the long-rich countries in modern, large-scale activities. Airplane manufacture is a fairly labor-intensive activity, but airplanes are not going to be manufactured in Bangladesh or Indonesia or Egypt or other obviously labor-rich economies. Korea and Taiwan have, over substantial time periods, entered world markets in big industries, but in general it is correct to say that most developing countries cannot. The approach that does have considerable hope is that of finding niches, finding relatively small, identifiable activities that can be exploited effectively. This will put a heavier burden on the entrepreneur to find such activities, but it also carries much the greatest hope. We need to know more about how to go about doing this.[10]

---

10. Perhaps the clearest case of an undervalued exchange rate is Taiwan over the past 15 or so years. In the early 1990s Taiwan had foreign exchange reserves equal to almost one year's imports. The figure was even higher in the late 1980s. In 1953 one US dollar would buy 350

Conclusion

A brief conclusion on the open economy. A country with built-in, indigenous productivity growth and considerable and increasing transformation capacity can profit greatly from foreign trade. A country without these characteristics can be very vulnerable to openness. And a developing country cannot import these characteristics. More generally, a country cannot import the basic conditions for growth. It cannot import a growth ethos, an ethos of searching and learning. It cannot import the Idea of Progress. It cannot import the institutions and social organizations that make it possible for a market mechanism to function as an effective instrument for generating increasing well-being. It cannot duplicate the North, and if it tries, such replication will not result in enhancing well-being. A people must really do these things themselves. A people can learn from abroad, can profit from contacts with other peoples, can profit from exports and imports—if it is really strong enough to be its own master.

Japanese yen and the exchange rate did not change until the early 1970s. If the 350 yen per dollar was right in 1953, then by 1960 or so and later, that rate surely represented an undervaluation. Brazil, Korea, Colombia, and other countries have had undervalued exchange rates over particular intervals of time. Botswana's supply of foreign exchange reserves now (the mid-1990s) amounts to almost 18 months' supply of imports. This is the largest amount of any country, except possibly some very small nations. Experiences of these countries do seem to lend support to the argument in the text.

CHAPTER 9

The Roles of the Government and the Market

Economic development is necessarily a normative notion. It implies a progression from one situation or environment or state to another which is, in some sense, presumed to be better. So evaluation is an intrinsic part of the very idea of development. I have argued that the appropriate evaluation criterion is well-being, and that well-being will be enhanced if—in broad terms—the following conditions are met:

1. Labor productivity grows routinely.[1]
2. Jobs that are themselves sources of well-being are created by the economy in numbers equal to the labor force. If this objective is met, then any poverty problem will be resolved over time.
3. The processes by which 1 and 2 are achieved do not destroy or undermine the institutions and traditions that are themselves representative, and that are carriers of the deeper values of the society.
4. The households of the society recognize the fundamental role of preference improvement and the extended version of basic needs combined with the Aristotelian Principle as sources of well-being.

In this chapter I discuss the role of the government and government policy in creating and maintaining an economic system where performance achieves these results.

The Present Policy Debate

During the years after 1980 or so there emerged a fairly widespread consensus for the appropriate development policy. The main characteristics of this policy include a great emphasis on the use of the market (to get prices right) in all

---

1. For reasons noted in chapter 3 it is labor productivity that must rise routinely. Whether this results in growing per capita GDP depends on how the population chooses to use its increasing productive capacity. There are of course many ways to use the growing capacity that do not appear in the conventional GDP accounts. Increased leisure is the most obvious such item. There are other matters as well, for example, improving environment, more interesting jobs, and jobs that contribute directly to well-being, that do not appear in GDP accounts but can be purchased with rising labor productivity.

sectors of the economy and therefore a minimal role for government, an economy open to the rest of the world in general with special emphasis placed on nontraditional exports, unhesitating acceptance of foreign direct investment in all areas of the economy, and balanced government budgets. The balanced budget seems to be partly an end in itself and, more often, the means to preventing inflation. If there exist public firms, the consensus view urges privatization at as rapid a pace as seems possible. There is no role for the entrepreneur that calls for anything more than managerial skills.

This consensus seems to have emerged, not so much because of new theoretical developments and insights or new empirical evidence, but rather because of the failure in many countries of previous approaches built around comprehensive planning of one sort or another and import substitution. The impressive economic performance of Japan, Korea, and Taiwan since the late 1950s and Malaysia and Thailand more recently are usually cited as examples of the successful application of this general approach.

This policy package is consistent with textbook general equilibrium theory in an economy where there is no ignorance, technology and preferences are given, and instantaneous adjustment processes are in place. It does not however tell us how growth occurs. This latter deficiency is corrected, in the opinion of some students, by the endogenous growth theory briefly summarized above. If this latter theory were adequate then we could have a general equilibrium situation accompanied by growth. I think however that most observers agree that endogenous growth theory does not yet offer that sort of service except at an extremely rarefied level of abstraction.

Virtually all parts of this approach have been under severe attack in recent years from a number of sources. Especially, more and more people are convinced that the success stories of the Far Eastern countries are much more complex and basically different from that which the consensus picture implies. The approach that I have worked out in this essay also disputes the consensus story in a number of ways. There is necessarily ignorance and, in the presence of ignorance, there can be no equilibrium for firm or economy. There is great diversity of knowledge and ignorance and productivity growth among firms, and so the idea of "right" prices loses much of its precision. Our understanding of the sources of productivity growth is so primitive as to make the endogenous theory quite sterile. That searching and tinkering and learning are major sources of productivity growth does seem clear, and this creates a distinct and crucial role for the entrepreneur in this way of thinking. We have also found reason to question unrestrained openness as an effective means of achieving continually increasing well-being.

Finally, we emphasized that the outcome of an "unfettered" market may not be consistent with society's preferences. A society may, for example, want to prevent huge firms from appearing, may wish to grow its own rice or yams and so on, may wish to have more leisure and less GDP, may believe that unfettered markets induce antisocial behavior, and so forth. These matters create an obvious problem of social choice for which, as emphasized, social scientists cannot offer a very convincing solution, much less a practical one.[2]

All this means that there is no general answer, no unique approach. There is, in particular, inevitably a role for the government. There is however a market. So the great task is to use the market and other instruments, including direct government action, to achieve what society deems to be growing well-being. One of the major sources of the apparent success of Japan, Korea, Taiwan, and Singapore has been the effective symbiosis of the state and market in pursuing the development objective. The term *development state* is often applied to a government for which the commitment to development is firmly in place. Development state is in contrast to a *predatory state* where government officials are indifferent to development and, in many instances, simply exploiting the people for individual gain.

I now turn to an examination of some aspects of how a development state might come into being and some aspects of its role in the development process as that process has been described in previous chapters.

Creating the Idea of Progress

As emphasized earlier the Idea of Progress is a characteristic of the ethos of the community. The private entrepreneurs are a part of that ethos. Now I discuss the role of the government and other elites in the emergence of an ethos of searching and learning.

The argument that somehow or other individuals and households could, in long-nongrowing economies, suddenly begin to think in terms of the role of preferences in their well-being without some kind of "exogenous" pressure or inducement is appealing, but, I think, not adequate in most countries. The public sector and other elites must be involved, especially at the very outset of the development effort. In addition to addressing the household preference issue, public sector and other elites also appear to be the principal agencies to insure that the deeper values of the society are recognized and, in some ways, protected. The role of the government is not to be seen simply as managing or finding ways to aggregate the preferences of the members of the community, but includes that of creating—or trying to create—an environment in which the members of the community appreciate, and therefore respond, to the idea that preferences can be better and must be better if well-being is to rise continually. In a similar way and for similar reasons the elites must "take sides" in the support of the continuation (and possibly the creation) of a

---

2. The argument that a perfectly working market results in a social optimum also implies that a social choice has been made, and this is rarely, if ever, the case.

nation, a culture, a tradition, a religion, and so on that, in effect, defines the community.[3]

All this is, of course, difficult and dangerous. *Elites* is not an especially endearing term, but it is difficult to see who other than they can perform these essential roles. Nongovernment elites here refer to the propertied, the well-educated, the religious leaders, community leaders in general, labor leaders, CEOs of big and small enterprises. Where such groups are alive to the issues of development, as that notion is defined in this book, and, by their activities and pronouncements, reveal the possibilities—the costs and rewards—that inhere in such a process they can serve as catalysts, instigators of the idea for endogenously inspired change and betterment. Some illustration may help.

Gustav Ranis (World Development 1989, 1443–63) suggests that "typical East Asian citizens think of themselves as having certain obligations to the state, feel the need to reach a consensus and not to make too many unreasonable demands on the government." This, Ranis notes, is in contrast to other countries where such recognized and accepted limitations are absent. Vernon Ruttan (World Development 1989, 1385, citing Ishikawa 1981) argues that the traditional moral obligation of the members of the Japanese village to cooperate in infrastructure maintenance makes it easier and less costly to organize such projects than (say) in South Asian villages where the caste system inhibits such cooperation. In these examples the institutions act on the economic system in a direct way. At the same time the institutions themselves also have direct effects on well-being. It is not always the case that these institutions evolved in response or even primarily in response to economic incentives. They emerged simply as the society evolved over its history.

Ronald Dore (in Gereffi and Wyman 1990, 360) suggests that in Latin America "there was a much more distinct differentiation between European-ized enclaves of the towns and countryside than was ever found within the Asian countries." He argues also that the higher income groups in Japan, Korea, and China created a strong demand for the output of domestic artisans, while higher income groups in Latin America concentrated on imports from Europe and the United States. He has evidence that the rent-seeking problem (discussed below) is less severe in countries where there is a shared national interest among all groups. A bureaucracy dominated by extremely able people will not only be more efficient in the usual sense but will create respect and acceptance of the government by the private sectors. Dore concludes that the

---

3. Charles Taylor (1992) develops this idea in detail and with great power. See also the discussion of Taylor's argument in the same volume by Amy Gutmann, Steven C. Rockfeller, Michael Walzer, and Susan Wolfe. These essays are only indirectly concerned with development as such.

great Confucian (and, in Japan, Shinto) traditions of these Eastern countries have given prestige and distinction to service for the public.[4]

In contrast with this picture of Japan and Korea consider Egypt under Mohammed Ali in the first half of the nineteenth century. Ali was eager for Egypt to imitate Europe. He hired foreign experts, imported capital goods, established training programs, sent Egyptians to Europe for training, and pursued many other devices available to him to imitate the Europeans. None of these devices worked because Egyptian society was unwilling to have imposed on it alien and not-understood ideas of the good life. Ali was apparently unable to appreciate that a development process built onto the existing Egyptian environment was possible, and indeed was the only kind that could so modify the economy in such a way that growth could become pervasive. The Shah of Iran made the same kind of mistake in the 1950s and 1960s. So too did Peter the Great in Russia much earlier.

Compare these latter stories with the one that Michio Morishima tells about Japan. Morishima (1982) argues that the ethical system that is Confucianism gave to the Japanese society a great cohesiveness and commitment. Japanese capitalism "started as state capitalism, an economy guided and driven by bureaucrats" (86–87). These government officials were part of this cohesive and committed society and thereby understood (and believed in) the deeper values and basic characteristics of the Japanese. The result, says Morishima, was that a "capitalist economy which was managed in an entirely different spirit from English capitalism—an economy combining Japanese soul and Western technology—was set up in Japan" (Morishima 1982, 87).[5]

Kenneth Boulding (1971, 49) has a helpful aphorism. It is not, he suggests, the survival of the fittest, but survival of the fitting that is relevant to countries seeking to enhance their well-being in the presence of a small group of economically rich and powerful nations. Japan and Korea have seemed to understand this, but many other countries have not. As noted earlier, the great dependence of Malaysia and Thailand on foreign investment, especially those

---

4. Contrast this sort of situation with one in which the government is dominated by people appointed for political reasons only and with huge numbers of people hired to prevent unemployment or to carry out a guarantee that all college graduates have a job. In this latter case the role that the government can play is extremely circumscribed. I discuss this issue below.

5. Morishima also argues that Confucianism was concerned primarily with mutual relationships among people rather than individual conduct vis-à-vis some specific behavioral yardstick. Individualism therefore was (and is) less potent in Japan than in the West. Such a view, however, he concludes was quite "rational" and did not impede the application of science and technology to economic activity. It probably does have some impact on the originality and independence of Japanese investigators. Morishima's book is, in my view, the most revealing of the really fundamental sources of Japanese development.

in the Free Trade Zones, suggest that their favorable growth is not very firmly based on indigenous sources.[6]

Consider a last example with two sides. The first side refers to foreign training. Since the early 1950s tens of thousands of nationals of developing countries have been sent or have gone abroad for training of a great variety of kinds. There are many examples where such training has been valuable both from the personal and social point of view. There is a lot of evidence that it has not. Of the latter the most obvious is the Brain Drain. People are trained abroad and never return to their home country to work.[7] The 1991 World Development Report discusses this issue briefly. That report argues (94) that the costs of the Brain Drain are mitigated, at least in part, by remittances of foreign exchange back to their home country by students who do not return home and by the possibility of facilitating the transfer of various kinds of technical information back to their home countries.

These arguments about possible mitigation represent a misunderstanding. The value of remittances, from the discussion in chapters 3 and 7, may well be quite low, and can even be negative if they distort the exchange rate to a substantial degree. There is, so far as I can ascertain, virtually no evidence that nationals of foreign countries who remain abroad constitute an important conduit for the sending of information back to their home countries. There is, however, a more important cost of the Brain Drain. If the more alert, more aggressive people go abroad to stay, the ethos of their home country is affected in fundamental ways. The effort to create the Idea of Progress is seriously damaged. Remittances cannot mitigate this kind of damage.[8]

The second side refers to the supplying of advice by outsiders, also discussed briefly earlier. I use a specific example. The World Bank has a great number of economists, a large number of them from countries sorely pressed

6. In his "Essay of Innovations," Francis Bacon writes, "It is true that what is settled by customs, though it be not good, yet at least it is fit; and those things which have long gone together, are, as it were, confederate with themselves; whereas new things piece not so well; but, though they help by their utility, yet they trouble by their inconformity; besides, they are like strangers, more admired and less favored. All this is true, if time stood still; which, contrariwise, moveth so round, that a forward retention of custom is as turbulent a thing as an innovation; and they that reverence too much old times, are but a scorn of the new: It were good, therefore, that men in their innovations, would follow the example of time itself, which indeed innovateth greatly, but quietly, and by degrees scarce to be perceived."

7. The *World Development Report* of the World Bank for 1991 (94) provides some readily available data. During the period 1962 through 1976 some 63% of students from the Republic of Korea remained in the United States after completion of their training programs. During the same interval, 49% of students from Jordan and 33% from Greece remained in the United States. More casual data from China indicate that the percentage of Chinese students who remain in the United States after training is even higher.

8. There are other problems with foreign training referred to earlier. The reason for bringing it up here is to try to help illustrate the nature of the task of creating the Idea of Progress.

for people of technical competence. The rationale of the Bank's accumulating such a large number of economists rests on the argument that such a group talking and researching together with ample data and computer resources will be able to determine the correct policies to achieve development. These policies would then be made available to the developing countries who will be, if necessary, induced, in one way or another, to follow them, and thereby development would be achieved. (This argument seems less generally applicable now than it did a decade or so ago.) The argument is surely misguided. Economic and social policies must be indigenous. They must be understood, must be really grasped by those who are to apply them. It is not possible to learn simply by being told, especially told by strangers from some mighty international organization. Again then we come back to the idea of indigenousness, of finding out, of making one's way, of searching and learning. It is this that the World Bank and other international organizations must help the countries to do. To think that a large group of economists sitting together in Washington, D.C. (or anywhere else) can draw up the blueprint for policies that will lead to the enhancing of well-being in a great range of specific countries is, again, to misunderstand the process by which such enhancement can come about.

In all these endeavors and activities both the government and nongovernment elites have strategic roles to play. The differences noted by Dore between Japan and the Latin American countries are startling. The dominant roles of foreign investment and Free Trade Zones in Malaysia and Thailand imply that government and business in these countries have not found it possible to accept the responsibility of a genuinely autonomous development effort. Their growth is surely much less firmly based and less likely to contribute to well-being than that in Korea and Taiwan. There have to be leaders, deciders, political and nonpolitical, and these are the people who create the development ethos, they become those who can be imitated, who can be learned from, who set legitimate and understandable examples, who show that it can be done. This is what elites do. This is how they earn the right to be elite. If they are just idle and rich, they are not elite, they are just idle and rich.[9]

I try to summarize. The idea is to accept the society and culture and language within which the people exist and express their values and goals and to recognize the customs, norms, and history that help to define boundaries and processes. Accept and appreciate all this, and then *within* it all, put in place the Idea of Progress. This is the great role for the government and

---

9. As already noted, *elites* usually is a pejorative term. Certainly there are many people classified as elites who deserve to be railed against and removed from such status. These are the idle rich, the absentee landlord, essentially parasites. The point in the text is that there must be people who stand out, who lead, and so on, and who earn their status by their commitment to the development idea. I have more to say about income distribution a bit later.

nongovernment elites. The articulation of a vision of the Idea of Progress put in the particular context of a specific society and, thereby, understandable to the population is perhaps the beginning of development in most countries at the present time.[10] This is the Development State.

Can such a state emerge? It did in Japan, Korea, and Taiwan. For other countries what can be offered? My brief general answer has already been discussed: create an economy with great and obvious opportunities for new activities of many kinds within the context of the existing institutional and cultural environment. This requires some protection and patience. It may require something more, and this I discuss later.[11]

I want now to consider a particular approach to policy-making, or, more accurately, a way of thinking about policy-making. Then I will examine rent seeking and the New Political Economy, two related ideas that have attracted a great deal of attention in recent years.

Policy-Making and Policy Change

Suppose now an economy which has failed to perform in a way that added significantly to well-being in the last 150–75 years. The policy task is to look at this nongrowing economy, armed with the ideas and arguments and assumed relationships and behavioral characteristics discussed from page 1 to here, and try to determine what, if anything, central policy-making agents or agencies can do to so modify the economy that it begins to contribute to the continuing enhancement of well-being. The policymakers approach this task with certain knowledge and a vast array of ignorance. The knowledge, perhaps "understanding" is better, arises in part from their position in society, their own individual histories, their awareness and interpretation of the history and traditions of their society. This understanding, plus some more specific information about the economy as such, provides them (the policymakers) with a view, a perspective about how the economy now functions. It also gives them a view of what is possible or feasible in the economy.

In the language and spirit of figures 2 through 11, they have some ideas about the barriers around which and the boundaries within which households and firms may search and learn and so add to their well-being. These well-being mazes, as we know, can represent a great number of things and are not

---

10. The vision may turn out to be unfeasible or just plain wrong. There is ignorance here as elsewhere. That this is the case is another reason why the capacity to adjust, to change, to adapt the vision, as learning takes place, is important to it becoming a guiding hand.

11. The role of elites as discussed here is different from that of entrepreneurs discussed earlier. Entrepreneurs are the action people, those who get things going, and reflect or implement the Idea of Progress. I may note, in passing, that Schumpeter placed great emphasis on the role of elites in a variety of ways.

known in detail, nor is it known how the economy will respond to various possible stimuli or any formal policy package. This latter condition means that a great deal of trial and error is necessary if desired changes are to be achieved. As noted earlier the capacity of a government to experiment, to recognize mistakes and back off is an important feature of effective government policy-making in the presence of ignorance.

I try now to examine in more detail how the government and civil servants might proceed, given this way of thinking. The effort is rather untidy, but untidiness is part of the inherent nature of the issues.

The general point of departure may be described as follows: What can be expected to happen in a particular economy at a particular time if it were essentially a free-enterprise economy, another Hong Kong say? The one major adjustment to be allowed is that the government may maintain an undervalued exchange rate as described in the previous chapter. Otherwise the government would limit itself to running the post office and providing national defense and police protection and little more. Then the policymaker reflects on the arguments and so on described here and reaches some sort of conclusion as to the outcome that such a *very* free market (combined with the undervalued exchange rate) will produce in that particular country. If the conclusion from this reflection is that the unfettered market will in fact achieve the objectives defined at the beginning of this chapter, the policymaker would then seek to move the economy as quickly as possible to that particular state, that is, would remove the government from whatever activities it was currently engaged in beyond the few basics of defense, policing, and so on. There may be, doubtless there will be, barriers to doing that, and these too the policymaker must recognize, but to get to that "Hong Kong cum undervaluation" state will be the guiding objective.

If, on the other hand, the policymaker concludes, on the basis of his/her understanding, that the Hong Kong model, modified by an undervalued exchange rate, will not yield the appropriate outcomes—even with the conventional textbook market failures recognized—then the approach is much more complex and less precise. The argument goes something like this: The policymaker appreciates that there is ignorance at every turn, even ignorance as to the specific content of well-being. The policymakers do understand well enough to know that things can be better and what better means immediately. They then look at their economy and society and try to identify the bottleneck or barriers—try to define the well-being maze—that presently block the achievement of this immediately identifiable improvement.

To remove a particular barrier may not be possible at a given moment. Then the task is to identify something that can be done that will matter, that is, that will move the system a bit in what now appears to be right direction. Even the direction may turn out to be wrong as more and more is learned about social choice and about how the various economic actors respond, as well as about the capacity of the bureaucracy and the government in general. The effective economist and policymaker are those then who can so "see" the economy in the context of the social environment that they have a pretty good idea where it makes sense to act. So the policy task, just as searching and learning, never ends.[12]

One should note that this way of thinking is very different from that which rests on the assumption that there are no barriers except the general limitation on resources and hence the Hong Kong model applies. There are several reasons why the present way of thinking is more helpful. Except in very particular circumstances—Hong Kong only, maybe—the unfettered market, even when working in the textbook manner, has not produced sustained growth. Previous arguments have shown why some "fettering" seems necessary. Thus a capital goods sector that violates comparative advantage will often be necessary. A thriving agriculture sector is usually necessary at the beginning of sustained growth irrespective of comparative advantage. Learning may require greater protection from foreign and domestic competition in excess of that provided by the undervalued exchange rate. Controls on foreign direct investment are probably necessary. Markets are necessarily incomplete, information is not always widely available, responses to price signals may be slow and misleading. The society may simply not want the large-scale activity that significant economies of scale can lead to. All these things create an environment in which there is room for some government activity along with the market.

In addition to these more growth-related categories of market failures, there are the institutions, values, mores, inherited from history or created to serve deeper needs that are relevant to the way that the market can and should function. These characteristics affect how the market can be expected to work and indeed how it should work to contribute to the well-being of the population. More generally the population may be convinced that the conditions that produce growth through the market violate some of its important preferences.

The government itself is an important actor. For example a finance minister may, for understandable or other reasons, oppose a change in the exchange rate, an increase in the government deficit, a raising or lowering of taxes, and so on, even though from a more narrow perspective, such changes may be in order. There may be corruption of a severe sort, but to prevent the corruption would create more problems still, and possibly great chaos. Governments can hardly be asked to do that which will force them from office or cause a riot or widespread revolt. In such cases the role of the government itself is circum-

---

12. C. E. Lindblom (1959), in a famous article on "The Science of Muddling Through," argues in a similar way. My point in the text is that "muddling through" is the only approach available to economic policymakers.

scribed and limited, and the effective civil servant must search for ways to maneuver and operate in order to make some headway. More on this latter point a bit later.

Unfettered markets simply do not exist. An argument, frequently encountered, is that if the government would just stop intervening in the economy, a perfect market would appear. This is not an acceptable argument. The question is then what government policy should be. Unfettered markets will rarely create the appropriate environment for growth to be put in place, but *there is a market,* and to act as if there were no market forces is as dangerous as acting as if there were only market forces. Then it is necessary to appreciate that the government cannot do many things; there is, as is often said, government failure. Just because there is market failure does not mean that the government can or should act. The choice may be (probably is) between reliance on a market that is not up to the task or relying on the government which also is not up to the task. The great policy task then is to find a way to use the market where possible and to find where and how outside agencies, usually the government, should have a significant role. In most instances, neither answer will result in a perfect solution. In these days of great emphasis on privatization, one should note that it may turn out that the most productive task at a given time is to try to improve the quality of the government bureaucracy and leadership. One can easily see why a policymaker must understand the economy as completely as he/she can rather than rely on abstract general formulations.[13]

The policymaker, even the most sincere and committed, faces a wide range of constraints and boundaries, and it is easy to conclude that nothing can be done, that change is impossible. Sometime this may in fact be true and almost all the time certain changes will be impossible or exceedingly unwise. Rarely however, is it the case that *nothing* can be done. Grindle and Thomas

---

13. The approach that I am trying to describe is consistent with an increasing number of comments and arguments of other observers. It is worth repeating that Gustav Ranis in *African Development* (1991) emphasizes that in Taiwan, policy was not made by mandarins sitting around announcing policies on a once and for all basis. Rather he says that there was a great deal of "bumbling and stumbling and going back and forth" in searching for policies that had the desired effects. In Korea numerous people have pointed out that the government was willing and able to modify policies that seemed not to be having the desired effects.

The New York Times for September 29, 1991, quotes Robert Solow as follows: "There is not some glorious theoretical synthesis of capitalism that you can write down in a book and follow. You have to grope your way." This statement is quoted by Roger L. Janeli (1993) where it first came to my attention.

My colleague Catharine Hill and I have developed this line of thinking in more detail in studying the roles that counterpart funds can play in a government budget. See Bruton and Hill (1991, 1992).

Perhaps the most thorough statement of the argument that nothing matters except the market is Little (1982).

(1991, 19) have a helpful list of five propositions that summarize an approach to policy-making that fits well with the way of thinking for which I am groping. I quote their summary:

a. Decision makers are not fully constrained by the interest of social classes, organized societal interests, international actors, or international economic conditions, but have *space* for defining the content, timing, and sequencing of reform initiatives.

b. Decision makers often have articulate and logical explanations of the problems they seek to resolve based on their experience, study, personal values, ideology, institutional affiliation, or professional training.

c. Decision makers may alter their perspectives on what constitute preferred or viable policy options in response to experience, study, values, ideology, institutional affiliation, and professional training.

d. Decision makers may often take active and formative roles in shaping reforms to make them politically acceptable to divergent interests in society or in government.

e. Bringing about changes in public policies and institutions is a normal and ongoing aspect of government and a normal and ongoing function of many officials.

The term *space* in item a is, I think, especially helpful and revealing. There are barriers and hurdles and boundaries, and there is also space. The policymaker searches for that space and there acts.

Another aspect of this way of thinking about policy-making is that it means that one or a small number of people can accomplish some things even if "the government" as such is uninterested. With some space, some freedom, a minister or even a person at a lower level may be able to get some changes made or some project going or some new policy in place that really matters. A person or two with interest and understanding can then make a difference. I find this a much more helpful and hopeful way to think than to limit one's thinking to general economy-wide policies that do require the government to act. Indeed, often the economy-wide policies fail because individuals or other components of the government do not cooperate. Evidently it is much easier and effective if there is full commitment at all levels. The point here is that it is not impossible without that.

Rent Seeking and the New Political Economy

When one gives a strategic role to the government (or to any one group), rent seeking[14] and the New Political Economy must be recognized. To discuss rent

---

14. There is of course an abundant literature on rent seeking, most of it highly critical. A

seeking is necessary because so many have condemned it and identified it as a major reason for "wrong" policies. I want to concentrate attention on why caution is necessary before one yields to the urge to make wholesale condemnations of these ideas and enjoys the luxury of concluding that a pure market approach is all that is required to solve our problem.

1. Good rent seeking. In an economy in which labor productivity is growing steadily, rent seeking is rampant among private sector firms. In the discussion of growth in earlier chapters, each firm sought rents by searching for new knowledge that would enable it to produce at lower costs than competitors or produce a new product for which a strong demand was found to exist. The very idea is to create something that allows monopoly profits (rents) before other firms find ways to compete them away. Thus rent seeking (or perhaps quasi–rent seeking) in the presence of competition constitutes an essential part of the mechanics by which growth takes place. This is of course the kind of argument that Schumpeter emphasized, but he added a business cycle component (and other things) and allowed the new knowledge to come from outside the system. So rent seeking of this sort is essential, is part of the growth process. It also is effectively hidden or ignored in most textbook analysis because of the concentration on static equilibria, static efficiency, and perfect competition. Clearly then one must qualify the term in most instances of its use.

2. Bad rent seeking. The rent seeking that is so widely condemned and blamed for wrong policies refers to the efforts of private sector firms to persuade the government to grant them some form or other of protection from competition (domestic or foreign) or a subsidy of one kind or other that allows a more or less permanent monopoly position. This position is maintained without the search-and-learn efforts that produce rising productivity and new products that are the sources of the growth of output and labor productivity. The very purpose of this rent seeking is to circumvent the process that has been described in previous chapters.

Such activity is facilitated by assumptions that government officials are themselves rent seekers who exploit their position by granting monopoly power in return for favors. Successful rent seekers not only avoid the pressures to search and learn, but also use resources in the unproductive activities of convincing government officials to grant their requests for some form of protection that will enable them to profit and continue to profit with little effort.

That this sort of thing has occurred and has imposed penalties on the development effort of many countries is surely correct, although the empirical

clear recent statement is Krueger (1990). More questioning discussions are Toye (1987, 122 ff) and Mosley et al. (1991, 13 ff) and Warren J. Samuels and Nicholas Mercurio in Colander (1984).

evidence is, so far as I can ascertain, ambiguous. There are however several things to note that make the usual arguments less open-and-shut than is usually implied.

a. The line between legitimate lobbying and rent seeking is not easily identified in many cases. It is in order for the members of the community to express themselves to the government, and providing such information is not always and everywhere rent seeking.

b. Most analysts seem to assume that rent seeking applies only to individuals who want gain that somehow penalizes the economy. If the poor manage to organize in such manner that the government takes action to relieve or compensate for that poverty, is that bad? This objective may also use resources and may involve offering civil servants some rewards.

c. To assume that all government officials are susceptible to rent seekers and are themselves simply rent seekers is surely inadequate. Such a cynical view is falsified by numerous examples and other evidence that many, maybe most, civil servants want to do a respectable job and are sincerely interested in carrying out their duties. This does not mean that these people are not interested in their own well-being, but it does mean that these people are, for the most part, not simply concerned with rip-offs.

d. It may also be noted that almost all countries of the North have, over their history, experienced what is now identified as rent seeking and the New Political Economy. So far as I can determine historians have given very little attention to the impact or role of such activity on the development of the North.[15]

e. It is frequently argued or implied that the way to prevent rent seeking is to have as minimal a role for the government as possible. This is a doubtful conclusion for several reasons. If government activity is itself lucrative, then *that* activity would presumably come into existence. The other major reason is that noted above, the argument that minimal government yields better results than more than minimal government is not convincing, indeed not really present.

One form of rent seeking is usually classified as corruption. Corruption by its definition is bad, but the definition of corruption is never very precise. In many countries, what appears as corruption to an outsider may be a way of

---

15. I think one reason for this is that historians pay little heed to "efficiency"—in the sense of the economist—and now that so much of development economics is concerned with efficiency, the rent-seeking argument seems more important than it did when more people accepted that development was and is something other than efficiency.

solving specific problems that could not, in the prevailing environment, be solved in any other way. Much of petty corruption is in this category in countries where the wages of bureaucrats are so abysmally low.

In some countries there are much more substantial forms of corruption that are virtually impossible to uproot. In fact to try to eliminate it would often create more problems than it would solve. In such an environment corruption may be looked upon as a fixed cost. Ways might then be found to pay this cost without any or with little additional cost to the development effort. If it can be paid and leave the economic policymaking and implementing more or less unaffected and in the hands of fairly disinterested agents, then corruption (or high-level indifference) may be effectively offset—not eliminated. Where political or personal gain can be acquired by force by some individual or group, the idea is to recognize that this is the way things are and seek for ways to pay and still have an effective policy.

Countries which have substantial oil revenues illustrate this argument. Oil revenue both creates the temptation to engage in efforts to get some of that revenue by damaging the economy and provides the means by which strategic people can be paid off easily, thereby allowing others to try to get policy reasonably appropriate for the achievement of development objectives. There are examples of both kinds of uses of oil revenues. Indonesia is often cited as a nation that has used its oil revenues fairly productively, including paying off—in one way or another—a substantial number of people who could otherwise cause a great deal of trouble. Iran and Nigeria have been much less successful in learning how to do this or to eliminate corruption, although, as will be discussed later, some parts of the Nigerian economy seem to be functioning in a hopeful way independently of the rest of the economy.[16]

All of this does not mean that rent seeking and New Political Economy issues can be ignored, even downplayed. It means rather that part of the task of achieving development is improving the government, just as improving the functioning of the market is part of the task. It means that ways must be found and can be found to get things done, but it is a constant trial and error, hunt and peck, seek and act where it is possible. The argument also illuminates again the importance of keeping productivity growth and employment in the forefront of the story, with efficiency of the textbook kind in some back room, but not buried.

---

16. One may note that in countries without oil (or another major source of immediate revenue) but with counterpart funds, the latter funds might profitably be used to keep people quiet who would otherwise cause trouble. It has also been suggested that foreign aid or World Bank funds used for this kind of purpose would be more productive than in some of the uses to which they are now put. Such recommendations can hardly be taken seriously, but they do help us to see the nature of the problem and to make the contrast with the idea of a free market, zero corruption, no rent seeking etc., clearer.

Policy Criteria

How does the policymaker and analyst know if the economy is on or approaching a sustained-growth status, given that some headway has or is being made toward instilling the Idea of Progress? Given the list of conditions at the very beginning of this chapter, the following are characteristics or variables to which the analyst and policymaker may give primary attention. The idea would be to create a picture or statement about the economy that addresses the following questions.

1. What has been happening to labor productivity over as long a period as possible? To the extent possible it is also necessary to have ideas as to why it is happening. Part of the answer to the latter question should be reflected in the capital-output ratio, because if it is rising, profit rates are probably falling. The data should cover as wide a spectrum of sectors of the economy as is possible.
2. What has been happening to the rate of growth of employment and of the quality of the jobs that are created?
3. What has been happening to the composition of output in general and to exports in particular?
4. What has been happening to the appearance and growth of new firms? Is there great turbulence in this sector?
5. To what extent has (and is) foreign investment a significant part of the answer to any of these questions?

The discussions in the preceding chapters should have made clear why these are the relevant questions for the policymaker to consider.[17] The list does not include the rate of growth of GDP or GDP per capita. Although I do not object to these series being included, I do not think that they are variables that tell us much about the real capacity of the economy to generate increasing well-being over long periods of time. Similarly the balance of payments and inflation are relevant only insofar as they affect one's response to the above questions. Many developing countries, strongly pushed by the international organizations, have in the last decade or so moved or made efforts at moving toward a much more market-ruled economy than prevailed in previous decades. The notion of government failure has been recognized and widely appreciated. The major areas where those who push these views recognize continued and practical and theoretical difficulties are with respect to the exchange rates and to the extent and manner of foreign influence and control. I

---

17. Certain issues—distribution of wealth and income, health levels, and so on—are considered in the following section.

have described a position on both of these issues in previous chapters, but prevailing opinion (and passion) is far from a consensus.

I try now to be more specific and more direct.

Analysis and Policy

I begin with some examples.

1. Suppose the data show that labor productivity has been rising over numerous segments of the economy for the past decade or more. Yet the employment picture is quite dismal and the rate of domestic private investment seems low given the rate of growth of labor productivity, a picture not unlike that for India in the 1960–80 period (see Ahluwalia 1985, 1991). The first question to ask is: What is happening to the capital-output ratio? Suppose one finds that it is rising rather sharply, as it was in India in the period noted. This probably means two things: it means that increased investment is the main source of the increased labor productivity and that the rate of return on investment is (almost) sure to be falling. Evidently such a situation cannot continue very long unless the government is able and willing to put very large amounts of funds into direct investment. Since the government is unlikely to be able to do this, one concludes that labor productivity will not continue to rise in these circumstances.

What now does the analyst or policymaker look for? The most obvious question is: Are factor price signals conveying information that leads entrepreneurs to search in the "wrong" direction, in the direction that induces producers to use more and more capital per unit of labor? So then why are factor prices "wrong"? The favorite answer is, due to "wrong" government policy. The careful analyst will, however, note that there are numerous other possible reasons and will check them out. Does the labor market not function well for institutional reasons, that is, reasons unrelated to government policies? There are ample reasons why, with a rising capital-labor ratio, wage rates would rise in the face of unemployment. The conclusion may be however that factor prices look reasonable. Where then does the analyst search? Now it is evident how valuable detailed and intuitive knowledge of the economy is. It helps one to know where to look to find the problem. Figure 9 on an earlier page may suggest where the difficulties lie. Maybe the entrepreneurs are unable or unwilling to search in directions that do not make use of "modern" technology, or they may have little confidence in their capacity to find underutilized indigenous technical knowledge. Would some kind of formal effort (government or otherwise) to disseminate information help or be just one more useless, make-work scheme? Are there reasons to think that a formal R&D institute would help entrepreneurs learn new knowledge to take advantage of the available labor? Would stronger incentives than the undervalued exchange rate provide the necessary inducement for entrepreneurs? The most obvious solution is perhaps an employment subsidy of some kind.[18]

2. Suppose that the rate of growth of productivity was essentially zero in most sectors of the economy and had been for a decade or more. What then should the analyst/policymaker look for? There are two obvious barriers. The first is that the profitability of increased output appears very dim even with the undervalued exchange rate. The second is that no new knowledge is in fact findable that will increase productivity. Evidently the appropriate policy or action by the government depends on which (if either) is the explanation.

When perceived profit opportunities are apparently too slight to elicit the search required, there are a number of possible ways to step up the inducements: further devaluation may be in order, a greater effort to spread more information about the state of the economy, a subsidy that rewards increased productivity in some way, making signals that the market generates accurate or more overt, and so forth.

Where the analyst concludes that the problem is not an absence of discerned profit opportunities, but rather that new usable knowledge is not findable, the difficulties are more severe. Is there really *no* underutilized knowledge that can be found and brought to bear on the production process? This is difficult to believe, but it could be the correct diagnosis in some instances. Would a step-up in aggregate demand by government spending have favorable effects on search-and-learn efforts, or would it lead *only* to inflation? Would an increase in investment, induced somehow, "embody" some new knowledge that would add to productivity? What are the barriers to increasing investment? And on and on.

3. Suppose the economy and political situation are in exceeding disarray. There is corruption, there is political unrest that borders on chaos, there is inflation, infrastructure is falling apart, and there is very little prospect that things will get better in the immediate future. Nigeria or Zaire might be in such a state at the moment. Is there nothing that anyone can do? Maybe not in

---

18. For the manufacturing sector a subsidy that gives a tax advantage to firms that achieve "high" values for the following ratio may work: consider

$$\frac{W_0 (E_1 - E_0)}{\Delta VA}$$

W_0 is the wage rate in the present year, E_1 and E_0 are employment in the present year and the preceding year, and ΔVA is the increase in value added for the firm over the two years. Evidently the higher this ratio, the higher is the increase in employment relative to value added. Where such a ratio can be effectively applied it will constitute a strong inducement to find ways to use more and more labor. Such an incentive is to be contrasted with the common practice of providing tax relief based on the size of the investment.

some instances, but maybe so in many. In Nigeria, for example, there are examples of successful activities (as of 1993) in which there is some kind of informal cooperation between a private sector firm and some government agency. The *Economist* (August 21, 1993, Survey section, 10) reports that Guiness Brewery has developed a stout brewed from millet and sorghum because the government had banned the importing of barley malt. The new stout has been a hit. Some farmers in Nigeria apparently proceed either independently of the government or possibly find a minister or lower-level bureaucrat who will help in some way or other. So some markets in many instances are well stocked with agricultural produce despite many problems, including that of getting access to fertilizer. This same article refers to estimates of the output of the informal sectors of Nigeria that add 20–30 percent to the usually cited estimates of GDP.[19] The study *Successful Development in Africa* (1989) describes seven cases in which projects and policies seemed to succeed despite, in most cases, little or no government support. All is not hopeless, even when it seems that all is hopeless. We recognize that we do not have to have everything more-or-less textbook perfect before things can happen.

4. Suppose that the "right" economic policy is impeded by a recalcitrant minister or president. Can technical economists do anything about that? As an example suppose that the undervalued exchange rate is not in place and that all signals indicate that a strong devaluation is very much in order, but the relevant minister refuses to consider such a move. The economy, she/he argues, will grow into the prevailing exchange rate, or a devaluation will force up prices of intermediate goods and will force an unbearable cutback in production and employment, or it will have adverse effects on the price of some basic food items consumed by the very poor, or (someone else hints) a major constituency of the minister's will be especially penalized by a devaluation. The technical economists can sit back and say that nothing else can be done and the problem is a political one, or they can look for other policy changes that could contribute to remedying the effects of a wrong exchange rate. Is such possible? It certainly is not possible without a major search effort and without an acceptance by the economic analysts that political issues are part of the environment within which economic policy must be made. There are a number of examples of how to devalue without "devaluing." One of the best-known is the Pakistan Export Bonus Scheme of the early 1960s, but there are others. These arrangements usually result in some form of a multiple exchange rate system. Defects of such a system are well-known, but they have

---

19. Evidently these examples do not mean that unfortunate government activities and roles do not matter. Of course they do; they matter greatly. The point here again is that something can usually be done that can help and serve as examples to be imitated elsewhere in the nation.

also had favorable effects and should not be ruled out because they are not, in some abstract sense, ideal.

Such ideas do not result in efficient resource allocation in the usual sense, but—and this is the main general point—it is possible to do something, to take measures that result in the economy contributing more to the policy objectives listed at the beginning of this chapter than not doing anything because the "right" thing is not possible.[20] In the language used above suggested by Grindle and Thomas (1991), there is always space. The great message is that the useful economist always looks for that space.

5. Suppose that the diagnosis is that the agricultural sector constitutes an important barrier for the economy at a given time. Suppose further that the government is indeed eager to remove this barrier. The question is how to do that. Is it adequate just to get prices "right" or just not to squeeze the sector, or is stronger medicine necessary? Consider two obvious alternative approaches: subsidies for the price of fertilizer and (where relevant) water, or no subsidies but a favorable guaranteed price for agricultural products. Even more potent than the latter would be a price that was higher, the greater the increase in yields that were obtained. A subsidized-fertilizer price induces farmers to use fertilizer (maybe too much fertilizer) and this may help although there are many examples of difficulties on the supply side. It tends—as do all subsidies on input prices—to dampen incentives to try to find ways to increase productivity. A price for the product that rises as yields rise—with no other inducement at all—might result in major (and successful) efforts to find ways to get yields up. Its effectiveness depends on many things (including the government's capacity to administer the price incentives) that could be found out only by trial and error. Clearly this kind of an incentive is much more conducive to productivity and yield growth than is a subsidy of the price of inputs.[21]

6. Suppose the analyst identifies an employment problem. The most obvious such problem is of course open unemployment, but a number of other kinds of employment problems were identified earlier. Suppose employment has been growing at an impressive rate over a decade or two and wages are rising for the good and sensible reason that the demand curve for labor has shifted into the region where the actual supply curve is rising. The jobs however are of little interest and provide no opportunity for learning in any way. What does it make sense for the government to try to do? The answer may well be "nothing," on the assumption that with a strong demand for

---

20. The term *second best* is often applied to this kind of situation, but I think that term is inappropriate. These kinds of policies are not second best. They are the best that can be achieved in the general environment prevailing at a particular time.

21. It may be noted, somewhat in passing, that counterpart funds provide an excellent means to finance an arrangement that would pay higher prices as yields rose. Not all developing countries have counterpart funds of course.

labor, people are able to pick and choose among jobs. If that were in fact the case, then those jobs that did offer considerable nonwork attractions would (presumably) get labor and those that did not would find it increasingly difficult to meet their staffing needs. This kind of argument puts the major burden on the workers for finding good jobs that create well-being; if workers want such jobs, they can find them in a market where the demand for labor is strong year after year after year.

This is an important argument. As indicated in the employment chapter, a strong demand for labor is surely a necessary condition for work to be rewarding in ways in addition to providing wage income. Whether or not it is a sufficient condition depends very much on the specific circumstances of the country and the labor force. There is, for example, much evidence that many jobs in the electronics sector in Southeast Asia have little appeal other than the income produced. It seems likely that the quality of these jobs is not going to change much even if the labor market gets tighter. There is also very little learning attached to such jobs.[22] The *Economist* for August 14, 1993 (18) reports that an International Labor Organization study shows that about 11 percent of the work force in some Asian countries are children, up to 17 percent in Africa and 25 percent in Latin America. Many of the jobs held by children are not only dreary, but do great harm to the child's health and provide little learning.[23]

Evidently legal restrictions against these jobs will have and have had little effect. Similarly more postsecondary education is not the answer. What then, in addition to the strong demand for labor, will have much of an effect? I have referred earlier to greater emphasis on apprenticeship arrangements as an approach with some hope. More effort on elementary schools and school attendance (and less on postsecondary) is in order in most countries. All these possibilities for solving child labor inequities require more than a market working well, but they will not be effective unless there is a strong demand for adult labor.

7. One of the major issues with which many developing countries are confronted is that of ethnic diversity. Although there are many sources of diversity, ethnic diversity seems to be the most difficult for a community to profit from, and the easiest for it to suffer from. If in such an environment the market were to function "perfectly" most in-groups would remain in, most out-groups remain out. At the same time, government leaders not infrequently favor their own ethnic group or tribe or region or linguistic or religious group.

---

22. Such jobs are held mainly by young women who work for several years and then are released. There is also some evidence that the eyesight of such women is harmed.

23. These percentages appear quite high, especially that for Latin America. Also it is not clear what the age is when one stops being a child and becomes an adult in these estimates.

Even with the most unbiased of governments, a specific "right" policy in this kind of situation is not available. Governments must stumble around, must expect trial and error, and must hunt and peck to try to find an acceptable way to go about achieving some enhancement of well-being.

8. Consider a final example. I have placed great emphasis on the existence of a turbulent small-scale sector. If one relied completely on "the market," then one takes what the market doles out, large scale, small scale, and so on. If however one finds reason and evidence that a small-scale sector is especially important, then specific (other than "right" prices) policies may be in order to encourage or induce or see to it that one exists and thrives.

The small-scale sector is closely identified, in many countries, with the informal—I prefer indigenous—sector. Such a sector appears to be especially important in Africa, but is also relevant elsewhere. As already noted, a dynamic indigenous sector helps resolve numerous problems: those related to regional matters, employment (both job quality and number), learning entrepreneurship, learning how to search for ways to increase productivity, identifying niches of production that permit exporting, and so forth. One key policy issue for the government in this area is to determine if the prevention of large-scale firms from usurping markets, will, in turn, result in the small-scale, domestic firms emerging. Whether the undervalued exchange rate environment will be enough, or something more is required, is an issue that can only be resolved by trial and error, by stumbling and bumbling.[24]

A particular barrier for small-scale firms that is being identified with increasing frequency is working capital. Small firms often can get started with their (or their friends' and family's) savings, but then run into problems meeting working capital needs. In some countries (and regions of countries) the finance infrastructure functions better in providing funds for the initial investment than for working capital.[25] This is an obvious example of a country's policy not acting directly on an immediately restraining barrier.

Policy Strategy

These examples are intended to help us appreciate some of the complications of policy design and implementation. I have noted a range of policies and projects and practices. This does not mean that a government (or firm) should try everything, pursue a sort of shotgun approach to policy-making.[26] The

---

24. Especially interesting examples of this argument are the Town and Village Enterprises of China and the Grameen Bank of Bangladesh mentioned earlier. There are also many examples in Africa.

25. There is some evidence that this is the case in Russia as that country makes efforts to use the market more effectively.

26. Several years ago the International Labor Organization sponsored a series of country

idea is that the analyst and policymaker understands the economy well enough, sees the well-being maze that obtains at a particular moment clearly enough, to know where and how to act. A major conclusion of the sort of approach that I am urging is that the government (or firm) should not, indeed cannot, do "everything." Then, to identify what *can* be done that will make some positive contribution to the basic objective is the great task of the analyst and policymaker. To repeat (again): To proceed in this way requires not only a working knowledge of micro and macro theory, but full acquaintance with the institutions, traditions, deeper values, ethnic make-up, and so on. That is what the well-being maze is meant to emphasize.

An especially valuable kind of knowledge is that which informs the policymaker about whether and how the private sector responds to various incentives. Such knowledge is necessary to determine the division of labor between the government and the private sector—enterprise and household. The widespread belief in the 1950s and 1960s that comprehensive planning was necessary to achieve development rested largely on the assumption that the private sector would not or could not respond to conventional market signals. This we no longer believe to be the case. Firms and households do respond to market forces, but within constraints and boundaries and within their knowledge and understanding.

In many cases government policies may seek to strengthen market forces, may make the market message clearer and more overt. This is a convenient and important objective of policy. It must also be appreciated that it may well be the objective of policy to offset or redirect market incentives. I have mentioned several examples of market results that can defeat the efforts to establish an economy that contributes to increasing well-being. Similarly, one may note again that market signals that are "right" for achieving an optimal situation in which there is long-run perfect competition, perfect knowledge, profit maximization, full employment, and so on, are unlikely to be "right" for inducing searching and tinkering and learning. So it is not a safe generalization to say that the role of government policy is limited to making the market work better—at least as that notion is usually used.

The Role of Crises

Economic and political crises often provide extra space for the policymaker. Grindle and Thomas (1991, passim) have an interesting discussion of the role

---

studies related directly to employment. These were carried out in every instance by economists of great stature in the profession. These studies, it is not unfair to say, have had little effect on the countries concerned. The main reason, I think, was the common practice of most studies to provide an exceedingly long list of things that the government should do, so long that governments had trouble knowing where to start.

that a crisis may play in effecting policy changes. The perception of a crisis by a strong government official can, as a minimum, put an issue on the agenda. Virtually by definition, a crisis cannot be hidden, cannot be ignored, so the policymaker must do something. One often hears the observation that "when things get bad enough, we *can* act." A crisis may convince groups (or ministries, or the population) that some action is necessary. Policymakers may be allowed more freedom to maneuver; the *space* available for action is increased.

Although the advantages offered by a crisis are widely recognized, few recommend inducing a crisis just to enable greater freedom of maneuver. The reasons are obvious: a crisis is open ended and can lead to unwanted results; a policy to solve a crisis issue may be a very unfortunate long-run policy, but be hard to change at the end of the crisis; a crisis forces quick action that may in fact exacerbate the situation; and so on. A crisis may elicit action—for example, obtaining foreign aid—that enables the government to continue the policies that produced the crisis initially.

The role of an extra-helpful analyst is that of identifying barriers that will at some later point produce a crisis and convincing the policymaker to act now, while a more careful examination of policy options is still possible. Such a role requires not so much "prediction of things to come" as it does understanding how the economy works. I want to illustrate this last point by asking the question: How does an economy get to the undervalued exchange rate position?

Suppose the exchange rate is now either overvalued or at what might be identified as the equilibrium rate. When should the policymaker move to the undervalued state? The general answer is, when the balance of payments is extra strong and the economy seems to be doing well. As argued earlier, the purpose of the undervaluation is not to correct a balance of payments problem. Rather it is to effect an environment which is conducive to the searching and learning that produces productivity growth. The idea then is to get to that position with the least disruptive effects, at a time when the economy is able to tolerate some marked change in direction. An unexpected devaluation almost always causes fewer difficulties than one widely anticipated. A relatively crisis-free situation has the further advantage of allowing the policymaker to give attention to longer-run issues rather than simply trying to eliminate the crisis. In particular it could help the analyst/policymaker to think in terms of establishing an economic environment which results in routine growth.

The difficulty is, of course, obvious. If the economy is doing reasonably well, why change? The *space* the policymaker has to effect change is less (than in a balance of payments crisis situation) for the reasons referred to earlier: the idea that change is necessary is not widely recognized and is therefore resisted. So the main pressures work largely to impede change, rather than to seek change. It is to be emphasized that this sort of situation is not the consequence of rent seeking or of the New Political Economy as such. Rather it falls out very much from the nature of societies and their organization and their functionings. The task then of government leadership is to create a milieu in which the sort of changes can be made that analysis dictates are appropriate. Policy-making rarely consists simply of a once-and-for-all change that puts the economy on a well-defined path.[27] Rather, as already emphasized, barriers and obstacles appear as the economy moves into new activities, as new evidence appears, new understandings are achieved, and so on. So there is a need for constant policy activity. It is the milieu that creates this sort of constant searching that is to be sought.[28] It is this sort of environment that is conducive to considerable flexibility in policy and that also serves as a deterrent to dogmatism and rampant ideology.

Government and Better Preferences

Are there any policy implications following from the arguments of chapter 2 that better preferences are an essential component of development and from John Rawls's "Aristotelian Principle"? One can easily argue that these are issues about which governments can and should do very little. This burden is one that is the responsibility of individuals and households. Such an argument is fundamental. At the same time, it is, I think, important to appreciate a number of issues that are relevant to how a government proceeds and how the division of labor between it and households should be made.

I suggest five categories of issues that relate to the preference question about which a role for the government seems to exist.

1. General atmosphere. I have emphasized often in previous pages the role of the general atmosphere, the ethos, of the community. It plays a role in creating and maintaining the searching and learning routines of firms, in the creation of dynamic small-scale activities in all parts of the economy, in the emergence and efforts of entrepreneurs, and in finding export markets. The Idea of Progress itself is of course a part, an essential part, of the atmosphere, and I discussed a few pages back the government's (and other elites') role in creating and sustaining that particular notion. I want now to consider briefly the role of the government in the efforts to create an atmo-

---

27. One would like to think that the achievement of the undervaluation is this sort of once and for all thing, but even this is doubtful as corrections for price level changes are necessary.

28. Both the World Bank and the International Monetary Fund usually impose some conditions on their loans. The idea of conditions is surely acceptable, but the notion that is often implicit in such arrangements is that once the policy is "right"—budget balanced, exchange rate at "equilibrium" level, no subsidies or price controls—then the policymaker has nothing more to do. This is surely not the way it is.

sphere to help the members of the community think hard about their preferences and the improvement of their ideas of the good life.

It seems legitimate to expect that in an economy where there is considerable searching and learning in production activities, there should be the same in the other activities of the society. A government that can bring itself to allow open discussion—especially a relatively free press—thereby contributes to the idea that questioning and probing is very much in order. In their work on famines Dreze and Sen (1989) argue that the free press in India was a significant factor in preventing famines in certain areas of that country. The acceptance of the idea that truth is not frozen in either edict or doctrine, but emerges and develops from experience and debate and reflection is facilitated by a free press. The general stance, general approach to issues by a government can help to create such an atmosphere. A government should be able to accept the notion that doubt and recognition of ignorance are necessary conditions for change and development and neither jeopardize their existence nor undermine their authority. Again, this is something for governments to learn, not only how to do it but why it is important to do so.

The role of a relatively free press is often considered a political threat, and hence must not be allowed by governments who doubt (implicitly) their legitimacy. A free press (or radio or television) that is concerned with other—nonpolitical—issues may still be allowed. To exploit such an opportunity may be an effective way for a good guy or two to proceed in an otherwise inhospitable climate. In the language used earlier, a space may exist that allows some activity that really matters. Preferences are an ideal topic for discussion.

Foreign advisors and consultants may have a useful role in this sort of an approach. Policymakers are often, usually I think, eager to find reasons why change is impossible, why certain changes, sometime any change, cannot be done. Foreigners can push as to whether something is really impossible, why certain consequences will necessarily follow if those things are done, and so forth. Foreigners however tend not to see barriers that are there, and policymakers tend to see barriers that are not there. Perhaps conversations between the two will lead to greater understanding of what is, in fact, there. The great danger of foreign consultants (on economic policy) is that they bring theoretical baggage and maybe ideological predilections that stand in their way of understanding how the various parts of a particular society function and of appreciating the full content of well-being in a particular country.

2. Elementary education. I have already emphasized the role of elementary education on the production and productivity growth side of things. It is equally important on the "preference development" side. Schools in which students learn to read and write extra well, gain some awareness and understanding of their nation's history and present status, and learn what it means to question, to value, to probe are in a strong position to reflect on their prefer-

ences and on the kind of society in which they want to live. The appeal of a university is strong, but until the elementary and secondary schools are in first-class shape, the role of the university is severely limited.

3. Employment. Attention to the quality of jobs is a useful way to help make the population aware of the role that work can play in the search for the understanding and reflection that are necessary for learning about preferences. A government that explicitly considers job quality (as well as job numbers) and seeks employment policies that reflect that concern will also help people appreciate that preferences and choice are fundamental to their well-being. The Adam Smith quotation in footnote 6, chapter 5 reminds us of the deadliness of uninteresting jobs. It is important that awareness of this fact be explicit in government policy and statement.

4. Time preference. Decisions are made by every government every day that reflect a time preference of some sort. There are few issues that do more to force a community to think hard about long-run matters—life styles, environment, communal and ethnic and family matters, social and political organizations, the content of the well-lived life, and doubtless other things—than does confronting the time preference question. Where it is possible to make such issues widely known and reflected upon, a community must necessarily come to grips with some basic ideas about individual and group preferences. Although academic economics offers formal solutions to some of these questions—present values, discount rates, and so on—the resolution of the ultimate question does not lend itself to this sort of formal approach. It is a matter of values, deep values, of preferences.[29]

The numerous issues associated with the great ecological questions have, somewhat as a by-product, brought to the front of attention, in an irresistible manner, how a community must think about its future. Something similar, but less overwhelming, applies to the building of large scale multipurpose dams and large "low-cost" housing arrangements, and other similar matters associated with development. A government and a community that bring themselves to discuss such matters openly may not only reach better decisions on the specific question at hand, but also become more aware of the basic question of preferences and their improvement.

Just as a general awareness of its history and tradition is a binding agent of great significance for a society, so too are reflections on its future.

5. Community. In all societies there are groups, sects, richer and poorer, tribes, and so forth. I have noted this fact throughout this study. One additional comment here is useful. Explicit recognition of such diversity and pluralism creates opportunities for reflection and discussion of the deep-seated

---

29. My colleague, Gordon Winston, has done much to convince me of the great role that time preference does play and can play in the development effort.

issues that reside in this diversity. Discussions of ways to understand and adapt to this kind of environment may also induce people to think about preferences and life-styles and right and wrong. Considering the role of women more explicitly is a specific approach that can help the people think harder about their society. Such discussions help the population appreciate the idea of a nation or national society.

One issue in particular is especially relevant in this connection: the search for the right mixture of individualism and communalism. Unbridled individualism is damaging both to the development effort and to the social and cultural environment. Yet it is necessary for a person to be somewhat independent of, to see over and beyond, the existing limits of social organization, of existing ideas of right and wrong, of the good life, and so on. To be able to do this is, of course, a condition for change of any sort, especially of preferences. The question is: how should individualism be bridled? The only point to make here is that this issue itself—community and individualism—can be made explicit and discussed, and learning and understanding can take place.[30] It is in this general context that distribution of income, of wealth, of political and economic power may best be discussed.

All of these suggestions are of course open to many doubts, and there are few examples of successful efforts readily at hand. I do insist, however, that improving preferences is an essential component of development and that the government can play a role in helping the population understand this. This is true even if it is recognized that the basic task must be performed in the household.

A Brief Conclusion

The great and unrelenting complexity of exploiting the market in the effort to put a growing economy in place is probably exceeded only by the complexity of finding the appropriate role of government. The latter complexity is made even greater because the space within which a government, even one that is more or less fully committed to serving the society, can maneuver is often small and, in many instances, difficult to identify. The complexity is added to again when the full content of well-being is recognized and appreciated, and the social-choice issue identified. Because of this latter argument and the central role of productivity and employment growth in the search for enhanced well-being, the notion of efficiency is necessarily and inevitably fuzzy. This last point gains in importance (and in intractability) as we remind ourselves that the role of the market and of prices is much more clearly defined

---

30. I do not mean to suggest or imply that the countries of the North have found the right mixture of these two notions. It is sometimes said that in the North individualism is harmfully unbridled, while in the South it is unduly limited. This is a useful idea, but difficult to appraise.

and understood when static efficiency, with a well-filled ceteris paribus, is the objective, rather than productivity growth, rewarding and illuminating jobs, and other components of increasing well-being. So, part of policy making includes learning about how and where the market serves well and where it cannot and where the government seems effective and where not. We must appreciate also that neither will ever work "perfectly" or even extra well, so we must continue to probe and search.

This point of view is supported by the recognition that market mechanisms—"capitalism"—have taken and continue to take many forms around the world, and have changed over time in most countries. One may turn the statement around to say that the role of government in economic activity has varied widely across countries and across time. These changes have occurred in response to changing ideas and values and institutions as well as to continued learning and trials and errors. There is of course no such thing as a market independent and separate from the institutions and values and ideas that, along with production and distribution of goods and services, define the society.

I have tried to illuminate these complexities and some of the ways of dealing with them in designing and implementing policy. In this area, as in all other areas of economics, dogmatism is surely the most effective way to prevent searching and learning, and therefore to prevent the enhancing of well-being.

Epilogue: Another Great Question and More Ignorance

The approach to development worked out in the preceding pages has built around several ideas. The basic idea is that development—the enhancement of well-being—means building from the institutions, values, technology, preferences that define the society seeking to develop. Development is necessarily an indigenous process. This approach is in contrast to that which emphasizes the replacement of these characteristics of the indigenous community by those from the North. This latter process is not, in my view, development. It is simply displacement.

In the approach of this book great attention has been given to ignorance and hence to searching and learning, to the existence of variety among firms and households and hence to an intractable and continuing social choice problem, to the importance of institutions and ideas of the good life and of what is right and what is wrong, and the importance of learning from the North without trying simply to imitate the North.

The displacement approach, on the other hand, intends specifically to make the country over in the image of the North. Complete openness to the North is paramount, foreign investment is actively encouraged, foreign advisors sought, foreign higher education is deemed vital, and technology is imported in order to make the economy internationally competitive. Market outcomes are always right or at least the best possible, so attention is given to getting and keeping prices right and the government minimal. There is no ignorance to worry about as the objective is imitating, not finding one's own way. (See footnote 12 in chapter 2 above.) Little attention is given to values and traditions and history and ethos because they interfere with the modernizing process. Foreign loans are to be sought from private banks and international organizations, and growth of the GDP per capita, with some attention to poverty relief, is given overwhelming prominence as the criterion of success.

This latter approach is well illustrated by Singapore. Foreign firms dominate the Singaporean economy. There is virtually no unemployment, very little poverty, no illiteracy, excellent health care, and a per capita GDP that is now among the highest in the world and still growing rapidly. The saving rate is over 40 percent of GDP. The government is in firm control, is staffed by well-trained, well-paid civil servants who have a clear vision of what Singapore should be. Singapore now has what many developing countries desperately seek, and what Singapore itself did not have a mere 40 years ago. Malaysia is a similar example, although not so spectacular as Singapore.

Why then should not all countries follow the "modernizing" strategy and accept whatever comes from the North? Indeed, as is sometimes argued, the long centuries of unrelieved mass poverty in many countries of the world suggest strongly that such nations simply cannot develop in their own image, so they must do as the North has done or they are doomed to continuing hopelessness and despair.

One of the main reasons that I wrote this book is that I find the displacement argument extremely disconcerting. It is an attractive, even alluring notion, but it is surely mistaken. I do accept it as worthy of attention and thought and study, and, of course, it is an argument pushed by highly responsible and astute students and policymakers and policy advisors. Thus the choice between the two approaches remains a great question about which we must still debate, for there remains great ignorance.

References

Abramovitz, Moses. 1989. *Thinking About Growth*. Cambridge: Cambridge University Press.

Adelman, Irma, and C. T. Morris. 1973. *Economic Growth and Social Equity*. Stanford: Stanford University Press.

African Development: Lessons from Asia. 1991. Proceedings of a seminar on Strategies for the Future of Africa. Washington, D.C.: Winrock International Institute for Agricultural Development.

Ahluwalia, I. J. 1985. *Industrial Growth in India*. Delhi: Oxford University Press.

Ahluwalia, I. J. 1991. *Productivity and Growth in Indian Manufacturing*. Delhi: Oxford University Press.

Amsden, Alice. 1977. "The Division of Labor Is Limited by the Type of Market." *World Development* 5:217–34.

Amsden, Alice. 1989. *Asia's Next Giant: South Korea and Late Industrialization*. New York: Oxford University Press.

Arkoun, Mohammed. 1984. *Pour une Critique de la Raison Islamique*. Paris.

Arndt, H. W. 1987. *Economic Development: The History of an Idea*. Chicago: The University of Chicago Press.

Arrow, K. J. 1951 (2d ed. 1963). *Social Choice and Individual Values*. New York: John Wiley and Sons.

Arrow, K. J. 1974. *The Limits of Organization*. New York: W. W. Norton.

Arrow, K. J. 1983. *Social Choice and Justice*, Collected Papers of Kenneth J. Arrow, Vol. I, Cambridge, Mass.: Harvard University Press.

Arrow, K. J., H. B. Chenery, B. S. Minhas, and R. M. Solow. 1961. "Capital Labor Substitution and Economic Efficiency," *Review of Economics and Statistics* 43:225–50.

Artz, F. B. 1953. *The Mind of the Middle Ages*. New York: Alfred A. Knopf.

Balasubramanyan, V. N., and Sanjaya Lall. 1991. *Current Issues in Development Economies*. New York: St. Martin's Press.

Banfield, Edward C. 1958. *The Moral Basis of a Backward Society*. Chicago: The Free Press.

Barnett, H. G. 1953. *Innovation: The Basis Of Cultural Change*. New York: McGraw-Hill Book Co.

Barr, A. M. 1995. "The Missing Factor: Entrepreneurial Networks, Enterprises and Economic Growth in Ghana." London: Center for the Study of African Economies, Working Paper 95/11.

Baumol, W. J., S. A. B. Blackman, and E. N. Wolff. 1989. *Productivity and American Leadership*. Cambridge and London: The MIT Press.

Becker, Gary. 1962. "Investment in Human Capital: A Theoretical Analysis," *Journal of Political Economy* 70 (5) (Supplement, October): 9–49.

Berlin, Isaiah. 1969. *Four Essays on Liberty*. Oxford: Oxford University Press.

Berlin, Isaiah. 1980. *Against the Currents*. New York: Viking.

Birch, D. L. 1987. *Job Creation in America—How Our Smallest Companies Put the Most People to Work*. London: Macmillan.

Blaug, Mark. 1985. *Economic Theory in Retrospect*. 4th ed. Cambridge: Cambridge University Press.

Blaug, Mark. 1992. "The Overexpansion of Higher Education in the Third World." In *Equity and Efficiency in Economic Development* (ed. Donald J. Savoie and Irving Brecher). Montreal and Kingston: McGill-Queen's University Press.

Boland, L. A. 1992. *The Principles of Economics*. London and New York: Routledge.

Boorstin, D. J. 1983. *The Discoverers*. New York: Random House.

Boulding, K. E. 1969. "Economics as a Moral Science." *American Economic Review* 59:1–12.

Boulding, Kenneth. 1971. "Ecology and Economy." In *Collected Papers*, Vol. 2. Boulder: Colorado Associated University Press.

Braudel, Fernand. 1984. *The Perspective of the World*. Vol. III of *Civilization and Capitalism. Fifteenth–Eighteenth Century*. New York: Harper and Row Publishers.

Bruton, H. J. 1965. *Principles of Development Economics*. Englewood Cliffs, N.J.: Prentice-Hall.

Bruton, H. J. 1985. "The Search for Development Economics." *World Development* 13 (10/11): 1099–1124.

Bruton, H. J., and C. B. Hill. 1991. "The Development Impact of Counterpart Funds." CAER Discussion Paper No. 6. Harvard Institute of International Development, Harvard University, Cambridge, Mass.

Bruton, H. J., and C. B. Hill. 1992. "The Role of Counterpart Funds in Economic Development." *IDS Bulletin* 23 (2): 29–35.

Buchanan, J. M. 1994. *Ethics and Economic Progress*. Norman and London: University of Oklahoma Press.

Bury, J. B. 1932. *The Idea of Progress*. New York: The Macmillan Company.

Cairncross, Alec, and Mohinder Puri (eds.). 1976. *Employment, Income Distribution, and Development Strategy*. London: Macmillan Press Ltd.

Chenery, H. B., Sherman Robinson, and Moshe Syrquin. 1986. *Industrialization and Growth*. Oxford: Oxford University Press. (Published for the World Bank.)

Chenery, H. B., and T. N. Srinivasan. 1988. *Handbook of Development Economics*. Vol. I. Amsterdam: North-Holland.

Chenery, H. B., and T. N. Srinivasan. 1989. *Handbook of Development Economics*. Vol. II. Amsterdam: North-Holland.

Chenery, H. B., and Alan Strout. 1966. "Foreign Assistance and Economic Development." *American Economic Review* 56:679–733.

Colander, D. C. (ed.). 1984. *Neo-Classical Political Economy*. Cambridge, Mass.: Ballinger Publishing Company.

Coleman, J. S. 1990. *Foundations of Social Theory*. Cambridge, Mass.: Harvard University Press.

Corden, W. M. 1985. *Protection, Growth and Trade*. Oxford: Basil Blackwell.

Cortes, Mariluz, Albert Berry, and Ashfag Ishaq. 1987. *Success in Small and Medium Scale Industries*. Oxford: Oxford University Press.

Csikszentmihalyi, Mihaly. 1989. *The Psychology of Optimal Experience*. New York: Harper and Row.

Dasgupta, P. 1990. Well-Being and the Extent of its Realisation in Poor Countries, *Economic Journal* 100 (Supplement): 1–32.

Davis, J. D. 1994. *Keynes's Philosophical Development*. Cambridge and New York: Cambridge University Press.

Domar, E. D. 1957. *Essays in the Theory of Economic Growth*. New York: Oxford University Press.

Dooley, M. P., J. A. Frankel, and Donald Mathieson. 1987. "International Capital Mobility—What Do Saving-Investment Correlations Tell Us?" *IMF Staff Papers* 34:508–30.

Dosi, Giovanni, Christopher Freeman, Richard Nelson, Gerald Silverberg, and Luc Soete. 1988. *Technical Change and Economic Theory*. London: Pinter Publishers.

Dosi, Giovanni, Keith Pavitt, and Luc Soete. 1990. *The Economics of Technical Change and International Trade*. Hemel Hempstead, Harvester Wheatsheaf.

Dreze, Jean, and Amartya Sen. 1989. *Hunger and Political Action*. Oxford: Clarendon Press.

Easterlin, R. A. 1981. "Why Isn't the Whole World Developed?" *The Journal of Economic History* 41 (1): 1–16.

Eisenstadt, S. N. (ed). 1987. *Patterns of Modernity*. Vol. II: *Beyond the West*. New York: New York University Press.

Elias, V. J. 1990. "The Role of Total Factor Productivity Growth on Economic Growth." Background paper for the *World Development Report*, World Bank, Washington, D.C.

Elster, J. 1989. "Social Norms and Economic Theory." *The Journal of Economic Perspectives* 3 (Fall): 99–117.

Etzioni, A. 1988. *The Moral Dimension: Toward A New Economics*. New York: The Free Press.

Evensky, Jerry. 1993. "Ethics and the Invisible Hand." *The Journal of Economic Perspectives* 7 (2): 197–206.

Evenson, R. E. 1975. *Agricultural Research and Productivity*. New Haven: Yale University Press.

Evenson, R. E., and Gustav Ranis. 1990. *Science and Technology*. Boulder: The Westview Press.

Feenberg, Andrew. 1991. *Critical Theory of Technology*. New York and Oxford: Oxford University Press.

Fei, John, and Gustav Ranis. 1964. *Development of the Labor Surplus Economy*. Homewood, Ill.: Richard D. Irwin, Inc.

Feldstein, Martin, and Charles Horioka. 1980. "Domestic Saving and International Capital Flows." *Economic Journal* 90:314–29.

Fischer, Stanley. 1991. "Growth, Macroeconomics, and Development." In *NBER Macroeconomics Annual*, ed. Olivier Jean Blanchard and Stanley Fischer. Cambridge and London: The MIT Press.

Fishlow, Albert, et al. 1994. *Miracle or Design? Lessons from the East Asian Experience.* Policy Essay No. 11, Overseas Development Council, Washington, D.C.

Foster, John. 1993. "Economics and the Self-Organization Approach: Alfred Marshall Revisited." *Economic Journal* 103 (July): 975–91.

Frank, C. R. Jr., and Richard C. Webb. 1977. *Income Distribution and Growth in Less-Developed Countries.* Washington, D.C.: The Brookings Institution.

Frankel, J. A, Michael Dooley, and Donald Mathieson. 1986. "International Capital Mobility in Developing Countries vs. Industrial Countries." NBER Working Paper No. 2043, Cambridge, Mass.: National Bureau of Economic Research.

Frankel, Stephen (ed.). 1993. *Organized Labor in the Asia Pacific Region.* Ithaca, N.Y.: ILR Press.

Freeman, R. B. 1993. "Labor Market Institutions and Policies: Help or Hindrance to Economic Development." *Proceedings of the World Bank Annual Conference on Development Economics,* 117–45.

Fromm, Erich. 1947. *Man for Himself.* New York: Rinehart.

Fuchs, V. R. 1967. "Redefining Poverty and Redistributing Income." *The Public Interest* 8 (Summer): 88–95.

Galenson, Walter (ed.). 1985. *Foreign Investment and Economic Development in the Newly Industrializing Asian Countries.* Madison: University of Wisconsin Press.

Gereffi, Gary, and L. D. Wyman (eds.). 1900. *Manufacturing Miracles.* Princeton, N.J: Princeton University Press.

Gerschenkron, Alexander. 1962. *Economic Backwardness in Historical Perspective.* Cambridge, Mass.: Harvard University Press.

Gifford, Donald. 1990. *The Farther Shore.* New York: The Atlantic Monthly Press.

Gray, John. 1991. "The Unavoidable Conflict." *Times Literary Supplement,* July 5.

Griffin, James. 1986. *Well-Being.* Oxford: Clarendon Press.

Griliches, Zvi. 1991. "The Search for R & D Spillover." Working Paper No. 3768. National Bureau of Economic Research. Working Paper Series, Cambridge, Mass.

Grindle, M. S., and J. W. Thomas. 1991. *Public Choices and Policy Changes.* Baltimore and London: The Johns Hopkins University Press.

Grossman, G. M., and Elhanan Helpman. 1991. *Innovation and Growth in the Global Economy.* Cambridge, Mass.: The MIT Press.

Haberler, Gottfried. 1959. *International Trade and Economic Development.* Fiftieth Anniversary Lecture, National Bank of Egypt, Cairo.

Harrison, Ann. 1991. Openness and Growth. Working Paper 809. Washington, D.C.: The World Bank.

Harrod, R. F. 1939. "An Essay in Dynamic Theory." *Economic Journal* 49 (March): 14–33.

Harrod, R. F. 1949. *Towards a Dynamic Economics.* New York: The Macmillan Company.

Hausman, D. M., and M. S. McPerson. 1993. "Taking Ethics Seriously: Economics and Contemporary Moral Philosophy." *Journal of Economic Literature* 31 (2): 671–732.

Hayami, Yujiro, and V. W. Ruttan. 1985. *Agricultural Development: An International Perspective.* Baltimore: The Johns Hopkins University Press.

Hayek, Frederick. 1960. *The Constitution of Liberty.* London: Routledge and Kegan Paul.

Hayek, Frederick. 1979. "Law, Legislation, and Liberty." Vol. 3: *The Political Order of a Free People.* Chicago: University of Chicago Press.

Helleiner, G. K. (ed.). 1992. *Trade Policy, Industrialization, and Development: New Perspectives.* Oxford and New York: Oxford University Press.

Helliwell, J. F. 1992. "Trade and Technical Progress." National Bureau of Economic Research Working Paper No. 4226, Cambridge, Mass.

Helliwell, J. F. 1992a. "International Growth Linkages: Evidence from Asia and the OECD." National Bureau of Economic Research Working Paper No. 4245, Cambridge, Mass.

Higonnet, Patrice, David S. Landes, and Henry Rosovsky (eds.). 1991. *Favorites of Fortune.* Cambridge: Harvard University Press.

Hirschman, A. O. 1958. *The Strategy of Economic Development.* New Haven: Yale University Press.

Hirschman, A. O. 1981. *Essays in Trespassing.* Cambridge: Cambridge University Press.

Honohan, Patrick, and Izak Atiyas. 1993. "Intersectoral Financial Flows in Developing Countries." *Economic Journal* 103 (418): 666–79.

Hughes, Helen (ed.). 1988. *Achieving Industrialization in East Asia.* Cambridge: Cambridge University Press.

Hughes, Jonathan. 1970. *Industrialization and Economic History.* New York: McGraw Hill Book Company.

Ignatieff, Michael. 1991. "The Ends of Empathy." *The New Republic,* April 29: 31–37.

Ignatieff, Michael. 1985. *The Needs of Strangers.* New York: Viking.

Inkles, Alex, and D. H. Smith. 1974. *Becoming Modern: Individual Change in Six Developing Countries.* Cambridge, Mass.: Harvard University Press.

Ishikawa, Shigeru. 1981. *Essays in Technology, Employment and Institutions in Economic Development.* Tokyo: Kinokuniya.

Jaki, S. L. 1974. *Science and Creation.* Edinburgh and London: Scottish Academic Press.

James, Jeffrey, and Susumu Watanabe (eds.). 1985. *Technology, Institutions, and Government Policies.* London: MacMillan.

Janelli, R. L. 1993. *Making Capitalism.* Stanford, Calif.: Stanford University Press.

Jones, L. P., and Il Sakong. 1980. *Government, Business, and Entrepreneurship in Economic Development: The Korean Case.* Cambridge, Mass.: Council on East Asian Studies, Harvard University.

Jorgenson, D. W. 1995. *Productivity.* Cambridge: MIT Press.

Keynes, J. M. 1935. *The General Theory of Employment Interest and Money.* New York: Harcourt, Brace and Company.

Knight, F. H. 1935. *The Ethics of Competition and Other Essays.* New York: Harper and Brothers.

Knight, F. H. 1956. *On the History and Method in Economics.* Chicago: University of Chicago Press.

Kohn, M. L., and Carmi Schooler. 1983. *Work and Personality: An Inquiry into the Impact of Social Stratification.* Norwood, N.J.: Ablex.

Koopmans, T. C. 1957. *Three Essays on the State of Economic Science*. New York: McGraw-Hill Book Co.

Krueger, A. O. 1990. "Government Failures in Development." *The Journal of Economic Perspectives* 4 (3): 9–24.

Kuran, Timur. 1992. "The Unthinkable and the Unthought." Working Paper No. 9305, Department of Economics, University of Southern California.

Kuznets, Simon. 1971. *Economic Growth of Nations: Total Output and Production Structure*. Cambridge, Mass.: Harvard University Press.

Landes, D. S. 1983. *Revolution in Time*. Cambridge: Harvard University Press.

Lane, R. E. 1991. *The Market Experience*. Cambridge: Cambridge University Press.

Lazonick, William, and Thomas Brush. 1982. "The 'Horndal' Effect in Early U.S. Manufacturing." In Discussion Paper No. 936. Harvard Institute of Economic Research, Harvard University, Cambridge, Mass.

Levine, Ross, and David Renelt. 1991. "A Sensitivity Analysis of Cross-County Growth Regressions." Working Papers, WPS 609. Washington, D.C.: The World Bank.

Levine, Ross, and David Renelt. 1991a. "Cross-Country Studies of Growth and Policy." Working Papers, WPS 608. Washington, D.C.: The World Bank.

Lewis, W. A. 1954. "Economic Development with Unlimited Supplies of Labor." *The Manchester School* 22:139–91.

Lewis, W. A. 1955. *The Theory of Economic Growth*. London: George Allen and Unwin Ltd.

Lindblom, C. E. 1959. "The Science of Muddling Through." *Public Administration Review* 19 (Spring): 79–88.

Lindblom, C. E. 1988. *Democracy and the Market System*. Oslo: Norwegian University Press.

Lindblom, C. E. 1990. *Inquiry and Change*. New Haven: Yale University Press and Russell Sage Foundation.

Little, I. M. D. 1957. *A Critique of Welfare Economics* (2d ed.). Oxford: Oxford University Press.

Little, I. M. D. 1982. *Economic Development*. New York: Basic Books, Inc.

Little, I. M. D., Dipak Mazundar, and John Page Jr. 1987. *Small Manufacturing Enterprises*. Oxford: Oxford University Press.

Loasby, B. J. 1976. *Choice, Complexity, and Ignorance*. Cambridge: Cambridge University Press.

Lucas, R. E. 1988. "On the Mechanics of Economic Development." *Journal of Monetary Economics* 22:3–42.

Maddison, Angus. 1962. "Growth and Fluctuations in the World Economy, 1870–1960." *Banca Nazionale del Lavoro* 62:3–17.

Maddison, Angus. 1970. *Economic Progress and Policy in Developing Countries*. New York: W. W. Norton and Co.

Maddison, Angus. 1987. "Growth and Slowdown in Advanced Capitalist Economies." *Journal of Economic Literature* 25:649–99.

Maddison, Angus. 1991. *Dynamic Forces in Capitalist Development*. Oxford: Oxford University Press.

Mankiw, N. G. 1995. "The Growth of Nations." *Brookings Papers on Economic Activity* I:275–327.

Marsden, Keith. 1990. *African Entrepreneurs: Pioneers of Development.* Washington, D.C.: The World Bank.

Marshall, Alfred. 1946 (1920). *Principles of Economies,* 8th ed. MacMillan and Co. Limited.

Mason, E. S., and Mahn Je Kim. 1980. *The Economic and Social Modernization of the Republic of Korea.* Cambridge: Council of East Asian Studies, Harvard University.

Matthews, R. C. O., C. N. Feinstein, J. C. Adling-Smee. 1982. *British Economic Growth.* Stanford, Calif.: Stanford University Press.

McPherson, M. S. 1983. "Want Formation, Morality and Some Interpretive Aspects of Economic Inquiry." In Norman Haan, R. N. Bellah, Paul Robinson, and William M. Sullivan (eds.), *Social Science as Moral Inquiry.* New York: Columbia University Press.

Mill, J. S. 1873. *Autobiography.* London: Longmans, Green, Reader, and Dyer.

Milner, Chris (ed.). 1990. *Export Promotion Strategies: Theory and Evidence from Developing Countries,* New York: New York University Press.

Mirza, Hafiz. 1986. *Multinationals and the Growth of the Singapore Economy.* New York: St. Martin's Press.

Mokyr, Joel. 1990. *The Lever of Riches.* Oxford: Oxford University Press.

Montaigne. 1958. *The Complete Essays of Montaigne* (trans. Donald Frame). Stanford: Stanford University Press.

Morishima, Michio. 1982. *Why Has Japan Succeeded?* Cambridge: Cambridge University Press.

Morley, John. 1917. *Recollections,* Vol. I. New York: The MacMillan Company.

Morris, M. D. 1979. *Measuring the Condition of the World's Poor: The Physical Quality of Life Index.* New York: Pergamon Press.

Morris-Suzuki, Tessa. 1989. *A History of Japanese Thought.* London: Routledge.

Morris-Suzuki, Tessa. 1994. *The Technological Transformation of Japan.* Cambridge: Cambridge University Press.

Mosley, Paul, Jane Harrigan, and John Toye. 1991. *Aid and Power.* London and New York: Routledge.

Nadiri, M. J. 1993. *Innovations and Technological Spillovers.* Working Paper No. 4423. National Bureau of Economic Research, Cambridge, Mass.

Needham, Joseph. 1956. *Science and Civilization in China.* Vol 2. Cambridge: Cambridge University Press.

Nelson, J. M. (ed.). 1990. *Economic Crisis and Public Choice.* Princeton: Princeton University Press.

Nelson, R. R., and S. G. Winter. 1982. *An Evolutionary Theory of Economic Change.* Cambridge: The Belknap Press of Harvard University.

Nisbet, Robert. 1980. *History of the Idea of Progress.* New York: Basic Books.

Nishimizu, Mieko, and J. M. Page. 1986. "Productivity Change and Dynamic Comparative Advantage." *Review of Economics and Statistics* 68:241–47.

Nordhaus, William, and James Tobin. 1973. "Is Growth Obsolete?" In Milton Moss (ed.), *The Measurement of Economic and Social Performance*. New York: Columbia University Press.

North, D. C. 1990. *Institutions, Institutional Change, and Economic Performance*. Cambridge: Cambridge University Press.

Nussbaum, M. C. 1986. *The Fragility of Goodness*. Cambridge: Cambridge University Press.

Nussbaum, Martha, and Amartya Sen. 1993. *The Quality of Life*. Oxford: The Clarendon Press.

O'Connor, Daniel, and Francis Oakley. 1969. *Creation: The Impact of an Idea*. New York: Charles Scribner's Sons.

Organization of Economic Cooperation and Development (OECD). 1990. *Implementing Change*. Paris.

Pacey, Arnold. 1990. *Technology in World Civilization*. Cambridge, Mass.: The MIT Press.

Pack, Howard. 1994. "Endogenous Growth Theory: Intellectual Appeal and Empirical Shortcomings." *The Journal of Economic Perspectives* 8 (Winter): 55–72.

Pasinetti, L. L. 1981. *Structural Changes and Economic Growth*. Cambridge and New York: Cambridge University Press.

Pasinetti, L. L. 1993. *Structural Economic Dynamics*. Cambridge: Cambridge University Press.

Pavitt, Keith. 1984. "Sectoral Patterns of Technical Change: Towards a Taxonomy and a Theory." *Research Policy* 13.

Pechman, J. A., and M. S. McPherson (eds.). 1992. *Fulfilling America's Promise*. Ithaca: Cornell University Press.

Penz, G. P. 1986. *Consumer Sovereignty and Human Interests*. Cambridge: Cambridge University Press.

Polanyi, Karl. 1944. *The Great Transformation*. New York: Farrar and Rinehart.

Power, J. H. 1963. "Industrialization in Pakistan: A Case of Frustrated Take-Off." *Pakistan Development Review* 3:191–207.

Prebisch, Raul. 1950. *The Economic Development of Latin America*, Lake Success, United Nations.

Putnam, R. D. 1993. *Making Democracy Work*. Princeton, N.J.: Princeton University Press.

Putterman, Louis. 1990. *Division of Labor and Welfare*. Oxford: Oxford University Press.

Putterman, Louis, and Dietrich Rueschmeyer (eds.). 1992. *State and Market in Development*. Boulder and London: Lynne Rienner Publishers.

Rahman, Fazlur. 1982. *Islam and Modernity*. Chicago: The University of Chicago Press.

Ramsey, Frank. 1928. "A Mathematical Theory of Saving." *Economic Journal* 38 (4): 543–59.

Ranis, Gustav. 1978. "Science, Technology and Development: A Retrospective View." In *Science, Technology and Development*, ed. William Beranek Jr. and Gustav Ranis. New York and London: Praeger Publishers.

Ranis, Gustav. 1990. "Science and Technology Policy: Lessons from Japan and the

East Asian NICs." In *Science and Technology,* ed. Robert E. Evenson and Gustav Ranis. Boulder, Colo.: Westview Press.

Rawls, John. 1971. *A Theory of Justice.* Cambridge: Harvard University Press.

Rawls, John. 1993. *Political Liberalism.* New York: Columbia University Press.

Reynolds, L. G. 1985. *Economic Growth in the Third World, 1850–1980.* New Haven and London: Yale University Press.

Riley, Jonathan. 1988. *Liberal Utilitarianism,* Cambridge: Cambridge University Press.

Robbins, Lionel. 1935. *An Essay on the Nature and Significance of Economic Science.* London: MacMillan and Co.

Rodrik, Dani. 1993. *Trade and Industrial Policy Reform in Developing Countries: A Review of Recent Theory and Evidence.* Working Paper No. 4417, National Bureau of Economic Research, Cambridge, Mass.

Romer, P. M. 1986. "Increasing Returns and Long Run Growth." *Journal of Political Economy* 94:1002–37.

Romer, P. M. 1990. "Endogenous Technological Change." *Journal of Political Economy* 98 (Part 2): S71–S102.

Rosenberg, Nathan. 1982. *Inside The Black Box: Technology and Economics.* Cambridge: Cambridge University Press.

Ruf, F. J. 1991. *The Creation of Chaos.* Albany: State University of New York Press.

Salter, W. E. G. 1966. *Productivity and Technical Change.* Cambridge: Cambridge University Press.

Samuels, Ernest. 1989. *Henry Adams.* Cambridge: Harvard University Press.

Samuelson, P. A. 1947. *Foundations of Economic Analysis.* Cambridge: Harvard University Press.

Schimmel, Annemarie. 1994. *Deciphering the Hand of God.* Albany: State University of New York.

Schumpeter, J. A. 1934. *The Theory of Economic Development.* Cambridge: Harvard University Press.

Scitovsky, Tibor. 1985. "Economic Development in Taiwan and Korea: 1965–81." *Food Research Institute Studies* 19(No. 3): 215–64.

Scitovsky, Tibor. 1986. *Human Desire and Economic Satisfaction.* New York: New York University Press.

Scott, M. F. 1989. *A New View of Economic Growth.* Oxford: Clarendon Press.

Sen, Amartya. 1975. *Employment Technology and Development.* Oxford: Clarendon Press.

Sen, Amartya. 1981. *Poverty and Famines: An Essay on Entitlements and Deprivation.* Oxford: Oxford University Press.

Sen, Amartya. 1981a. "Public Action and the Quality of Life in Developing Countries." *Oxford Bulletin of Economics and Statistics* 43 (4): 287–319.

Sen, Amartya. 1984. *Resources, Values and Development.* Cambridge: Harvard University Press.

Sen, Amartya. 1987. *The Standard of Living.* Cambridge: Cambridge University Press.

Sen, Amartya. 1987a. *On Ethics and Economics.* Oxford: Blackwell.

Sen, Amartya. 1991. "Markets and Freedom." The Development Economics Research Programme, London School of Economics, London, Dep. No. 31.

Shackle, G. L. S. 1958. *Time in Economics*. Amsterdam: North Holland.

Shackle, G. L. S. 1988. *Business Time and Thought*. (Selected Papers, ed. S. F. Frowen). New York: New York University Press.

Shionoya, Yuichi. 1990. "The Origin of the Schumpeterian Research Program: A Chapter Omitted from Schumpeter's *Theory of Economic Development.*" *Journal of Institutional and Theoretical Economics* 146:314–27.

Shove, G. F. 1942. "The Place of Marshall's *Principles* in the Development of Economic Theory." *Economic Journal* 52:294–329.

Singer, H. W. 1950. "The Distribution of Gains between Investing and Borrowing Countries." *American Economic Review* 40:473–85.

Smith, Adam. 1937 (1776). *The Wealth of Nations*. New York: Random House (Modern Library Edition).

Solow, R. M. 1956. "A Contribution to the Theory of Economic Growth." *Quarterly Journal of Economics* 70 (February): 65–94.

Solow, R. M. 1957. "Technical Change, and the Aggregate Production Function." *Review of Economics and Statistics* 39:312–20.

Solow, R. M. 1994. "Perspectives on Growth Theory." *The Journal of Economic Perspectives* 8 (Winter): 45–54.

Stern, Nicholas. 1989. "The Economics of Development: A Survey." *The Economic Journal* 99 (September): 597–685.

Stewart, H. C. 1989. *Taking Goals Seriously: A Reconsideration of Rationality in Economics*. Unpublished Ph.D. Dissertation, Harvard University.

Stewart, Hamish. 1995. "A Critique of Instrumental Reason in Economics." *Economics and Philosophy* (11): 57–83.

Stobaugh, Robert, and L. T. Wells (eds.). 1984. *Technology Crossing Borders*. Boston: Harvard Business School Press.

Streeten, Paul, and Associates. 1981. *First Things First*. Oxford: Oxford University Press (published for the World Bank).

Successful Development in Africa. 1989. "EDI Development Policy Case Series." Analytical Case Studies Number 1. Washington, D.C.: Economic Development Institute of the World Bank.

Swedberg, Richard. 1990. *Economics and Sociology: Redefining Their Boundaries*. Princeton, N.J.: Princeton University Press.

Taylor, A. M. 1994. "Domestic Saving and International Capital Flows Reconsidered." Working Paper No. 4892. Cambridge, Mass.: National Bureau of Economic Research.

Taylor, Charles. 1985. *Human Agency and Language*. Cambridge: Cambridge University Press.

Taylor, Charles. 1989. *Sources of the Self*. Cambridge, Mass.: Harvard University Press.

Taylor, Charles. 1992. *Multi-culturalism and the Politics of Recognition*. Princeton, N.J.: Princeton University Press.

Taylor, Lance. 1988. *Varieties of Stabilization Experience*. Oxford: Clarendon Press.

Taylor, Lance. 1991. *Income Distribution, Inflation, and Growth*. Cambridge, Mass.: The MIT Press.

Tocqueville, Alexis de. 1856. *The Old Regime and the Revolution.* New York: Harper and Brothers.

Tokunaga, Shojiro (ed.). 1992. *Japan's Foreign Investment and Asian Economic Interdependence.* Tokyo: University of Tokyo Press.

Toye, John. 1987. *Dilemmas of Development.* Oxford: Basil Blackwell.

Tsao, Yuan. 1985. "Growth without Productivity." *Journal of Development Economics* 18:25–38.

United Nations Development Programme. 1991. *Human Development Report 1990.* New York: Oxford University Press.

Vernon, Raymond. 1977. *Storm Over the Multinationals.* Cambridge: Harvard University Press.

Viner, Jacob. 1952. *International Trade and Economic Development.* Glencoe, Ill.: The Free Press.

Wad, Atul (ed.). 1988. *Science, Technology and Development.* Boulder, Colo.: Westview Press.

Wade, Robert. 1990. *Governing the Market.* Princeton, N.J.: Princeton University Press.

Wahid, A. N. M. (ed.). 1993. *The Grameen Bank.* Boulder: Westview Press.

Wallace, J. D. 1978. *Virtues and Vices.* Ithaca and London: Cornell University Press.

Watt, W. M. 1988. *Islamic Fundamentalism and Modernity.* London: Routledge.

Weale, Martin. 1993. "A Critical Evaluation of Rate of Return Analysis." *Economic Journal* 103 (418): 729–37.

Werhave, Patricia. 1991. *Adam Smith and His Legacy for Modern Capitalism.* New York: Oxford University Press.

Westphal, L. E. 1982. "Fostering Technological Mastery by Means of Selective Infant Industry Protection." In *Trade, Stability, Technology, and Equity in Latin America* (ed. Moshe Syrquin and Simon Teitel). New York: Academic Press.

Westphal, L. E. 1990. "Industrial Policy in an Export Propelled Economy: Lessons from South Korea's Experience." *Journal of Economic Perspectives* 4 (3): 45–60.

Wiggins, David. 1987. *Needs, Values, Truth.* Oxford: Basil Blackwell.

Wilber, C. K., and K. P. Jameson. 1980. "Religious Values and Social Limits to Development." *World Development* 8 (July/August): 467–79.

Williams, Bernard. 1985. *Ethics and the Limits of Philosophy.* Cambridge: Harvard University Press.

World Bank. 1987. *World Development Report.* Oxford: Oxford University Press.

World Bank. 1989. *Sub-Saharan Africa: From Crisis to Sustainable Growth.* Washington, D.C.: The World Bank.

World Bank. 1990. *The Long-Term Perspective Study of Sub-Saharan Africa.* Three Volumes. Washington, D.C.: The World Bank.

World Bank. 1991. *World Development Report.* Oxford: Oxford University Press.

World Bank. 1993. *The East Asian Miracle.* New York: Oxford University Press (for the World Bank).

World Development, Special Issue, 1989. "The Role of Institutions in Economic Development." 17 (September).

Index